100 THINGS
CAPITALS FANS
SHOULD KNOW & DO
BEFORE THEY DIE

100 THINGS CAPITALS FANS
SHOULD KNOW & DO
BEFORE THEY DIE

Ben Raby

TRIUMPH
BOOKS

Library of Congress Cataloging-in-Publication Data available upon request

This book is available in quantity at special discounts for your group or organization. For further information, contact:
   Triumph Books LLC
   814 North Franklin Street
   Chicago, Illinois 60610
   (312) 337-0747
   www.triumphbooks.com

Printed in U.S.A.
ISBN: 978-1-62937-338-6
Design by Patricia Frey
Photos courtesy of Washington Capitals Photography

To my wife, Allyssa, the best teammate I could ask for.

*And to my parents, Alice and Joel, the
best two coaches I ever had.*

Thank you all for the love and support.

Contents

Foreword *by Craig Laughlin* xi

Acknowledgments xiii

1 Save the Caps 1

2 Ovechkin Debuts 5

3 NHL Comes to Washington 9

4 Juneau Sends Capitals to 1998 Stanley Cup 14

5 Poile's Bold Move 20

6 That Was Classic 27

7 Dale Hunter's OT Winner vs. Flyers 31

8 Alexander the Greatest 36

9 Capitals Move to MCI Center 40

10 Capitals Win 2008 Southeast Division 44

11 Retired Jerseys: Labre, Langway, Hunter, Gartner 48

12 Capitals Discover Bondra 55

13 Winning the Lottery 60

14 Holtby Ties Brodeur 64

15 The Canadiens Challenge 68

16 First Playoff Appearance 74

17 The King Is Dead 79

18 Growing Pains for Early Prospects 84

19 Saint Nick 88

20 Nicklas Backstrom Time Line 92

21 Natural-Born Leader 94

22 The Captaincy 98

23 Workaholic Caps Break on Through 104

24 Maryland Native Makes the Capitals 109

25 Druce on the Loose............................. 114

26 A Brouwer-Play Goal 119

27 The Swedish Embassy........................... 122

28 See the Capitals on the Road..................... 125

29 Tommy McVie 129

30 Could Pat Quinn Have Coached the Capitals? 134

31 Barry Trotz First Meets the Capitals 138

32 Dale Hunter Trade 144

33 Holtby Emerges as Fourth-Round Gem 149

34 Veterans Bellows and Tikkanen Join '98 Capitals......... 153

35 Roger That 158

36 The Goal..................................... 161

37 Olie the Goalie 164

38 The Stanley Can 170

39 Easter Epic 173

40 Deadline Blockbuster 180

41 Attend Practice at the Kettler Capitals Iceplex........... 185

42 Joel Ward's Unlikely Journey 187

43 Stevens Checks In.............................. 191

44 Ace Bailey.................................... 195

45 Caps Deal Can't-Miss Kid 200

46 The Feisty George McPhee........................ 204

47 King of Capitals Broadcasts....................... 208

48 Early Trips to Philadelphia 210

49 Snowvechkin................................... 213

50 Ovechkin's 50-Goal Seasons 216

51 See the Hershey Bears 221

52 Game Over Green. 223

53 Bedeviled: Caps Let One Slip Away in '88 227

54 Halak, Canadiens Upset 2010 Capitals. 233

55 Mike Marson's On- and Off-Ice Battles 238

56 After Olie: The Kid Goalies 244

57 Attend Capitals Prospect Development Camp 248

58 The Original Voice. 249

59 A Comeback 13 Years in the Making 253

60 The Forgotten 60-Goal Scorer 256

61 Niskanen and Orpik Come to Town. 262

62 The Wild Thing 267

63 That's a Stretch 270

64 Tim Taylor's Skate in the Crease 273

65 Play Poker with the Capitals 277

66 Ovechkin "Nose" Goal Scoring. 279

67 Best Men. 282

68 Jagr Bombs 287

69 To Russia with Love 293

70 Holtby's Coming-Out Party 296

71 Washington's First Taste of Pro Hockey 301

72 Mr. Outdoors 304

73 Japan Trip. 307

74 Comeback Kids Go Streaking. 312

75 Fan Favorites Move On. 315

76 Brian MacLellan's Long-Awaited Promotion. 321

77 Capitals Deal Bondra for Laich 325

78 The Capitals' Miracle on 33rd Street 329

79 Island Time for the Big Cheese 333

80 Unleash the Fury 336

81 McVie's Weight Scale and the Capital Mile 338

82 A Mystery Fit for a Net Detective 342

83 See the Capitals Play Outdoors 346

84 Capitals Go 3-D 350

85 Holtby Pays the Price of Success 352

86 20/20/20 Vision 354

87 Listen to *Hockey Diaries* 357

88 Capitals Host 1982 All-Star Game 359

89 Capitals All-Star Game Highlights 361

90 Hunter's Cheap Shot 365

91 Fedorov Joins Capitals in 2008 368

92 The Loch Ness Monster Arrives 372

93 Baltimore's Bid for the NHL 376

94 The Dueling Hat Tricks 378

95 Five Alive for Gusty and Bonzai 382

96 Esa Tikkanen's Game 2 Miss 384

97 Visit the Capitals' Hat Trick Display 387

98 20 Minutes of Fame 391

99 The Chimeracle on 34th Street 394

100 See the Capitals Win the Stanley Cup 397

Sources 401

Foreword

It was September 10, 1982. A day that I remember like it was yesterday....

It was a beautiful, sunny, brisk morning in Montreal, Quebec, Canada, and I was preparing for my third NHL camp with the Montreal Canadiens. I was heading to the Montreal Forum, one of the greatest and most iconic hockey arenas in the world. It was the first day of training camp, and I was nervous and had butterflies swirling in my stomach as I stepped into the ice rink. This, I thought, was my chance to prove that I belonged here—in the NHL and with the Canadiens. I wanted to make the team right out of training camp.

Before practice I was told to go upstairs to meet with general manager Irving Grundman. This was unusual. So many thoughts ran through my head. Was I getting a new deal? Was I being sent to Halifax before our first day of camp even started? Why was I meeting with the GM?

As I stepped into the office, my mind was swirling. And little did I know that this next conversation would change my life forever. "Craig," Mr. Grundman said, "we have traded you to the Washington Capitals, and wish you well there!" This ended up being one of the biggest blockbuster trades in NHL and Washington Capitals history—and a trade that changed my life forever.

It's now been 35 years since that day, and here I am still residing in Washington, D.C. I spent the majority of my NHL playing career with the Capitals, and stayed on with them even after I retired, becoming the color analyst in the broadcast booth, where I have been ever since. Since my time here in D.C., I have been around to witness the "Save the Caps" campaign back in the early

'80s, the tear-down-and-rebuild era, the Jaromir Jagr experiment, numerous coaches, the first pick of Alex Ovechkin the Great 8, the "Rock the Red" campaign, and the change of ownership and new buildings.

Having been around this organization for more than 30 years, I'd like to think that I have seen and heard it all when it comes to the Washington Capitals. But boy, am I wrong! Ben Raby has been able to capture not only my stories and the stories of other former players, but also the evolution of this organization and then some in this book.

There are a ton of die-hard Caps and hockey fans alike out there, and in this book Ben delves into the stories, the players, and the fans of this '70s-era expansion franchise to the present day. There have been good times and there have been some bad, all of which are captured throughout this book. It's an adventure you will not want to miss!

—Craig Laughlin
June 21, 2017

Craig Laughlin's NHL career spanned 13 seasons, including playing right wing for the Capitals from 1982 to '88. He is currently the Capitals' color analyst for CSN Mid-Atlantic.

Acknowledgments

The writing of this book would not have been possible without the support of many colleagues, friends, and family members.

Longtime NHL reporter Chuck Gormley introduced me to the folks at Triumph Books in July 2016, and within days I was signing paperwork to author *100 Things Capitals Fans Should Know & Do Before They Die*. I spent five seasons working alongside Chuck on the Capitals beat and always appreciated his insight and friendship. He is among the best in the business.

Throughout the writing process, I worked closely with Triumph Books editor Michelle Bruton. I owe a great debt of gratitude to Michelle for her encouragement and patience with a first-time author. Her flexibility made for a smooth and rewarding experience.

Among the highlights in producing this book were the interviews of more than 60 former players. This book was somewhat reliant on their stories and memories, and I'm appreciative that so many Capitals alums were happy to accommodate. Additional interviews were conducted with current Capitals players, as well as past and present coaches, broadcasters, and team executives.

Special thanks to former Washington general managers David Poile and George McPhee and to Capitals team president and minority owner Dick Patrick for their generosity and candidness.

Thank you to Sergey Kocharov, Pace Sagester, and Megan Eichenberg from the Capitals' media relations department for assisting with interviews and photographs.

Capitals.com senior writer and the team's unofficial historian, Mike Vogel, was a great resource for perspective and research. Ditto for members of the CSN Mid-Atlantic broadcast crew, including Joe Beninati, Al Koken, and Alan May. Few former players are as passionate about Capitals history as CSNMA color analyst Craig

Laughlin, who did an outstanding job writing the book's foreword. Thank you, Locker!

I'm fortunate to have worked with such talented writers in Washington, D.C., as Zac Boyer, Brian McNally, and Stephen Whyno and am lucky to call them all great friends. I appreciate the proofreading and the feedback they all provided as I navigated through *100 Things*.

A stick-tap as well to Dan Steinberg and Scott Allen with the *Washington Post*'s D.C. Sports Bog. They are two terrific storytellers and many of their articles came up during the research process. Someday they should write a book. On anything. I'll buy a copy, fellas.

Thanks to a great group of teammates I get to work with on the Capitals Radio Network, including John Walton, Ken Sabourin, and Mike Callow. Between them, I must have been asked 100 times during the writing process if I was finished. They knew I wasn't, but they'd ask. It became a bit of an ongoing joke. On some long days I spent both writing and broadcasting, they made coming to work a blast.

And seeing as this is my first book, I'd like to acknowledge Mitch Melnick and Montreal's TSN 690 (formerly the Team 990), who gave me my first job in sports media when I was 19 and helped me grow.

Finally, thank you to my family. They recognized my passion for sports journalism at an early age and encouraged me to chase my childhood dream. I couldn't have asked for better role models growing up. Thank you to my parents, Alice and Joel, and to my sister, Stephanie.

And a special thank you to my wife, Allyssa, for all her support and patience (and coffee runs!) during the writing process. Writing a book can be a lonely endeavor, with many nights and weekends sacrificed, but Allyssa's support never wavered. Thank you, Allyssa. You're the best!

1 Save the Caps

It's hard to blame some Capitals fans for taking the whole experience for granted. They have been spoiled for much of the last decade by a perennial Stanley Cup contender that is led by one of the greatest goal scorers in NHL history (Alex Ovechkin) and one of the best playmakers of his generation (Nicklas Backstrom).

Their favorite hockey team has built a home sellout streak north of 360 consecutive games. All but one of those home games have been played at a privately funded arena in a once desolate but now vibrant part of downtown Washington, D.C. The other home game over that stretch was staged before a capacity crowd of 42,832 at Nationals Park, where the Capitals—during their 40th-anniversary season—hosted one of the NHL's marquee events at the 2015 Bridgestone Winter Classic.

Washington has become a desirable destination for free agents and one of the NHL's most successful U.S. markets. For the modern-day Capitals fan, this is normal. In some cases, it's all they know.

But during the early 1980s, the whole thing would have seemed like a pipe dream.

In fact, if not for a series of events in the summer of 1982, none of it would have been possible. Back then, the Capitals were essentially on life support, a miserable team on the ice with eight consecutive losing seasons since its inception and a struggling club off the ice, with more than $20 million in losses, according to owner Abe Pollin.

In their first eight years, the Capitals went through eight coaches, three general managers, and five captains. They missed the playoffs in each of those eight seasons, the last three of which saw 16 of 21 teams qualify.

Attendance was also thin at the Capital Centre in Landover, Maryland, where the Capitals averaged 10,726 fans during their first eight years (59 percent capacity). Of their first 320 home games, only 19 were sellouts.

"The Capitals to date have been the major disappointment and the major failure of my business career," Pollin told the *Washington Post* in November 1981.

According to Pollin, the team couldn't survive for much longer. So, in conjunction with the NHL, he looked at his long-term options during the 1981–82 season. Relocating and folding the franchise were real possibilities, as was merging (and relocating) with an existing club.

Perhaps following the lead of the Atlanta Flames, who moved to Calgary in 1980, Pollin scheduled a meeting with government officials in Saskatoon, Saskatchewan, in June 1982. The meeting was cancelled at the last minute, though, and never rescheduled.

"I take full responsibility for the sorry state of the Washington Capitals to date, and I underline *to date*," Pollin said. "It has not been for lack of commitment, lack of effort, or lack of pouring bucks into the team, many millions of bucks."

On July 20, 1982, Pollin revealed four conditions that had to be met to ensure the club's viability in Washington.

The criteria included the sale of at least 7,500 season tickets for the 1982–83 season, complete sellouts for the first 10 home games, a reduction in the Capitals' rent to the Capital Centre from 15 percent to 10 percent, and a reduction of the Prince George's County entertainment tax.

Pollin wanted the PG County amusement tax reduced from 10 percent to one-half of one percent over the next three years.

If the conditions could be met within 30 days, Pollin had a group of investors on standby that would purchase a share of the team and help keep it in Washington. Dick Patrick, who has remained with the organization for more than three decades, was among those investors.

"The challenge is laid down to all segments of the community," Pollin said.

Spearheaded by a small group of season-ticket holders, a "Save the Caps" campaign grew into a tremendous monthlong endeavor as local fans, businesses, and media did their part to ensure that the team would stay.

Save the Caps telethons were held from the Capital Centre and broadcast on WRC-TV with legendary sportscaster George Michael emceeing the events. Local celebrities, including Washington Redskins head coach George Allen, stopped by the makeshift set and urged fans to support the ticket drive.

The goal of selling out the first 10 games was reached when a group of businesses stepped up and agreed to buy any unsold tickets for each of first 10 games of the season.

A rent reduction of 33 percent was granted at the Capital Centre and although the season-ticket drive fell about 1,900 tickets short, Pollin let that slide when two other businesses stepped up and ensured two more home sellouts.

The only question mark remained the necessary entertainment tax break from PG County.

If the Capitals did not receive the tax relief, plans had already been put in place by August 1982 for the team to merge with the New Jersey Devils for the 1982–83 season.

"We will definitely make the deal if Abe Pollin doesn't get what he needs," Devils owner John McMullen told the *New York Times.* Negotiations for such a move had been ongoing for weeks.

But on August 24, 1982, Pollin made one final push before the PG County Council.

"At this time, Prince George's County is effectively without a hockey franchise," Pollin said. "My new investors and I are trying to, in effect, bring a new hockey team to Prince George's County.... With passage today of CB-143-1982, my investors and I will consider all four conditions as having been met. A favorable vote today will result in the Washington Capitals taking the ice against the Philadelphia Flyers on October 9 at our regularly scheduled home game."

The council soon voted 10-to-1 in favor of the tax break. The Capitals were staying put.

"I'm pleased, very pleased," Pollin said. "This has been my most difficult month as a sports franchise owner."

A difficult chapter in Capitals history had passed, but nobody could have predicted at that time the sudden turn the franchise would soon take on the ice.

Patrick came on board as an investor, but, by design given his hockey background, was soon involved in the Capitals' hockey operations. Patrick's grandfather, Lester Patrick, was the longtime head coach and general manager of the New York Rangers, and his father, Muzz, played for the 1940 Stanley Cup champion Rangers.

"Looking back, it's amazing that it ever happened," Dick Patrick said in 2017. "I wasn't involved with the Caps previously. I didn't know Abe Pollin, really. I knew that they had played eight years and I knew that they had never made the playoffs.

"I think Abe had just enough with hockey and the people he was working with. So, he asked me to be executive vice president and have the hockey people report to me. I thought that was great. Today, I don't think that would ever happen. He barely knew me. His franchises were so valuable, and it took so many people to run them. So, he said, 'Why don't you get a new general manager?' So, I was basically given the green light."

Within a week, Patrick hired Calgary Flames assistant general manager David Poile as the Capitals' new GM. Ten days later, Poile completed the biggest trade in franchise history, acquiring Rod

Langway, Brian Engblom, Doug Jarvis, and Craig Laughlin from the Montreal Canadiens for Rick Green and Ryan Walter.

The deal went a long way in changing the identity of a team that would reach the Stanley Cup Playoffs in each of the next 14 seasons.

There was a regular season Patrick Division title in 1989 and a maiden trip to the Wales Conference Final one year later. In 1998, months after an in-season move to the MCI Center in downtown Washington, D.C., the Capitals reached the Stanley Cup Final for the first time in team history.

And by the start of the 2005–06 season, the player who would emerge as the greatest in franchise history was on board in the form of Alex Ovechkin.

As the memories and success stories, many of which you will read about in this book, continue to pile, it is worth remembering that if not for a successful *Save the Caps* campaign in 1982, it's possible that they might not have happened at all.

2 Ovechkin Debuts

There's a scene in the movie *Slap Shot* where Charlestown Chiefs captain Johnny Upton is introduced to his new teammates, the Hanson brothers.

"They're fucking horrible looking!" Upton says of the goofy-looking trio with their thick glasses and long hair.

The scene played out in Jeff Halpern's head when he first met prospect Alex Ovechkin in August 2005. Halpern was one of several Capitals players skating in Laurel, Maryland, that summer in the weeks leading up to training camp.

"I remember the first time he shows up, he was wearing cut-off Daisy Duke jean shorts that would have been too short on a girl," Halpern said. "And he had these monstrous, Incredible Hulk legs sticking out of them. His shirt was too tight, he was wearing flip flops, and it didn't look like he fit into his clothes.

"And with all the billing of this guy being the savior of our franchise, I'm looking at him thinking, 'Seriously? This is the guy? He's going to carry us?'"

His English was raw and his fashion sense limited, but Ovechkin quickly showed that he could play. He impressed at training camp and capped off the preseason with five goals in the final two games.

"It wasn't just that he was scoring in the preseason games," said general manager George McPhee, "but the goals were coming easily for him. We just thought, even in the preseason, he was scoring some big goals—like real goal-scorer's goals. We thought, 'Boy, this guy sure looks like a special player.'"

After netting a hat trick in the preseason finale against the Pittsburgh Penguins, Capitals fans eagerly anticipated Ovechkin's regular season debut.

The Capitals returned to the MCI Center on October 5, 2005, for their first regular season game in 550 days after a lockout wiped out the entire 2004–05 campaign. There was a curiosity factor coming into the season with the NHL implementing a series of rule changes to help boost scoring, plus so many fresh faces with new teams.

Nine players were making their Capitals debuts on opening night, but with no offense to incoming veterans Matt Bradley, Andrew Cassels, or Chris Clark, the 16,325 fans in attendance were mostly there to witness the most-talked-about NHL debut in team history.

"Capitals fans were buzzing about Alex Ovechkin on their way to the rink that night," said CSN Mid-Atlantic play-by-play voice

Joe Beninati. "Hockey fans were thinking about it because they had drafted Ovechkin in the summer of 2004 and the whole time, you had this great new toy that you wanted to try, but that you'd been told you had to wait to play [with]."

But once the puck dropped on the 2005–06 season, fans didn't have to wait long to see what all the fuss was about. Skating on a line with Halpern and Dainius Zubrus, Ovechkin was in the starting lineup against the Columbus Blue Jackets and created a lasting memory on his first career shift.

As Columbus defenseman Radoslav Suchy went into his own zone to retrieve the puck, Ovechkin skated past veteran Adam Foote, who was playing in his 800th career game, and crushed an unsuspecting Suchy into the end boards. Forty seconds into his NHL career, Ovechkin delivered a thunderous hit that was so hard it dislodged the stanchion between two pieces of Plexiglas. The game was delayed for a few minutes as repairs were applied, but the crowd helped pass the time with a standing ovation.

"That first game stands out," Zubrus said. "I remember, here we are all thinking that he's a goal-scoring guy who can put up a lot of points, and obviously, he was, but then on that first shift he runs the guy through the glass and we just looked at each other, like, 'Oh wow. What do we have here?'"

Halpern admits that he had his concerns going into opening night, not only because of the off-ice culture shock Ovechkin was dealing with but also because of how he carried himself on the ice. The opener against Columbus was less than a week after Ovechkin scored twice in a preseason game against the Philadelphia Flyers and riled them up in the process.

"He scored a goal and he skated by their bench and winked," Halpern said. "And Philly had a really tough team at the time. So, we felt he was clueless. I guess he didn't realize how excited he was to score goals at the time, but we were just hoping not to get killed after that. So, going into opening night, I thought he was a good player, but you wanted to know that he could [fend for himself]."

The first hit of his career, which came at the end of a hard 40-second shift, quieted some of those initial concerns.

"He just exploded from that first shift," Halpern said. "Physically, you don't expect a rookie to come in like that. And not only did he steamroll everyone he faced that year, but anyone that tried to hit him would get knocked down. Real strong, sturdy guys would try to run him, and he'd just knock them down. That first game, he laid out the Columbus defenseman right off the bat and just how easily the goals came to him was impressive. It was like, 'Wow, this guy can do everything.'"

In the second period, Ovechkin opened his personal scoring account, netting the Capitals' first goal of the season. Twenty-three seconds after Columbus took a 1–0 lead, Ovechkin was parked in the high slot when he blasted a one-timer from Zubrus and beat Columbus rookie Pascal Leclaire for his first career NHL goal.

Less than five minutes later, Ovechkin scored on the power play with Halpern feeding him from in close for the quick finish. Ovechkin became the first player in Capitals history to score twice in his NHL debut. He was also the first No. 1 pick with two goals in his first career game.

"That's how the whole season was," said Zubrus, who scored the game-winning goal in an eventual 3–2 Capitals win. "He surprised everybody. We knew that he was good, but I don't know that we all knew how much of a game-changer he was going to be."

Forward Brian Willsie, who played all 82 games during the 2005–06 season, also remembers the first game against Columbus setting the tone for Ovechkin's memorable rookie year.

"He was ultra-competitive all the time," said Willsie, "and he was always going 100 miles per hour. And then during the first game, it's like, 'Oh, wow.' He's finishing every check, putting guys through the wall, and you're asking, 'Can he really keep this up all year? Can he score goals at this rate? Can he hit guys at this rate?' And he did. He had no trouble keeping up at that pace, and it was amazing to be a part of it and watch him grow."

3 NHL Comes to Washington

Abe Pollin had never seen an NHL game before. And yet, here was the Washington businessman drumming up support from U.S. Senators and House representatives in the early 1970s to bring an NHL franchise to the nation's capital.

Pollin already owned the NBA's Baltimore Bullets and wanted to move the team closer to Washington. Having made his fortune in construction, Pollin planned to build a new arena in Landover, Maryland, about 10 miles from D.C.

The Bullets would fill some dates, but the owner needed another tenant. Bringing pro hockey to an area that hadn't even housed a minor league team in more than a decade was suddenly very appealing.

Enter the expansion-happy NHL, which ballooned from six teams in 1967 to 16 by 1972.

On June 9, 1972, the NHL added two more clubs with expansion bids from Washington and Kansas City beating out such markets as Cleveland, Indianapolis, Phoenix, and San Juan.

The Washington team was later nicknamed the Capitals, a decision made by Pollin after he vetoed the original results from a name-the-team contest. The most popular choice among more than 12,000 votes was Comets, but Pollin preferred Capitals. Other names under consideration included Cyclones, Domes, and

Pandas. Imagine for a moment if the Capitals-Penguins rivalry had instead been a battle of Pandas and Penguins.

Pollin paid the $6 million expansion fee, saw the Capital Centre go up in 15 months, and watched from afar as the Capitals took shape before their inaugural season in 1974–75. Perhaps he would have been better off not watching them at all.

To put it mildly, the expansion Capitals had a rough time. More than 40 years later, their 1974–75 season remains the worst in NHL history.

Washington won eight times in 80 tries. Their 8–67–5 record produced 21 points—the fewest by a team that played at least 70 games.

They lost four games by double digits and allowed 10 or more goals seven times.

"The losing just snowballed," said defenseman Yvon Labre, whom the Capitals selected from Pittsburgh in the 1974 expansion draft. "It was very difficult."

The Capitals set futility records across the board. No team has had a lower points percentage (.131), allowed more goals (446), or had a worse goal differential (-265). Along the way, they set new league benchmarks with a 17-game losing streak and a 37-game *road* losing streak.

They are the only NHL team to have been shut out (12 times) more often than they won (8 times). They're also the only team to have had more coaches (3) than road wins (1).

"That first year was something else," forward Mike Marson said in 2016. "Some nights you wondered, 'Do we even have a chance to keep the game competitive?' Every game was a tremendous challenge."

The Capitals' original lineup was a collection of castoffs, minor league journeymen, and not-yet-ready-for-prime-time prospects.

Pollin hired Hall of Famer Milt Schmidt as the Capitals' first general manager. Schmidt came recommended from Pollin's longtime friend Red Auerbach, the architect of the Boston Celtics' NBA dynasty in the 1960s. Schmidt spent 38 years with the Boston Bruins as a player, coach, and GM.

"Why inherit someone else's problems when I can start something for myself?" Schmidt told reporters at his introductory press conference.

In due time, Schmidt had plenty of his own problems, starting with the roster he built through the expansion draft.

"Mr. Pollin paid $6 million for the franchise and there wasn't one major league player made available," he told the *Washington Post* in 1983.

Schmidt was tasked with building a team that could contend within three years. Given the available lot of players, it was like asking an interior decorator to furnish a chic home with materials from a yard sale.

"There wasn't any kind of nucleus," he said. "If you had four or five guys as a nucleus, it wouldn't be so bad, but the players we got originally, nobody wanted them."

Expansion drafts were held in 1970 for Buffalo and Vancouver and in 1972 for Atlanta and Long Island. Established clubs complained that they were losing too many talented players to the new teams. So the rules were changed ahead of the 1974 expansion draft for Washington and Kansas City.

Teams were now allowed to protect up to 16 players, leaving the Capitals and Scouts to choose from the scraps of the talent pool. Throw in the rival World Hockey Association trying to fill rosters and the challenge for Washington's thin scouting department was made even tougher.

On June 12, 1974, Schmidt tried his best. He chose 24 players from the 16 existing NHL clubs, including goaltenders Ron Low of the Toronto Maple Leafs and Michel Belhumeur of the Philadelphia Flyers.

Belhumeur went 0–24–3 in 35 appearances with the first-year Capitals, setting an NHL record for most games played without a win.

The 22 skaters the Capitals selected had combined for 40 career NHL goals.

"We just told ourselves we're in the NHL," said forward Gordie Smith, a former Rangers prospect, who spent four years in the minors before making his NHL debut with the expansion Capitals.

"A lot of us were just happy that we had a chance to play. Was everyone good enough to be there? Probably not."

The Capitals survived the preseason, highlighted by a 4–4 tie with the Montreal Canadiens and a pair of wins over Kansas City.

"I remember my awareness of everything being so brand-new," said Marson, Washington's 19-year-old rookie forward. "There was a feeling of excitement, everyone was looking forward to a great campaign and to a team that could be a winner. It was very exciting."

After opening with back-to-back losses in New York and Minnesota, the Capitals made their home debut on October 15, 1974. A crowd of 8,093 gathered at the Capital Centre, where the Capitals tied the Los Angeles Kings 1–1. Labre beat future Hall of Famer Rogie Vachon for Washington's first goal at home.

Two nights later, the Capitals earned their first win, beating the Chicago Black Hawks 4–3 before 9,471 fans in Landover. Denis Dupere scored twice, Jack Eagers scored the first game-winning goal, and Low made 33 saves.

"I remember thinking to myself, 'You know, maybe we're not so bad,'" Marson said.

Think again. Over the next 26 games, the Capitals won once. As many pundits had predicted, the expansion Capitals were a miserable bunch.

"I started the year in Pittsburgh," recalled forward Ron Lalonde, "and I remember, maybe 20 games into the season, we were at the

Caps Centre and I'm sitting on the bench on the Pittsburgh side and I'm looking over and seeing my good friend Yvon Labre. We beat them 6–0, and I remember looking over and thinking 'Geez, I feel sorry for Yvon. It's going to be a long year.' Then two weeks later, the Penguins traded me to Washington, so I got to experience it firsthand!"

By mid-February, Washington's first head coach, Jimmy Anderson, was fired with a 4–45–5 record. Head scout Red Sullivan took over behind the bench, which longtime Capitals beat reporter Robert Fachet of the *Washington Post* found appropriate.

"It is perhaps fitting that the weight fell on Sullivan," Fachet wrote. "As chief scout, his recommendations weighed heavily in the draft selections. This can be interpreted as his punishment."

Sullivan went 2–16–0 as head coach and lasted just 40 days before Schmidt took over.

"My stomach just couldn't stand it," Sullivan said at the time. "The old stomach was all buggered up. I wasn't eating and sleeping properly, and at my age, that isn't good."

The Capitals lost 5–0 to Atlanta in Schmidt's coaching debut, after which he called the season "the biggest embarrassment of my life."

"I have been sitting upstairs cursing all year," he said. "And since I'm the reason things are the way they are, I had to go down to the bench and try to do something about it."

Schmidt was behind the bench for Washington's first and only road win of the season—a 5–3 triumph over the California Seals in Oakland. The Capitals celebrated by parading a trash can around the ice as if it was the Stanley Cup. For many of the players, it's as close as they'd get.

Veteran Tommy Williams led the original team in scoring with 22 goals and 58 points. He also had a minus-69 rating, the second worst in NHL history behind Capitals teammate Bill Mikkelson. Mikkelson, a defenseman, had a minus-82 rating in 59 games.

"They were tough times," Labre said. "I always thought we could have won more games. But the same way winning builds confidence, once you lose so many games, the guys get down and it was impossible to recover."

4 Juneau Sends Capitals to 1998 Stanley Cup

It wasn't aesthetically pleasing, but for a franchise that waited 24 years to play for the Stanley Cup, style points didn't matter.

So, when Joe Juneau finished off a goalmouth scramble by jamming a rebound past Buffalo's Dominik Hasek in Game 6 of the 1998 Eastern Conference Final, the celebration was on. Juneau's overtime winner, 6:24 into the extra session, sealed a 3–2 victory and secured the Capitals' first conference title.

The team that couldn't get out of its own way during its first eight seasons, and later developed a reputation as playoff underachievers, had earned the right to compete for the most famous trophy in sports.

"You don't believe it at first," goaltender Olie Kolzig recalled in 2016. "You're waiting for something to happen—maybe for the goal to be overturned—but then it hits you and you're thinking, 'We're going to the Stanley Cup Finals. We're going to the Stanley Cup Finals.' That's all I could think of. It was crazy."

There is no denying that the 1997–98 Capitals surprised many on their way to the NHL's biggest stage. They entered the playoffs as the No. 4 seed in the Eastern Conference, a year removed from missing the postseason altogether. But when the top three seeds— New Jersey, Pittsburgh, and Philadelphia—were all upset in the first round, the Capitals suddenly found themselves as the top team in the East.

"A lot of times the playoffs are about getting the right matchups," said general manager George McPhee. "Maybe a few things fell into place for us that spring, but we had a good veteran team, we got a break in the first series [with a disallowed go for the Boston Bruins in an eventual Capitals win] and we had outstanding goaltending."

After knocking off the Bruins in six games in Round 1, the Capitals made quick work of the No. 8 Ottawa Senators in five games in Round 2.

The Senators outshot the Capitals in all five games, but Kolzig was the difference. He allowed a total of three goals in Washington's four wins and stopped all 65 shots he faced in earning back-to-back shutouts in Games 4 and 5 to close out the series.

"That series I was probably more in the zone than at any point in my career," he said. "It's weird how that works as an athlete—you wish you could be in that zone all the time. But those two weeks, I was as locked in as ever. I remember [Game 4] in Ottawa, we were outshot 36–11 and we won 2–0. Playing playoff games in Canada, it's hockey central up there, maybe just being in that atmosphere helped. But it was great. I just felt right."

The Capitals would need more of the same from Kolzig if they had any chance of beating Hasek and the Sabres in the conference final. "The Dominator" was arguably the best goaltender in the world in 1998, fresh off an Olympic gold medal in Nagano and on his way to becoming the first goalie in NHL history to win the Hart Trophy in consecutive seasons as league MVP.

"Hasek was in his prime," McPhee said. "But Olie had a better series."

"You can't say enough about Olie Kolzig when you talk about that run," said forward Kelly Miller. "More than anything, Olie was just outstanding. We really fed off of him, he gave us a lot of confidence and he covered a lot of our warts. To have a goaltender playing as well as Olie played in those games was probably more than anything what got us to the finals."

Kolzig had a 30-save shutout in Game 4 in Buffalo as the Capitals beat the Sabres 2–0 to take a 3–1 series lead. It was Kolzig's team-record fourth shutout of the playoffs.

The Capitals couldn't close out the series on home ice—the Sabres won Game 5 at MCI Center 2–1—so the teams returned to Marine Midland Arena for Game 6. The Capitals rallied from 1–0 and 2–1 deficits to force overtime.

Just over six minutes into OT, Sabres defenseman Darryl Shannon turned the puck over to Juneau at the Buffalo blue line. Juneau then fed linemate Brian Bellows as he was entering the zone with speed.

"I remember getting the puck and just driving wide," Bellows said in explaining his strategy to beat Hasek. "My thinking is, I'm basically going to try to get a couple of guys into the net. I knew I wasn't going to score. So, the thought becomes, 'Just take it to the net.' You're hoping to cause a commotion or some chaos and maybe the puck will just be laying there. And that's what happened. Joey came in and Dominik was down on the play and that's how he scores."

Bellows did in fact drive to the net and had three chances to beat Hasek from in close. Hasek stopped them all, but along the way he fell to the ground, sprawled out trying to retrieve the loose puck. With the puck just out of Hasek's reach, Juneau was able to bang in the winning goal.

"That brings back some great memories," Juneau said. "That goal was one great moment, but we had a lot of special nights. It was a wonderful time, the whole spring of '98. The run we had for the Cup that spring, it was amazing. It was great team that just gelled and had a good push."

Juneau played 12 seasons in the NHL and never had more than three game-winning goals in a single campaign. His overtime goal in Buffalo was his fourth game-winner in the 1998 playoffs.

"It all came together at the time right time," he said. "That's what happens when you reach the finals."

The moment was especially gratifying for those who waited the longest. The club's original owner, Abe Pollin, did not attend Game 6 in person, but received a congratulatory phone call from McPhee outside the Capitals dressing room.

Pollin then asked McPhee to put Dale Hunter on the phone so the owner could congratulate his captain. Hunter was 37 and in

Defenseman Brendan Witt (left) and forward Craig Berube (right) skate with the Prince of Wales Trophy after the Capitals beat the Buffalo Sabres in the 1998 Eastern Conference Final on June 4, 1998. The Capitals eliminated the Sabres in six games to advance to the Stanley Cup Final.

his 18th NHL season. After 1,345 career games (and 163 more in the playoffs), Hunter had reached the Stanley Cup Finals for the first time.

"It's a big thrill because it's a long time coming," he told reporters. "In 18 years, I've been to the conference finals three times and [lost] all three times. Now, to be in this situation—to be playing in June like this—is unbelievable."

At the time, nobody had played more games in a Capitals sweater than Miller, who had been acquired more than 11 years earlier and was also moving on to the Stanley Cup Finals for the first time in his NHL career.

"Those are great memories and it was just a joy to be a part of it all," said Miller, who would retire one year later. "For me, it was kind of a nice way to put a semi ending to a really nice career in Washington. Such great memories along the way and to have the chance to play for the Stanley Cup at the end was a nice thing."

As part of the postgame celebrations, Hunter accepted the Prince of Wales Trophy awarded to the Eastern Conference champions. The Capitals paraded the trophy around the ice and later posed for pictures with it in the dressing room. Since the turn of the century, some teams have refused to touch the conference championship trophy, suggesting it will jinx their chances at winning the big prize.

"We let loose," Kolzig said. "We didn't even think about that. We looked at it like, 'We have to beat one more team.' For some teams, some individuals, that bothers them, but not us. I mean, hey, it was the first time in franchise history. It was great when Dale got presented the trophy—all the guys were so pumped for him."

Hunter made a toast on the team's charter flight back to Baltimore and word began to spread that thousands of fans were waiting to greet them at the Piney Orchard Ice Rink.

"I remember that night like it was yesterday," said coach Ron Wilson. "We came back and the place was packed. They actually opened the building and when we arrived back from the airport at two in the morning, about two miles from Piney Orchard, fans and cars were everywhere lining the streets. We realized at that point how special it was."

"The day after we won the third round was one of the happiest days of my life," said team president and minority owner Dick Patrick. "It was like euphoria. [That] day, I felt for sure that we were going to win the Stanley Cup."

The Capitals ultimately fell to the Detroit Red Wings, swept in four games, as Detroit repeated as Stanley Cup champions. The first three games of the series were all decided by one goal.

"Looking back, I still think that we had a good enough team to win," said Bellows, a Stanley Cup champion with Montreal in 1993. "Detroit had the advantage of being there before. If we had been there before, the same team, I think it eases the nerves and makes a real difference in how you play."

Still, the experience of reaching the Stanley Cup Final remains a fond memory and one of the greatest achievements in team history.

"It was fun for me," Miller said, "after all the years of [general manager David] Poile essentially trying to get to the Stanley Cup Final, to finally see some of the pieces come together and to at least get to the final dance. It certainly wasn't the outcome that we wanted, but it felt good to at least get to that final stage and give ourselves a chance to win the Stanley Cup."

5 Poile's Bold Move

Capitals owner Abe Pollin made a bold move in 1982 when he hired a 32-year-old first-time general manager. Ten days later, David Poile made a bold move of his own, completing a blockbuster trade that would forever change the course of the franchise.

In a six-player deal, Poile acquired Rod Langway, Brian Engblom, Craig Laughlin, and Doug Jarvis from the Montreal Canadiens for Rick Green and Ryan Walter.

The trade wasn't necessarily on Poile's to-do list so soon after he was hired, but barely a week on the job, Poile was seated next to Canadiens GM Irving Grundman at the 1982 Board of Governors meetings in Toronto.

"By chance, or by fate maybe, we were next to each other," Poile said three decades later. "But that got us talking."

Grundman had plenty to say. Few players back then would not have wanted to play in Montreal, but Langway was an exception and had asked to be moved.

"When a player tells you that he doesn't want to play for you, that's not the way you build a team," Grundman said. "The Montreal Canadiens weren't built by keeping players that didn't want to play for them."

Langway was turned off by Quebec's high taxes and wanted to play for a team based in the United States.

"The Canadiens had built a reputation and an atmosphere in the dressing room that speaks for itself," Grundman said. "So, when a player tells you outright that there's no way he's going to play for you, what are you supposed to do? You can't put handcuffs on him and say, 'No, you're playing here.' So, I made the trade and I thought the trade was good for both teams."

The quartet of former Canadiens had a combined seven Stanley Cup rings between them, but they were largely viewed as complementary pieces in Montreal behind future Hall of Famers Guy LaFleur, Bob Gainey, Larry Robinson, Guy Lapointe, and Serge Savard.

In Washington, both Green and Walter had been highly touted prospects—Green the first overall pick in the 1976 draft, Walter the No. 2 overall pick in 1978.

"Ryan Walter was the heart and soul of the Washington Capitals," said Bob Gould, who played 600 games with the Capitals in the 1980s.

By the start of the 1979–80 season, a 21-year-old Walter had become the youngest captain in NHL history. During his four years with the Capitals, only Dennis Maruk scored more often.

"I can still remember to this day being up in Toronto when I made the trade and calling Mr. Pollin," Poile said.

"I told him I have a trade—and again this is only 10 days after taking the job—and he says, 'Okay, what is it?' So, I said, 'We've traded Ryan Walter'—who at the time was Mr. Pollin's favorite player—and I remember he yelled back on the phone, 'You did what?!' So, I told him again and after I got Ryan Walter's name out of my mouth, he just said, 'Well, you better know what you're doing.'"

Poile still remembers the uneasy feeling he had pacing in his room at Toronto's Royal York Hotel soon after hanging up with Pollin. He mumbled to himself and eventually shouted out the words Pollin had relayed to him a few minutes earlier: "You better know what you're doing!"

More than 35 years later, it is clear that Poile knew something. The 1982 trade with the Canadiens is arguably the biggest in Capitals history, and it is widely viewed as a move that went a long way in changing the perception of, and the culture around, the organization.

"We got to Washington and all over the newspapers it was all about the 'Save the Caps' campaign," said Laughlin, now a Capitals television analyst with CSN Mid-Atlantic.

"So, we go from an established and elite team in the Canadiens that are right up there with the New York Yankees and are looked at as one of the premiere franchises in all of sports, and we go from there to a team that has very little recognition. With Montreal, we were the center of attention. Then we land in Washington, and it was like, 'Who are these knuckleheads with their sticks?'"

After eight years in the NHL, the Capitals were still searching for their first winning season and filling the Capital Centre in Landover, Maryland, was an ongoing challenge.

Over those same eight seasons, the Canadiens were the model of consistency, winning eight consecutive division titles and raising the Stanley Cup four times. The Canadiens routinely filled the Montreal Forum and in 43 lifetime meetings against the Capitals, Montreal lost just three games. A better example of two polar opposites in the NHL could not be found.

"I remember getting on the plane with our equipment and then heading to Hershey [for Capitals training camp]," Langway recalled, "and that's when we got the scoop on the 'Save the Caps' campaign and how players like Dennis Maruk were selling season tickets. We got on the phone with our agents and said, 'Are we sure that we want to be here? This is going to be some transition.'"

Soon after joining the Capitals, Langway heard that he might be on the move again, possibly headed to the Boston Bruins. He confronted Poile and was assured that he wasn't going anywhere. Instead, he was told, he and his Capitals teammates were going to be part of a tremendous turnaround in Washington.

The message to all the newcomers was clear from Poile and head coach Bryan Murray: anything less than a playoff berth in 1983 was unacceptable.

"It can't be underestimated how much Bryan Murray and David Poile believed in us," Laughlin said. "We wanted to prove everyone wrong."

"They worked hard at creating a winning culture," Engblom said of Murray and Poile. "The playoffs were a big thing."

Before the 1982–83 season started, Langway was chosen to replace Walter as team captain. The "Secretary of Defense," as he would become known in Washington, would wear the "C" for 11 seasons with the Capitals.

"I truly believe that when he stepped in and took over the leadership of that hockey club," Gould said, "and established the work ethic and the team workmanship and so forth, that was to me the turning point where that organization started to become for real."

Langway established himself as a leader both on and off the ice, becoming the first Capitals player to earn an individual NHL award when he won the Norris Trophy in 1982–83 and 1983–84. He remains the only Washington blue-liner to be named the league's top defenseman.

"Langway was a good player; nobody can say that he wasn't," Grundman said. "But was he Bobby Orr? No, he wasn't Bobby Orr. Maybe it wasn't the best deal in the world [for Montreal], maybe we felt the players we traded for had more potential than they showed, but we felt we were getting equal value in return."

Poile saw tremendous value in Langway and Engblom, who he believed slipped under the radar with the Canadiens.

"I think we were lucky that Montreal had the 'Big Three' on defense in Larry Robinson, Serge Savard, and Guy Lapointe," Poile said. "Langway and Engblom played behind three Hall of Famers and maybe didn't get the recognition they deserved. Those are the deals you love to make. Langway wasn't totally happy with his situation [in Montreal] so it was the perfect time to make a deal."

In addition to the four newcomers from Montreal, the Capitals roster also included a rookie defenseman named Scott Stevens and a 24-year-old speedster in Mike Gartner. The pieces were slowly coming together for a team on the rise.

Washington went 39–25–16 in 1982–83 for its first winning record and their first of 14 consecutive postseason appearances. Only the Capitals, Bruins, Chicago Blackhawks, and St. Louis Blues qualified for the playoffs every year from 1983 through 1996.

"We made a run of it and we had fun," Langway said. "We didn't want superstars. We wanted guys that came to play every night. For Craig and [me] and Brian Engblom and Doug Jarvis, we weren't superstars in Montreal, but we were part of the organization and we saw the way in Montreal they taught and stressed team play."

By the 1983–84 season, the Capitals emerged as legitimate contenders in the Patrick Division, finishing in second place for the first time and earning their first series win in the Stanley Cup Playoffs.

From 1982 through 1989, only the Edmonton Oilers and Philadelphia Flyers won more regular season games than the Capitals, who also established a franchise record with a 10-game winning streak in 1984 that would stand for a quarter century. Other milestones followed, including the club's first 50-win season in 1985–86 and a Patrick Division title in 1989.

"By the end of the 80s, only Langway remained [from the Montreal deal]," Poile said, "but the players we acquired and the experiences they brought with them helped give us an identity."

"We were all experienced players," said Jarvis, who spent parts of four seasons in Washington. "We had been through the playoff battles working our way to the Stanley Cups in Montreal. So, as your career moves on, that's part of being a player—that you have experiences that you can share with others and make a positive impact with a new group."

Laughlin only played 36 games with the Canadiens as a rookie before being traded to Washington, but he also recognized the differences in how the clubs operated in the early 1980s.

"People underestimate sometimes that there is a foundation set in these iconic franchises that they do things that are maybe different from franchises that lose," he said. "It was a totally different culture in Washington, but we embraced it and built something."

The Capitals retired Langway's number in 1997 at the final game at the Capital Centre—a 6–5 loss against Montreal—and he was inducted into the Hockey Hall of Fame in 2003. He remains a team ambassador and represents the team at community and charitable events.

Laughlin made the Washington area his permanent residence, purchasing a home in Annapolis, Maryland, soon after joining the Capitals in 1982 and returning to the region once his NHL playing career wound down in the late 1980s.

"I elected in '82 that is was where we were going to stay," he said. "I didn't want to move from this area, so it's been a real blessed thing that I've been able to hang around the Capitals and watch them grow."

In addition to Langway twice winning the Norris Trophy, Jarvis won the Frank Selke Trophy as the league's best defensive forward in 1983–84. He is now an assistant coach with the Vancouver Canucks.

"He was a winner," Poile said of the NHL's iron man, who played in 964 consecutive games from 1975 through 1987. "He could win key faceoffs, he killed penalties, and he could be trusted late in games. He did the little things that you need on a winning team."

Of the six players involved in the trade, only Engblom spent fewer than four seasons with his new team.

"It was a good first step and it was the start of a successful era in Washington," said Engblom, who was traded to the Los Angeles

Kings early in the 1983–84 for future Hall of Fame defenseman Larry Murphy.

"It was so different from Montreal where every move you made was dissected. In Washington, we started at the bottom of the ladder. But we built something, the fans rallied behind us and without that success who knows what would have happened with the franchise?"

In Montreal, Green and Walter became key cogs with the Canadiens, winning the Stanley Cup in 1986 against the Calgary Flames before falling in the rematch in 1989.

After spending the first six years of his NHL career with struggling clubs in Washington, Green embraced the chance to play in Montreal.

"I paid my dues, so to speak, with the growing years with the Capitals," Green said. "Then you go from a team that really struggled for quite a few years to one of the best franchises in all of pro sports, it's a real jolt for the career. Ryan and I were given a chance to step into a really special environment in Montreal."

While Green welcomed the change, Walter was at first shaken up by the news. Coming off the best season of his career in 1981–82 with 38 goals and 87 points in 80 games, Walter believed he was going to be part of the Capitals' eventual turnaround. Just months before the trade, Walter and his wife, Jennifer, had purchased a suburban home they were looking forward to settling into longterm.

"I would have loved to stay in Washington for my whole career," said Walter, who went to play more than 1,000 NHL games with the Capitals, Canadiens, and Canucks.

"When David told me that I had been traded, he called at 7:00 AM, and soon after the call I was still digesting the news, still feeling upset when I got a call from Abe Pollin. And he said, 'Ryan, I feel bad about this, but it's the direction our organization has to go in and I'm going to support it.'"

Pollin and Walter had a special bond; a picture of the captain was hanging in the owner's office.

"I'm so thankful to have spent my nine seasons in Montreal and to win a cup and always be in the playoffs," Walter said, "but I had a special spot in my heart, not only for Abe Pollin, but for the entire Washington organization. How many times in a player's career do you get a call from an owner after you've been traded? That never happens. So, it was a special thing and I really honor Abe. It was a pleasure working for him."

Poile would remain in Washington for 15 years, before taking the same position with the expansion Nashville Predators in 1997. He is the only executive in NHL history to serve as GM of two teams for at least 1,000 games each.

While the 1982 trade with the Canadiens was the first of Poile's career, it was among the last for Grundman, who was replaced in Montreal within months of the deal. Grundman eventually moved into municipal politics and has not worked in hockey since.

"I think making a trade of that magnitude certainly was a great building block for me in gaining Abe's trust," Poile said. "I was able to show him that even though I was young that I did in fact know what I was doing."

That Was Classic

On a sunny afternoon in July 2010, NHL Commissioner Gary Bettman and select members of the Capitals and Penguins stood on the 50-yard line at Pittsburgh's Heinz Field and imagined the possibilities.

They imagined taking one of the game's best rivalries outdoors and playing before more than 65,000 fans. They imagined two of the game's biggest stars, Alex Ovechkin and Sidney Crosby, meeting in the NHL's marquee midseason event—the Winter Classic on New Year's Day.

Amid all the positivity, though, Capitals team president and minority owner Dick Patrick had his doubts.

"I remember looking up at the far reaches of the stadium and thinking to myself, 'Who the hell is going to come out here to watch hockey if it's freezing?'" he said in 2017. "I was skeptical."

Patrick went to Pittsburgh thinking of everything that could go wrong. Warm temperatures and a rainy forecast on January 1 didn't ease those concerns as the game was delayed from a 1:00 PM start to 8:00 PM.

"You can build it up and hype it up, but you want to make sure you can actually play it," he remembers thinking.

Hours later, Patrick and the entire Capitals organization breathed easy. Not only was the game played under the lights in prime time, but the Capitals beat the Penguins 3–1 in one of the more memorable regular season games in franchise history.

It may have just been Game 40 of the 2010–11 campaign, a game worth the same two points as any of the first 39, but this one had the feel of something bigger.

"It was comparable, not to winning a championship, but it was something close," forward Jay Beagle recalled in 2015. "It's a huge game, so when you get the job done, it's almost a relief. Just a collective sigh of relief thinking, 'We did it.'"

From the weeks of buildup and hype—which included HBO's four-part *24/7* series—to the game-day tailgating, to the police escort the Capitals received for their ride to Heinz Field, to the elaborate pregame introductions, there was no mistaking that the game carried a big-production feel.

"It's a special moment when you think of where you came from and the stage you're about to play on," said Brooks Laich, who years earlier played in a half-empty MCI Center as the Capitals began to rebuild.

On this night, the Capitals and Penguins played before a standing-room-only crowd of 68,111 fans at Heinz Field. The Capitals quickly sold out their allotment of 20,000 tickets, with Capitals fans purchasing more tickets on the secondary market.

They yelled "Red" and "O" during the singing of "The Star-Spangled Banner," as had become tradition at home games in Washington.

"From a personal standpoint, it may be the most fun I ever had as a manager and maybe the most fun I ever had in my hockey life," said general manager George McPhee. "It was just a fabulous experience. It was a *Field of Dreams* thing—build it and they will come. You show up to this massive stadium, 70,000 people are there and 30,000 of them are from Washington. That was extraordinary."

"It was one of the best experiences of my life," said Ovechkin, who took a game-high six shots on goal but didn't register a point. "When you see it's sold out, it's like, I can't imagine when football players play every game like this. It's unbelievable and it's the kind of thing you want to do all the time."

The playing conditions may have been suboptimal as a light rain came down in Pittsburgh, but the atmosphere was terrific.

"It was pretty cool," said head coach Bruce Boudreau. "When you walk out and see those people out there, whether they're booing or cheering, it's an experience I'll never forget.... It was more than just a game to everybody. Don't let anybody fool you."

Among the highlights from a scoreless first period was the first fight at a Winter Classic. Washington's John Erskine and Pittsburgh's Mike Rupp dropped the gloves early, proving that no matter the setting, the Capitals and Penguins didn't much care for each other.

Evgeni Malkin opened the scoring for Pittsburgh in the second period, but the Capitals answered with a Mike Knuble power play tally from atop the crease. Eric Fehr then scored twice in one of the best games of his NHL career. Semyon Varlamov made 32 saves and was named the game's first star.

"There was about an inch of water on the ice, so you couldn't do anything with the puck," said defenseman Karl Alzner. "On the bench, we kind of knew we were going to win the game 3–1 because the play had become so poor that there probably wasn't going to be much offense. If you just managed the game, you could keep it 3–1 and we could ride it home. So halfway through the third, we kind of knew that we were going to win, which actually made it very enjoyable."

Soon after their postgame celebration on the ice, the Capitals gave their fans a stick salute from center ice.

"It felt like a seminal moment for this franchise," McPhee said. "I thought it was a special and unique night in many ways that put this team over the top in terms of popularity. It was a really neat thing to experience. It's neat that Washington had embraced this team."

The win was especially gratifying for the Capitals, who went through an eight-game losing streak in December—their first losing month in more than three years—with HBO's *24/7* production crew following their every move.

"For us, it was a monthlong build up where it didn't start very good at all," Boudreau said at the time. "But for us, this is as close to the Stanley Cup as we've gotten. We're not denying that it was more than just two points. It was a fabulous game. We came in wanting to win the thing."

"When I look back at it," forward Matt Hendricks recalled in 2016, "it was all the buildup that came along with the HBO *24/7*. The Penguins had been playing very well, we had been playing very poorly, we went on that big skid and we just couldn't seem to find ourselves. It was almost the story of two different teams finally coming together in a big game.

"Obviously, the weather wasn't perfect, the hockey wasn't perfect, the ice wasn't perfect, but it felt great to have a win and it felt like the perfect night and the perfect way to end that whole HBO ordeal."

Dale Hunter's OT Winner vs. Flyers

By the late 1980s the Capitals had emerged as a perennial Stanley Cup contender. From the 1982–83 season through 1987–88, only the Edmonton Oilers and Philadelphia Flyers had a better cumulative regular season record than Washington.

The Oilers won the Stanley Cup four times over that stretch, while the Flyers twice reached the Cup Final. The Capitals, though, were developing a reputation for their playoff shortcomings.

In 1985, Washington blew a 2–0 series lead in the best-of-five Patrick Division semifinal against the New York Islanders. One year later, the first 50-win team in Capitals history let a 2–1 second-round series lead slip away against the New York Rangers.

Nothing compared, though, to the 1987 collapse against the Islanders. With the NHL adopting a best-of-seven format for the divisional semifinals, the Capitals watched a 3–1 series lead evolve into a seven-game defeat. The season ended in devastating fashion with Washington losing Game 7 at home in *quadruple* overtime in a game that would become known as the Easter Epic. It was heartbreaking for the franchise and its increasingly suffering fan base.

"From my perspective, we seemed to be so unlucky in the playoffs," former general manager David Poile said in 2017. "So many things seemed to happen that didn't go our way and I think that was certainly beginning to wear on the franchise, the fans, and our ownership."

Players who had been through the prior playoff disappointments could also sense that these were golden opportunities missed.

"The playoffs are all about the timely goals or the timely saves, and we never seemed to get those," said former Capitals defenseman Larry Murphy. "We'd have good seasons, but when it mattered most, we couldn't find that somebody to step up to score that huge goal or make a big play that could make the difference."

That was the backdrop when Poile acquired Dale Hunter in a 1987 draft-day deal with the Quebec Nordiques.

A proven playoff performer in Quebec, Hunter was expected to provide leadership, grit, and timely goal scoring come springtime. He checked off all three boxes in his maiden postseason in Washington in 1988.

"That series was vintage Dale," said Kelly Miller, who played with Hunter for his entire 12-year tenure with the Capitals.

Facing the Flyers in the Patrick Division semifinals, the Capitals were actually on the verge of elimination after surrendering a 4–1 lead in an eventual 5–4 overtime loss in Game 4 in Philadelphia. The defeat left the Capitals staring at a 3–1 series deficit.

Washington, though, would rally with a 5–2 win in Game 5 at the Capital Centre and a 7–2 win in Game 6 at the Spectrum in Philadelphia.

That set the stage for another Game 7 in Landover, nearly a year to the day after the 1987 Easter Epic.

"The collective mentality was that we were going to find a way to win," said forward Greg Adams, "especially when we started coming back [in the series] and we won a game and then another game. Then it's Game 7 and it's like 'We're not going to be denied this time.'"

The Capitals may have been a confident bunch, but an uneasy feeling quickly set in as the Flyers built a 3–0 lead early in the second period. Making matters worse, the Capitals were down to just five defensemen after Grant Ledyard was ejected for spearing Philadelphia's Rick Tocchet in the first.

"To me," Poile said, "that whole season was just about getting back to the playoffs and to do better and to redeem ourselves. But then at that moment, it becomes a feeling of, 'Well, here we go again'—a seventh game, at home, and we're behind 3–0. 'Here we go again.'"

After the game captain Rod Langway conceded that he feared the worst.

"When it was 3–0, I thought we'd be blown out of the rink," he told the *Washington Post*. "Some guys were quiet, some were semi-scared. I'm sure some were semi-confident. You look at the young guys and you can't tell what they're thinking at a time like that. As a veteran, you know you're scared, but you try to look and act confident."

If Hunter was scared, he didn't play like it. He was the catalyst to the Capitals' comeback, beginning with the primary assist on a Garry Galley goal at 6:42 of the second period to pull Washington within two.

Hunter picked up speed in the neutral zone coming down the left wing, drew two defenders along the half-wall in the Flyers' zone, and then made a perfect cross-ice pass to the defenseman Galley, who was trailing the play. Galley then beat Ron Hextall as Bob Gould drove to the net to provide a screen.

Miller and Kevin Hatcher also scored in the second period, allowing the Capitals to tie the score at 3.

Hunter then gave Washington its first lead of the game with a power-play goal in the third, before Philadelphia defenseman Brad Marsh beat Pete Peeters just 1:02 later. The game remained tied at 4 through 60 minutes.

For the second consecutive year, the Capitals were heading to overtime in Game 7 on home ice.

"It weighs on you," Mike Gartner said in 2017 of the pressure to rewrite history. "You don't want it to, but it does become something that you think about more than you should. You should really just concentrate on the game and the series at hand, but it is there in the back of your mind—that idea of getting the monkey off your back."

Gartner had the best chance early in overtime, but hit the crossbar from in close.

"I thought 'Are you kidding me? Is this how it's going to end again? Missing it like that?'" he said.

Gartner hitting the crossbar in overtime could have been the lasting image of another premature playoff exit, but minutes later, Hunter would instead provide one of the greatest moments in team history.

After receiving a stretch pass from Murphy in the neutral zone, Hunter split two Flyers defensemen and found himself on a breakaway on Hextall. Hunter faked a shot, at which point Hextall provided just enough of an opening between his legs for Hunter to go five-hole for the series-clinching goal. The Capitals won 5–4 in overtime.

"Ron Hextall needed one more 10-bell save to keep this game alive," color analyst Bill Clement said on the ESPN broadcast.

"But on a breakaway right up the middle, the man that has the heart just about as big as this Capital Centre, Dale Hunter, puts it by Ron Hextall."

Less than a year after Hunter was acquired at the 1987 draft, he became the first player in Capitals history to score a series-clinching goal in overtime.

"That's when we won this series," head coach Bryan Murray said after the game. "The Dale Hunter trade we made at the draft table: that's what won it for us. We felt if we got in a tough, physical series with a team like the Flyers he'd really come through."

Hunter's childhood friend and Capitals teammate Bob Gould knew all along that Hunter was made for moments like this.

"I remember him hopping up and down the ice after he scored the goal," Gould said, "and I remember David Poile coming down to the dressing room afterward. David shook everyone's hand, and I said, 'That's exactly why you wanted Dale Hunter on your hockey club.' He's a clutch hockey player. I knew David knew the competitiveness that Dale had and that's exactly why they acquired him—he could score big goals."

Hunter had two goals and an assist in Game 7 and recorded his fourth career playoff overtime goal. At the time, only Maurice Richard had more (six).

"We showed that we're not chokers," Hunter told reporter Jeff Rimer on the Home Team Sports broadcast that night.

"Overcoming [a deficit] and having to battle through, I think, was more than satisfying, especially against a team like Philadelphia, which was a huge rival," Miller said. "Just a great series, a great rivalry, and to be a part of just that alone was something special, but to be able to battle back and end up on time—because that was a pretty good Philly team we were playing—was a pretty special feeling to win that series."

"We weren't big fans of that team, but we respected them," Langway said. "And it was so gratifying to be on top once. Murph and I were playing every other shift and it was a great play by Murph to [feed Hunter]. It was a special night, really. And Dale showed everyone he wouldn't quit."

8 Alexander the Greatest

Few players exude as much joy from scoring as Alex Ovechkin. And nobody has scored more often in a Washington uniform than the Great 8.

Since 2005–06, when he became the first Capitals rookie to score 50 goals and 100 points, Ovechkin has turned the franchise record book into an amplified personal resume.

Twelve years into his NHL career, Ovechkin was the Capitals' all-time leader in goals, points, power-play goals, game-winning goals and overtime goals.

He is also the only Capitals player to record 500 goals and 1,000 points.

"We have a once-in-a-generation player here," Capitals majority owner Ted Leonsis said in 2016.

Long considered the greatest goal scorer in team history, Ovechkin made it official on April 2, 2015, at the Bell Centre in Montreal. Ovechkin scored twice that night, including the 473rd goal of his career, to break Peter Bondra's team record.

"It's a huge accomplishment," Ovechkin said. "But records are to be beaten. Sooner or later, somebody is going to break my record. It's nice to [make] history."

Before Ovechkin, Bondra was the Capitals' most dynamic offensive player. From 1990 through 2004, he set the standard with 472 goals and 825 points in 961 games. Ovechkin needed just 691 games to pass Bondra in points and 756 games to pass him in goals.

"Bondra was star, but Ovi is a superstar," said former Capitals captain Jeff Halpern, who played with both. "Ovi has the capabilities where if he's not scoring, he can run somebody over, he can

Alex Ovechkin scored twice in his NHL debut and seemingly never stopped. During the 2014–15 season, Ovechkin passed Peter Bondra as Washington's all-time scoring leader and he later became the first Capitals player to record 500 goals and 1,000 points.

dominate the game physically. Nothing to take away from Peter, but it's an element with Ovi that makes him a true superstar."

Bondra was traded four months before the Capitals drafted Ovechkin in 2004. The top two scorers in club history were never teammates, but they played against each other seven times in Bondra's final two seasons.

"As soon as he stepped onto the ice and I played him for the first time, I told myself, 'Wow, this is a special player,'" said Bondra, who returned to Washington after his playing career.

"He changed everything around here. We can arguably say D.C. is now a hockey town and Alex basically did that himself. He's brought excitement, he's brought in the crowds, and he's brought energy to the building."

Beginning in 2007–08—Ovechkin's third season—the Capitals won five division titles in six years, highlighted by a Presidents' Trophy in 2009–10 and a second straight Eastern Conference regular season title in 2010–11.

Ovechkin's 500th Goal

The buzz at Verizon Center was palpable as the Capitals prepared to face the Ottawa Senators on January 10, 2016. With two goals, including an overtime winner, a day earlier in New York, Ovechkin returned to D.C. one goal shy of 500 for his NHL career.

The capacity crowd on this Sunday evening was ready to watch history. Ovechkin delivered. On a Washington power play late in the second period, Ovechkin wired a wrist shot past Ottawa's Andrew Hammond. The Capitals' bench emptied as Ovechkin's teammates mobbed him at the Ottawa blue line.

"I got goosebumps," Nicklas Backstrom said. "It was a special feeling."

Ovechkin became the fifth-fastest player to score 500 goals, hitting the plateau in his 801st game. Only Wayne Gretzky (575 games), Mario Lemieux (605), Mike Bossy (647), and Brett Hull (693) did it quicker.

Attendance records were shattered in the District, where the Capitals entered 2017–18 having sold out more than 360 consecutive home games.

Along the way, Ovechkin won the Hart Trophy three times as the NHL's Most Valuable Player and the Maurice "Rocket" Richard Trophy six times as the league's leading goal scorer.

"We used to have something we called 'S.O.S. nights,'" said Brooks Laich, who spent parts of 13 seasons with the Capitals. "Those were sold-out-section nights. If we were on the bench and we could look into the stands and find a section that was full, we were high-fiving each other, saying 'Boys, it's an S.O.S. night!' But then Ovi just explodes onto the scene. He's the marquee attraction, the face of the Capitals. Everyone wanted to see him and it became a hot ticket."

Fans were drawn to the goals, the jubilant celebrations, and Ovechkin's ability to take over a game. But they embraced the total package, which, in Ovechkin's case, included the physical play and a knack for delivering big hits not often seen from a high-end forward.

"He does everything at a high speed," Bondra said. "He's so powerful, and when he's on the ice you have to keep your head on a swivel because he's coming. He's like a train and he'll hit you and he'll hit you hard. As a fan, you need to acknowledge that. He's hard to miss."

In January 2008, the Capitals signed Ovechkin, then 22, to a 13-year, $124 million contract. Team president Dick Patrick admits that there was concern whether their investment would hold up given his rough-and-tumble style of play.

"He's so big and strong, but what if he gets hurt?" Patrick said. "It's hard to contemplate someone playing that style of game for so long without missing lots of games because of injuries. But he hasn't."

From 2005–06 through 2014–15, only three forwards delivered more hits than Ovechkin. At 6'3" and 245 pounds, Ovechkin has played through many bumps and bruises, including a broken foot in the 2013 playoffs and a nagging back injury during his 50-goal season in 2015–16.

"What I've been surprised at," said Leonsis, "is that he's continued his physical play and has still remained a great goal scorer. His durability has really positioned him as a really historic player."

In his first 12 years in the NHL, Ovechkin missed more than five games just once (he played 72 games in 2009–10 and still scored 50 goals).

In a career spent obliterating the Capitals' record book, Ovechkin is in position to hit another milestone as early as 2017–18, when he could become the first Capitals player to skate in 1,000 games with the franchise.

"It's incredible," said longtime teammate Nicklas Backstrom. "It's like they said after he signed the contract; he's the Russian machine that never breaks."

9 Capitals Move to MCI Center

When Abe Pollin first unveiled plans for the Capital Centre in Landover, Maryland, in 1972, the real estate mogul presented a futuristic facility complete with skyboxes and the world's first scoreboard capable of showing instant replays.

By the 1990s, though, the home of the Capitals and the Washington Bullets had grown obsolete. Across both the NBA and NHL, teams were upgrading their home facilities with even more luxury suites and amenities.

If the NHL's Boston Bruins, Chicago Blackhawks, and Montreal Canadiens could move from their historic home arenas—as all three did in the mid-1990s—surely the Capitals could relocate from their suddenly outdated home.

In the summer of 1995, Pollin announced his intent to privately finance a $200 million facility that would house both the Capitals and the Bullets, who would be rebranded as the Wizards in the new building.

This meant that after playing all of their prior home games in the state of Maryland, the Washington Capitals would at long last play within the city's limits. Pollin wanted his new arena built in an otherwise desolate part of downtown at Seventh and F streets NW.

Construction took 25 months and it wasn't without its challenges, with the discovery of contaminated soil and asbestos among the early obstacles. There was also a successful lawsuit from the Paralyzed Veterans of America to increase the number of seats for wheelchair-bound spectators.

Through it all, Pollin remained confident that his life's work had prepared him for the biggest business venture of his career.

Washington-based MCI Communications Corp. helped ease some of Pollin's financial burden, agreeing to a $44 million, 13-year deal for arena naming rights.

"I walk through that building [and] I get tears in my eyes," Pollin told the *Washington Post* days before the MCI Center opened in 1997. "It's unbelievable. I've got everything I've ever done in my life on the line. I've pledged everything. My advisors think I'm nuts. But I wanted to do something special for my town."

Pollin was born in Philadelphia but moved to Washington with his family when he was eight. He graduated from George Washington University in 1945 and became a D.C. lifer in the historically transient region. But for all the pride Pollin held for his hometown, he was also well aware of its diminishing reputation.

Despite Metro accessibility and the proximity to the Capitol Dome and National Mall, venturing downtown for a social night on the town, for example, didn't appeal to locals during the 1980s and early 1990s. Crime was rampant, and by 1989, Washington held the dubious title of murder capital of the United States.

"When we played at the Caps Centre way out on the Beltway," said onetime Capitals captain Ryan Walter, "we'd practice around the city and in Fort DuPont and different places, but downtown was pretty scary in those days. We were specifically told *not* to go downtown."

By the mid-1990s, Pollin wanted to change that. The arena would stand in the Penn Quarter neighborhood of Chinatown, but offered little in the form of nearby restaurants or entertainment when ground was broken in October 1995. Pollin, though, had dreams of a revitalized downtown with his arena as the centerpiece.

"Mr. Pollin always had the vision for Washington," said former Capitals general manager David Poile. "His background was in building and in real estate and he saw this. I remember coming downtown to the area where they were talking about putting the building and at that time I couldn't see it all. I couldn't see how it was going to work out and how it was going to be a destination place."

Ultimately, it would in fact turn into a $6.8 billion redevelopment project with restaurants, condominiums, and businesses now lining the once-vacant lots.

On December 3, 2007, Pollin celebrated his 84th birthday, with Mayor Adrian M. Fenty unveiling F Street between 6th and 7th Streets NW as "Abe Pollin Way."

"When you look at it years later, it's fabulous down there," Poile told the Capitals Radio Network in 2009. "It is exactly what someone with a vision, someone who could see these things, would think of. That was his vision."

Two years after the MCI Center first opened its doors, the D.C. Council unanimously approved a $46 million financing package that went towards construction of a $195 million entertainment, retail, and housing complex atop the Gallery Place Metro station, next to the arena.

Today the complex is home to such establishments as Regal Cinema, Lucky Strike, Bar Louie, and Clyde's of Gallery Place, all of which have become popular pregame or postgame destinations.

"Now, it's just so beautiful," Walter said. "To be able to walk through Chinatown and the Verizon Center is just spectacular."

"I have tremendous respect for the man and for what he did for Washington and what he did in terms of building the MCI Center and what it did for the area," said Kelly Miller, who played for the Capitals in 1997–98, when they moved downtown midseason.

"It's cool to go back now and see that area and see how it's grown and developed around that rink. When they first built that rink, there wasn't a whole lot going on down there. But to see now how it's gone up and what a wonderful area it's become around the rink, that's a credit to Mr. Pollin and his vision and the contributions that he made to the Washington, D.C., area and to redeveloping that entire area."

The MCI Center opened its doors on December 2, 1997, with the Wizards hosting the Seattle SuperSonics—the same opponent the Bullets played to open the Capital Centre in 1973. The Wizards christened the new building with a 95–78 win before a capacity crowd of 20,674 fans.

Three nights later, the Capitals won their first home game in the District, beating the Florida Panthers 3–2 in overtime on December 5, 1997. Richard Zednik and Chris Simon scored for the Capitals in regulation, with Jeff Toms beating Florida's John Vanbiesbrouck for the game-winning goal in the extra session.

Toms scored five goals over parts of three seasons with the Capitals but the overtime winner in the MCI Center opener tops the list.

"I remember [Panthers defenseman] Paul Laus was trying to get the puck by me and I blocked it," Toms recalled in 2017. "Then I went down and just tried to get Vanbiesbrouck to give me a little bit of the five hole and put it home.

"It was just such a big game. There was a lot of excitement and there was a lot of emotion; there was a lot of energy in the building so it was an exciting night. And it was good to get a win that first game. That was important for us. I remember the energy, how excited the fans were and even the organization and the owners, it was just a great night of hockey."

10 Capitals Win 2008 Southeast Division

The task was simple as the Capitals prepared for the 2007–08 regular season finale at Verizon Center: Beat the Florida Panthers, and the Capitals would be Southeast Division champions, playoff bound for the first time in five years. A loss in the final game of the year and the Capitals' furious late-season rally would be for naught.

Months earlier, the possibility of the Capitals even sniffing the postseason seemed remote, with the club sitting in last place with a 6–14–1 record by Thanksgiving. Bruce Boudreau replaced Glen Hanlon as head coach at that time and, despite a gradual uptick in their play, the Capitals remained in last place on December 30. By the midpoint of the regular season, the Capitals were in 14th place in the 15-team Eastern Conference.

Caps' 2007–08 Season

Although the Capitals were eventually eliminated by the Philadelphia Flyers with an overtime loss in Game 7 of their first-round series, the 2007–08 Capitals laid the groundwork for years of success.

The Capitals went 37–17–7 after Bruce Boudreau's hiring on November 22 as he went on to capture the Jack Adams Award as the NHL's Coach of the Year.

Alex Ovechkin won the Hart Trophy as the NHL's Most Valuable Player for the first time in his career, while leading the league with 65 goals and 112 points. Ovechkin's 65 goals are the most in one season by a left winger in NHL history.

Mike Green led all defensemen with 18 goals and Nicklas Backstrom set a Capitals rookie record with 55 assists.

The 2007–08 Southeast Division title was the first of four consecutive first-place finishes for the Capitals, who also finished as Eastern Conference regular-season champions in 2009–10 and 2010–11.

But buoyed by Boudreau's up-tempo style and the acquisitions of veterans Matt Cooke, Sergei Fedorov, and Cristobal Huet at the trade deadline, the Capitals found themselves in a playoff hunt down the stretch.

For the first time in their careers, players such as Alex Ovechkin, Nicklas Backstrom, Mike Green, Alexander Semin, and Tomas Fleischmann were playing meaningful games at the NHL level.

"It was a bunch of young professionals that didn't know any different than to chase after it," Brooks Laich said in 2016. "We really didn't know pressure, we really didn't know defeat. The game was really played at a pure and passionate level. We were the underdog the whole way, so maybe it was good timing, because we were able to fly under the radar. Once we got so far behind by November, people wrote us off and thought our year was over. It was like, 'Okay, let the media talk about everybody else and let's just push a little bit each day.' We started making waves, we started having winning streaks and all of a sudden it started to become real."

Following a late-March 5–1–0 road trip—during which Ovechkin established a new Capitals single-season record with his 61st goal of the season—the Capitals returned to D.C. for a three-game homestand against the Carolina Hurricanes, Tampa Bay Lightning, and Florida Panthers.

The Capitals dispatched Carolina on April 1 and beat Tampa Bay on April 3, extending their win streak to six games. Washington then received some necessary help on the out-of-town scoreboard when the Hurricanes dropped their regular season finale to Florida on April 4.

"I remember the night before our last game," Laich said, "Florida beat Carolina, and if Carolina had gotten two points, they would have been in the playoffs, and I remember thinking, 'Oh my God, the thing that we've been chasing for all season long is now in our hands. It's up to us to win a hockey game.' That's when it really became real. That's when our goal was in our hands. It was right in front of us and achievable."

Before a red-clad sellout crowd at Verizon Center, the Capitals didn't let the moment pass them by. They beat the Panthers 3–1 for their seventh consecutive win. Fleischmann, Fedorov, and Semin all scored and Huet made 25 saves to secure Washington's first division title in seven years.

As the seconds ticked down, Joe Beninati had the final call on Comcast Sportsnet:

"If the NHL is having a fairytale end to its regular season, hockey has its Cinderella! [Horn sounds] Southeast Division champions!"

Years later, Beninati reflected on the Capitals' improbable late-season surge, which included an 11–1–0 record down the stretch capped off by the final win of the year against Florida.

A furious late-season rally allowed the 2007–08 Capitals to clinch a playoff berth on the final day of the regular season. The Capitals beat the Florida Panthers 3–1 in the season finale on April 5, 2008, with Sergei Fedorov scoring the game-winning goal. Washington won seven consecutive games to end the regular season.

"I will never forget the reaction of the bench in the final 15–20 seconds," Beninati said in 2016. "As Verizon Center was going nuts all around them to cap off this extraordinary run to end the regular season, we were watching grown men behaving like little kids. It was spectacular. I specifically remember all of the reactions, all of the dog-piling that was being done on the bench. The guy behind the bench with his coaching staff, ear-to-ear grins jumping up and down. It was a magical moment."

"We went out and won the hockey game," said Laich, who finished third on the team that season with 21 goals. "The building was packed, everyone was rocking the red, they had the banner up [that read] Southeast Division Champions, and at that moment, hockey became cool in D.C. It became the hot ticket in town, and I think we won a lot of fans at that time."

General manager George McPhee has similar memories of a young team that played with an entertaining style and was quickly grabbing the attention of a fan base starved for a winner.

"That final stretch was really something," McPhee said in 2017. "I think it's what galvanized our fan base. That's when everything turned in Washington and the Washington Capitals became a popular team. That stretch of games for those three weeks caught everyone's attention. Whether the casual sports fan or the avid Caps fan, everyone was dialed in. And when we won that last game, I remember catching myself, because it almost felt like we had won the Stanley Cup. It was such a rush and the place was that loud and excited. And I said, 'Oh geez, all we've done is make the playoffs.' But it was spectacular, it was quite the feat, and I don't know too many other teams that have done that."

11 Retired Jerseys: Labre, Langway, Hunter, Gartner

At any point during a morning skate or practice at the Kettler Capitals Iceplex in Arlington, Virginia, players can look to the east end of the arena and find four oversize banners hanging on the wall, each one highlighting a key figure in franchise history.

The 20-by-30-foot murals overlook the ice rink and feature the images of former Capitals players Dale Hunter, Rod Langway, Mike Gartner, and Yvon Labre.

The quartet represents an exclusive group in Capitals history: the only players to have their numbers retired by the organization.

In numerical order, Langway's No. 5, Labre's No. 7, Gartner's No. 11, and Hunter's No.32 are not only prominently displayed at KCI, but all four are hanging from the rafters at Verizon Center.

Of the more than 1,600 home games the Capitals have played since 1974, only four have been preceded by a jersey retirement ceremony.

The first, Yvon Labre's, occurred on November 7, 1981.

No. 7: Yvon Labre

Labre was a member of the inaugural Capitals during the 1974–75 season and scored the team's first goal at the Capital Centre in a game against the Los Angeles Kings on October 15, 1974.

The stay-at-home defenseman served as Washington's captain from January 1976 through November 1978 and was the last player from the original Capitals to remain with the team. Injuries forced a 31-year-old Labre to retire prematurely in 1981.

Labre played 334 games over parts of seven seasons with the Capitals, recording 12 goals and 96 points while racking up 756 penalty minutes.

He is not in the Hockey Hall of Fame, and he is the only Capitals alum to have his jersey retired despite never representing the club at the NHL All-Star Game. Labre's jersey retirement is more a token of appreciation from the organization for the grit and dedication he brought to the team during its trying first few seasons.

The jersey retirement ceremony itself was not even promoted. In fact, Labre didn't even know about it until the ceremony was under way. Labre was brought out to center ice for a pregame ceremony, which he was told was to honor radio broadcaster Ron Weber as he approached his 500th consecutive game.

"I was asked to be on the ice with him," Labre recalled in an interview with the Capitals' official website in 1999. "I was told that Mr. Pollin wanted me out there, so I said, 'Okay, no problem.' I

Yvon Labre scored the Capitals' first goal on home ice when he beat Hall of Famer Rogie Vachon of the Los Angeles Kings at the Capital Centre on October 15, 1974. Seven years later, Labre became the first Capitals player to have his number retired.

remember being out there, and the lights had all dimmed and the spotlight was on. It was supposed to be on Ron, who was already in his broadcast position. So, the spotlight is on Ron, and I'm like, 'Great, let's get out of here.' But Ron pulls this jersey out that he'd been hiding in his jacket and he starts reading this spiel about me and retiring my jersey. I had no idea what to say at that time. It caught me totally off guard and by surprise. All I could manage, shaking in my boots, was 'Thank you.' It was heartfelt, but this was all I could get out.

"Not in a million years would I have thought that could happen, yet it was happening to me. I don't fit into the category with Bobby Orr and Bobby Hull and Phil Esposito and those guys. No way. But here it was, happening to me."

After his playing career, Labre wore many different hats with the Capitals, including assistant coach, color commentator, director of community relations, and director of special programs. He continues to play an active role with the Capitals Alumni Association, and seeing his No. 7 hanging from the rafters at Verizon Center remains a great source of pride.

"It's one of the greatest highlights of my career," Labre said in 2016. "Let's face it—I never thought that that would ever happen to a player such as myself. So I dedicated it to all the guys that played the game the same way I did—night in and night out playing hard. They're never going to get the chance that I did here in Washington, having been the last player from the original team."

No. 5: Rod Langway

The Capitals reached out to Rod Langway during the 1997 off-season and told him of their plans to retire his No. 5 sweater. Langway was living in Hilton Head, South Carolina, at the time, so the team gave him the courtesy to pick a date that would be most convenient for him to make the trip.

Langway chose the Capitals' home game against the Montreal Canadiens on November 26. The game was appealing because it featured both teams he played for during his NHL career. By coincidence, this just happened to be the Capitals' 977th and final game at US Airways Arena (née Capital Centre).

"I was fortunate enough that Abe [Pollin] and Dick [Patrick] allowed that to happen," Langway said in 2017. "I thought it was a perfect way to come back to the Capital Centre one final time and honor both Montreal and the Capitals for my playing days.

"These were the only two teams I played for in the NHL so it was ideal for me. Rejean Houle was the Canadiens' general manager at the time and he had been my roommate when I played in Montreal, so everything worked out that night."

A sellout crowd of 18,130 in Landover took in the final game, which the Canadiens won 6–5. Before the opening faceoff, Langway was presented with a golf cart, a set of golf clubs, a portrait, and a commemorative silver hockey stick.

Langway was the Capitals captain during his entire 11-year tenure in Washington, and he is the only player in team history to win the Norris Trophy as the NHL's best defenseman in consecutive seasons (1982–83 and 1983–84).

No. 32: Dale Hunter

Less than a year after Dale Hunter was traded to the Colorado Avalanche for one last run at the Stanley Cup, the Capitals celebrated their former captain by raising his No. 32 to the rafters at MCI Center. The ceremony took place March 11, 2000, before a home game against the New Jersey Devils.

At the time, Hunter had played the second-most games in franchise history (872) and was the club's third all-time leading scorer (556 points). His 2,003 career penalty minutes with the Capitals remain a team high.

"I'm not a Wayne Gretzky," he said during the ceremony. "I just tried to give my all every night. That work ethic is what the Caps have always been about."

Hunter remains the only player in NHL history with 300 career goals, 1,000 points, and 3,000 penalty minutes.

"I was in there quite a few days," he said of his frequent trips to the penalty box.

As part of Hunter's jersey retirement ceremony in 2000, the Capitals made sure he and the penalty box would remain close, even though his playing career was over.

In addition to presenting Hunter with an all-terrain vehicle and a horse trailer as part of the pregame ceremonies, the club also gave him the penalty box from the old Capital Centre.

"I've made it into a bar and that's how I get in," he told the Capitals Radio Network in 2009.

"The penalty box is when you go get a beer from the back for your company coming. So definitely, it's being used. It's in my basement, it's used as a bar, so the door is still being opened and I'm still getting into it—even more often than I did during my playing days!"

The Capitals blew a 2–0 lead against the Devils that night and entered the second intermission tied 2–2.

Chris Simon addressed his teammates during the intermission, urging them to win the game for Hunter.

"He mentioned that you can't have a night like this honoring one of the organization's greats and come out flat and lose the game," goaltender Olie Kolzig told the *Washington Post* later that night.

"It was really important to win it for Dale."

Ulf Dahlen scored the eventual game-winning goal 78 seconds into the third period, with Steve Konowalchuk adding an empty-net goal to secure a 4–2 win.

For one final time, Hunter was named the game's No. 1 star.

"It was a big night," defenseman Ken Klee told the *Washington Post*. "[Hunter] is a hero for all of us that played with him, as well as guys who just know him. Anyone who knows anything about hockey knows Dale Hunter. You gotta love him."

No. 11: Mike Gartner

When Mike Gartner retired from the NHL after a 19-year career in 1998, he was one of five players in NHL history with at least 700 goals. Although Gartner played for five teams, more than half of his 708 lamp lighters came in a Capitals sweater during the first ten seasons of his career.

The Capitals selected Gartner fourth overall in the 1979 draft, and he scored at least 35 goals in each of his first nine years in Washington. (He had 26 goals when he was traded 56 games into the 1988–89 season.)

When Gartner was dealt to the Minnesota North Stars on March 7, 1989, he was the Capitals' all-time leader in games played, goals, assists, points, power play goals, and game-winning goals.

"I look back at my time in Washington as a Capital very fondly," Gartner said in 2016. "I'm so glad that I played there, that I began my career there and that my jersey is hanging from the rafters there." The Capitals retired Gartner's No. 11 on December 28, 2008.

Gartner was introduced during the pregame ceremonies by his former Capitals teammate and longtime business partner, Wes Jarvis.

"He put us on the edge of our seats every time he swooped down that right wing and took that big slap shot," Jarvis told the crowd. "We saw his puck-handling and passing skills evolve to make him an all-star. What stood out to all of us, though, was his passion and enthusiasm for the game of hockey.... No. 11 in my day. No. 8 with today's team [Alex Ovechkin]—two passionate players."

Team president Dick Patrick presented Gartner with a framed No. 11 jersey, an engraved silver puck, and an oil painting by artist Michel Lapensee. Labre, Langway, and then–Capitals captain Chris Clark assisted with the presentation.

The Capitals wore retro jerseys with Gartner's No. 11 during pregame warmups, and wore their white jerseys at home for the game—just as Gartner's teams did at Capital Centre during the 1980s. Ovechkin and Brooks Laich scored twice each in a 4–1 win over the Maple Leafs (another one of Gartner's former teams).

"It was a great feeling," Gartner said nearly nine years later. "It was kind of surreal. It had happened a number of years after I had played in Washington, but having my family and friends there, it was a great experience. The Caps did a great job with it and made us feel very welcome and part of the rich history of the Capitals. I classify it as one of the top moments in my career."

12 Capitals Discover Bondra

Peter Bondra was prepared to have the game of his life. He was 22, and although he was content to spend his entire hockey-playing career in Czechoslovakia, he was intrigued that an NHL scout would attend one of his upcoming games.

Long before he became a 500-goal scorer in the NHL, Bondra was passed over at the NHL Draft for four consecutive years. Without the Internet or advanced scouting, he was an unknown. Bondra was born in Ukraine and raised in Czechoslovakia, but a citizenship quirk kept him from competing in heavily scouted international tournaments.

Then, in 1990, Bondra read in the newspaper that Capitals director of scouting Jack Button was scheduled to attend his next Czech-league game in Vitkovice. This was going to be his one chance.

Button was making the trip not to watch Bondra but to watch Vitkovice defenseman Richard Smehlik. Smehlik would become a serviceable NHL defenseman and had an 11-year career. But Button left the game most impressed with a speedy forward on the other team.

"My thinking going into the game was, 'Hey, maybe I can show the scout something,'" Bondra said in 2017. "And that's what happened. I scored twice and we won the game. Then he came to our next game and that was just to watch me."

Months later, on Button's recommendation, general manager David Poile selected Bondra with Washington's eighth-round pick (No. 156 overall). He was a player most NHL teams had never heard of, but he may have been the steal of the 1990 draft.

Over the next 14 seasons, Bondra emerged as Washington's all-time scoring leader. He was a five-time All-Star, a two-time 50-goal scorer, and very quietly one of the NHL's best players in the 1990s. For a four-year stretch from 1994 through 1998, Bondra scored more goals than any other NHL player.

"He's got the credentials to get into the Hall of Fame," said former captain Rod Langway.

Other than Button, though, nobody in the Capitals organization knew anything about Bondra when they drafted him. He came to Washington weeks later speaking little English and having never even watched an NHL game.

Poile hosted Bondra and fellow prospect Jiri Vykoukal at his Washington home late that summer. They spent time by the pool one afternoon before lacing up their Rollerblades, which was all

Before Peter Bondra emerged as a five-time NHL all-star and a 500 goal scorer, he wasn't a highly touted prospect. In fact, Bondra was passed over in the NHL draft in four consecutive years before the Capitals finally selected him in Round 8 (No. 156 overall) in 1990.

the rage in the early 90s. Bondra thought it would be a good idea to Rollerblade down Poile's sloped driveway. Poile wasn't so sure.

"The driveway was steep and then turned," Poile recalled in 2017. "If you went down on Rollerblades, you'd have to go slow and side to side."

Bondra insisted.

"So, we put on the Rollerblades," Poile said, "and I'm going cautiously down and Jiri is going cautiously down and Peter just put those things on and went flying down the driveway and made the turn. And it was like, no big deal. So, I'm thinking, 'Okay, well, maybe this will translate onto the ice.' And it certainly did. He loved the speed and he could fly."

On the first day of training camp in September 1990, the Capitals got an early taste of what was in store.

"I remember the year before," said former teammate Alan May, "during the conditioning skate, I crushed everybody in the 45-second skate drill. I was lapping players in my group. Well, the next year, Peter Bondra skates in my group to do this fitness test and he laps me! He never took his feet off the ice. He just had these huge legs, a tiny upper body, a huge ass and thighs, and he could flat-out fly. We had no idea who he was, but this kid could skate."

Bondra skipped the minors and made the Capitals right out of his first training camp. He was named the NHL's Rookie of the Month in November 1990 and finished his freshman campaign with 12 goals and 28 points in 54 games. Bondra was paired for much of the season with Czech center Michal Pivonka, who served as his interpreter, roommate, and mentor early in his career. Pivonka defected from Czechoslovakia in 1986.

"He helped me out a lot with my career, and I'm really thankful for that," Bondra told the Capitals' official website in 2007. "He helped me to learn the game. It wasn't easy to adjust from European style—the big ice rinks—to come to smaller rinks and try to play a little bit different game. He had a lot of influence on my career. I was really lucky to have him."

Before Alex Ovechkin became Washington's all-time goal-scoring leader and before Nicklas Backstrom was the club's all-time assist leader, Bondra and Pivonka held the honors, having contributed a great deal to the other's success.

"They're like bacon and eggs," Capitals general manager David Poile told the *Baltimore Sun* in 1994. "They just go together. Each can be successful on his own, but together they appear to be much more."

Following his rookie season, Bondra scored at least 20 goals in each of his final 13 seasons with the Capitals. He led the NHL with 34 goals in 47 games during the lockout-shortened 1994–95 season and, had a league-high 52 goals in 76 games in 1997–98.

He eventually mastered English and became one of Washington's most popular athletes. He was a sharpshooting speedster whom teammates nicknamed "Bonzai" because of his unpredictable and at times reckless nature on the ice.

"There were times we'd have to rein him in," said former teammate John Druce. "He'd shoot the puck over the net or it would hit the glass, but that was Bonzai—a little all over the place. But you saw that talent and that early potential."

Langway was at the end of his Hall of Fame career just as Bondra was coming into his own, but the former Capitals captain remembers how much easier things became when No. 12 was on the ice.

"You didn't have to pass the puck to him," Langway said. "You could just pass it in front of him because you knew he'd outskate somebody. He was similar to Mike Gartner. His top-end speed was incredible."

"He lit it up," said longtime teammate Kelly Miller. "He could skate like the wind and cut on a dime, and he had a tremendous shot. You put those two together, now you've got something special. The way he could shoot the puck, at full speed, was amazing."

Bondra was traded to Ottawa in February 2004 as part of the Capitals' 2003–04 fire sale. At the time, he was Washington's all-time leader in goals (472), points (825), power play goals (137), game-winning goals (73), short handed goals (32), and hat tricks (19).

"I grew up here," he said. "I grew up as a player and I grew up as a person."

13 Winning the Lottery

The Capitals were coming off their worst season in 26 years—a forgettable 2003–04 campaign in which they won 23 of 82 games—when their fortunes forever changed with the bounce of a Ping-Pong ball on April 6, 2004.

Despite owning the third-best odds of winning the 2004 NHL Draft Lottery at 14.2 percent, a Washington ball emerged from the hopper. For the third time in franchise history, and for the first time since 1976, the Capitals would pick first overall.

A Russian teenager named Alexander Ovechkin had burst on to the international scene two years earlier and had long been the projected No. 1 pick. His countryman Evgeni Malkin was expected to go second overall—not a bad consolation prize for the Pittsburgh Penguins—but Ovechkin was really considered a generational talent.

The Capitals had indeed hit the jackpot.

"We hope today is the first day in a new era for the Capitals," general manager George McPhee said that afternoon.

These days the NHL Draft Lottery has become an elaborate made-for-TV production, but back in 2004, the lottery was conducted privately at the NHL's offices in New York.

It wasn't exactly the type of the thing the Capitals could closely monitor as it was happening.

"I was at the practice facility at Piney Orchard," McPhee recalled in 2017, "when [NHL Senior Vice President] Colin Campbell called. He didn't tell me right away, but I had a feeling that he was calling me for a reason. But we were talking socially for five, six minutes and then he just said, 'Oh, by the way, you won the lottery. Congratulations.'"

McPhee quickly shared the news, calling Ross Mahoney, the team's director of amateur scouting, and team president Dick Patrick.

"It was sort of an odd call," Patrick said, "because we both pretty much had the same reaction, just kind of, 'Oh, really? That really happened?' Ovechkin was already on everybody's radar back then, but so was Malkin. We knew we were getting a good player. We just didn't know how good.

"It was a great feeling. It took all kinds of pressure off in a way, because we just had to take the best player. We didn't have to worry about anything happening in front of us that could potentially impact us. It was in our control."

McPhee was preparing for his seventh draft with the Capitals, but only once before did he have a top-10 pick. In 1999, the Capitals selected Kris Beech seventh overall. It was no comparison to what awaited in 2004.

"It was a very interesting moment," McPhee said, "because we knew at that point that the top two guys in the draft were elite players. On our list, we had Ovechkin and Malkin there."

Mahoney was at his home in Regina when McPhee called. The draft was still 81 days away, but Mahoney didn't hesitate when McPhee asked for his initial impression.

"It's got to be Ovechkin," Mahoney told him.

"We still discussed it in a lot of detail," McPhee said, "because Malkin is a hell of a player. But we thought that the combination of goals and physical play and enthusiasm that Ovechkin brought, that he had to be the guy."

NHL scouts were first introduced to him at the 2002 World Under-18 Championships in Slovakia, where a then-16-year-old Ovechkin crushed the competition. Ovechkin was the tournament's leading scorer with 14 goals and 18 points in eight games. Russia finished with a silver medal.

Months later he led Russia to a gold medal at the 2003 World Under-20 Championships in Halifax, Nova Scotia. Ovechkin had six goals in as many games.

"Most of us were at least a year or two older than him," said Brooks Laich, who played for Team Canada at the 2003 World Juniors. "He was still wearing the full-cage helmet, just a young kid, but you knew he was going to be a special player. He had a great World Junior tournament so I was aware of his abilities. He was a guy who could score big goals, but could also dominate the game physically, and for a player at that young age, you don't see that very often."

In addition to his international experience, Ovechkin had also played parts of three professional seasons with Dynamo Moscow of the Russian Superleague. His goal, though, was to play in the NHL. With the Capitals winning the lottery, the team with the best chance to select him was now known.

Laich was among some of Ovechkin's future teammates, who were preparing for the American Hockey League's Calder Cup Playoffs with the Portland Pirates, the day the news spread through the organization.

"I remember being surprised," Laich said. "I got a text message from a friend saying 'Wow, you guys got the No. 1 pick.' And I was very surprised, but also very excited because I knew who was coming. What a pick! I didn't think we were going to get it, but when we did get it, the cards just fell perfectly."

"We knew we could only go up," said Brian Willsie, who played 49 games for the last-place Capitals in 2003–04. "We were a basement dweller at that time. But after getting that No. 1 pick, we were all excited for what the future held. You could see it right away with Alex, how amazing he was. But then the other guys that were coming in—Shaone Morrisonn, Brooks Laich, Tomas

Could Alex Ovechkin Have Been a Phoenix Coyote?

The five teams with the five worst records from the 2003–04 season each had a shot at winning the 2004 draft lottery. The teams' chances were weighted based on where they finished in the standings.

Below is a look at the teams involved, the odds they each carried, and how the picks played out:

No. 1: Washington Capitals (14.2 percent)—Alex Ovechkin: Ovechkin is the Capitals' franchise scoring leader and the first player from the draft class to record 500 goals and 1,000 points.

No. 2: Pittsburgh Penguins (48.2 percent)—Evgeni Malkin: Malkin is a two-time Stanley Cup champion, the 2009 Conn Smythe Trophy winner, the 2012 Hart Trophy winner, and a two-time NHL leading scorer.

No. 3: Chicago Blackhawks (18.8 percent)—Cam Barker: The No. 3 pick recorded 21 goals and 96 points in 310 career games with four teams. He last played in the NHL during the 2012–13 season.

No. 4: Columbus Blue Jackets (10.7 percent)—Andrew Ladd: The Carolina Hurricanes acquired the fourth overall pick from Columbus for the eighth pick and the 58th pick. Carolina selected Ladd at No. 4. He played 17 postseason games as a rookie for the 2005–06 Stanley Cup champion Hurricanes.

No. 5: Phoenix Coyotes (8.1 percent)—Blake Wheeler: Wheeler did not sign with Phoenix, instead making his NHL debut with the Boston Bruins in October 2008.

Fleischmann, Mike Green, and some of those guys. You could see the bright years that were ahead for Washington."

Ovechkin was the headliner of the Capitals' 2004 draft class, but he was also one of Washington's *three* first-round picks. Thanks to trades completed during Washington's 2003–04 fire sale, McPhee acquired first-round picks from the Boston Bruins (27th overall) and Detroit Red Wings (29th overall).

The picks were used on defensemen Jeff Schultz and Mike Green, who combined to play 874 career games with the Capitals.

14 Holtby Ties Brodeur

It was the exclamation point in what was arguably the best season of Braden Holtby's career. In his final start of the 2015–16 campaign, with the Capitals having already clinched the top seed in the Eastern Conference and the NHL's best overall record, Holtby took his place in the history books.

On April 9, 2016, Holtby made 19 saves in a relatively routine 5–1 triumph in St. Louis to earn his 48th win of the season and tie Martin Brodeur's single-season NHL record.

"I don't focus too much on records, but this one is different," Holtby said. "This is a neat one to accomplish because it's a team sport and in a team sport, the best measure is wins and losses.

"It's not an individual thing. When you come back for alumni things years in the future, you can share it with the same guys that have been part of it and look back on it together."

On the night of the milestone, Holtby's teammates showered him with high fives and congratulatory chants in the victorious Capitals' dressing room.

It was also a special night for goaltending coach Mitch Korn, who had spent the previous two years rebuilding a goaltender who struggled with consistency during a turbulent 2013–14 season.

Shortly after the win in St. Louis, Korn was riding the elevator down to the event level at Scottrade Center when he ran into Brodeur. By coincidence, Brodeur happened to be on site when Holtby tied his record, because of his role as the Blues' assistant general manager.

"You talk about the hockey gods," Korn said, "well, the hockey gods lined it up perfectly for Braden to tie the record with Marty in the building."

Brodeur congratulated Korn, but Korn told him that he was congratulating the wrong guy. Korn suggested that Brodeur track down Holtby and pass on the kudos himself, which he did, minutes later, outside the Capitals' dressing room.

"It was pretty cool the way it worked out," Holtby said. "[Former NHL goalie and Blues television analyst] Darren Pang was telling me that when Marty broke the record [in 2007] in Philadelphia, [previous record holder] Bernie Parent was there, so it was kind of neat. A story to tell, I guess."

"It was a fantastic night," Korn told National Public Radio's *Hockey Diaries*. "It really was. And for Braden to do it in front of Brodeur, and then for Brodeur to come down, and the cameras caught a nice little conversation, it doesn't get any better than that. You can't top that."

Brodeur originally set the mark with a 48–23–7 record in 78 appearances in 2006–07, but a case can be made that Holtby was more economical, going 48–9–7 in 66 starts nine years later.

The Capitals ran away with the Presidents' Trophy and established a team record with 56 wins that season as Holtby joined Jim Carey (1995–96) and Olie Kolzig (1999–2000) as the only Capitals to win the Vezina Trophy.

"That's the one position that gives your team confidence—goaltending," head coach Barry Trotz said late that season. "He makes big saves and just gives you confidence—you have a strut or a little bit of swagger and that's the one position in our sport that can do that."

Before Trotz and Korn arrived in Washington in 2015, Holtby had lost some of his own swagger with a subpar 2013–14.

In the middle of that year, Holtby found himself part of a three-goalie rotation with Michal Neuvirth and rookie Philipp Grubauer. At one point, Holtby started just three times (posting a 0–2–1 record) in a 17-game stretch; hardly the workload expected for a typical No. 1.

Holtby not only saw limited playing time over that stretch, but with three goalies sharing two nets at practice, his between-game preparation was affected. The coaching staff in place at the time suggested that Holtby alter his game and adopt a less-aggressive style. Holtby's game suffered, and years later he acknowledged that it was the most challenging time in his professional career.

"It's always difficult when you don't play," he said in 2016. "It seems like the more time in between starts, the more pressure you put on yourself in those games that you do play and that never really turns out well."

Holtby and the Capitals missed the playoffs in 2014, but with the trust of a new coaching staff and with the chance to work with Korn, Holtby reestablished his confidence and took his game to another level.

NHL Single-Season Wins Leaders
T1: Braden Holtby, Washington, 2015–16: 66 Games, 48–9–7
T1: Martin Brodeur, New Jersey, 2006–07: 78 Games, 48–23–7
T3: Bernie Parent, Philadelphia, 1973–74: 73 Games, 47–13–12
T3: Roberto Luongo, Vancouver, 2006–07: 76 Games, 47–22–6
5: Evgeni Nabokov, San Jose, 2007–08: 77 Games, 46–21–8

Braden Holtby Capitals Goaltending Records
Most Appearances: 73 (2014–15)—tied with Olie Kolzig (2000–01)
Most Starts: 72 (2014–15)—tied with Olie Kolzig (2000–01)
Most Wins: 48 (2015–16)
Most Shutouts: 9 (2014–15)—tied with Jim Carey (1995–96)
Lowest Goals-Against Average: 2.07 (2016–17)—minimum 20 starts
Most Playoff Wins (Career): 29 (through 2016–17)

He was the undisputed No. 1 goalie in 2014–15 and appeared in 73 games that season—the most by a goalie in franchise history. His 42 wins that year were also a new team record as Washington returned to the postseason.

Holtby signed a five-year contract in the off-season, before turning in his 48-win campaign in 2015–16. Korn was among the first people he thanked when he accepted the Vezina Trophy at the NHL Awards Night in Las Vegas.

"Right from the start he had a game plan and we implemented it right away," Holtby said. "Just tightening up my game and limiting some erratic movement that I had in the past. I didn't really know how to fix it but Mitch came up with a plan and it worked great."

Korn, who is known in hockey circles as the "goaltending guru," had previously worked with the likes of Grant Fuhr and Dominik Hasek in Buffalo and Tomas Vokoun and Pekka Rinne in Nashville. He followed Trotz to D.C. after working together with the Predators for 15 seasons.

Among the areas that Korn sought to improve in Holtby's game was his body control. Early in their first year together, Korn noticed Holtby doing the full splits "guaranteed, four or five times a game."

Korn told Holtby that as a goaltender, he could make one of three types of saves—a normal save, an urgent save, or a desperate save. Although Holtby was capable of making the highlights with his raw athletic ability, Korn wanted to limit the "desperation" in those efforts.

"One of the things he's done extremely well is that he's improved his body use and as a result, he's a lot less busy."

The changes have allowed Holtby to emerge as one of the NHL's top goalies.

"You thrive on trying to be the best you can be, the best in your profession," Korn told NPR's *Hockey Diaries*. "And to be in the same breath and the same sentence as Marty Brodeur, that will be special as you look back on it during and following your career."

Holtby agrees.

"It's almost even cooler to be sharing the record with him than to have it yourself because he's a legend. He's arguably the best goalie that ever lived, and to be beside him, that's a huge honor."

15 The Canadiens Challenge

It's not often that the owner of a pro sports franchise will bribe his players before a scheduled game against a divisional opponent. But when it came to the Capitals searching for an elusive win over the Montreal Canadiens in the late 1970s, owner Abe Pollin was willing to try just about anything.

As the Capitals prepared to host the Canadiens on February 4, 1979, it was time, Pollin said, for Washington's drought against Montreal to come to an end. In their 26 previous meetings with Montreal, the Capitals' best result was a tie. The other 25 games all ended in defeat.

"It was a mental hurdle," former Capitals forward Tom Rowe said of beating the Canadiens. "So, Abe Pollin came into the room that night and said, 'If you beat the Canadiens, everyone gets $500.' That got our attention."

That much was evident, as Dennis Maruk, Guy Charon, and Rolf Edberg all scored in the first 2:25 of the game to give the Capitals a 3–0 lead and the fastest start in team history. The rest of the night, though, followed a familiar script. The Canadiens rallied to win in Landover 8–4, improving to 26–0–1 lifetime against the Capitals.

"They were so strong talentwise," Maruk recalled in 2016. "They had three, four good lines and we had maybe one and a half. You just hoped your goalie would play well to even have a chance. There was no way we could compete with that regularly. To be close was an accomplishment."

Other than in the alphabetical listing of the NHL's member clubs, the Canadiens and Capitals were never close during the 1970s. In fact, they could not have been further apart.

The Capitals were a historically bad team. The Canadiens were historically good. In 1975–76, the Capitals went 11–59–10 during the regular season. That same spring, the Canadiens went 12–1 in the postseason, en route to the first of four consecutive Stanley Cup titles.

The Canadiens of the 1970s were littered with such future Hall of Famers as Guy LaFleur, Steve Shutt, Larry Robinson, Serge Savard, and Ken Dryden. The Capitals, some would say, were simply litter.

"It was real tough," said former Capitals forward Gordie Smith. "We ended up playing Montreal always at the end of the year and it was always a shootout at the end of the year with guys like LaFleur and Shutt and all those guys going for total points or *x* amount of goals so they could hit their bonuses. If you look back at most of those games with Montreal at the end of the year, there were some lopsided games. Our guys were almost bailing out."

With Washington already eyeing the off-season and the Canadiens preparing for the Stanley Cup Playoffs, the Capitals played their final road game of the season at the Montreal Forum three times in their first five seasons. The Canadiens beat the Capitals by scores of 10–2, 11–0, and 10–3 in those games.

"We had guys at the end of the year who were looking at their plus/minus and didn't want to play the game," said Smith. "Guys suddenly coming up with the flu or a pulled muscle. You knew when we went in to face these clubs that we just didn't have the talent."

Making matters worse for the Capitals, they were placed in the Norris Division for their first five seasons, where they were joined by the Canadiens, Detroit Red Wings, Los Angeles Kings, and Pittsburgh Penguins.

This meant that as the Capitals went through the inevitable challenges as an expansion team, they would have to face the Canadiens at least six times a season. The results were both ugly and predictable.

Forward Dave Kryskow, the first skater the Capitals selected in the 1974 expansion draft, recounted Washington's first visit to Montreal in a 2013 feature in *The Globe and Mail*.

"I remember standing at center ice in the Montreal Forum," Kryskow said. "[Canadiens defenseman] Larry Robinson was there and he looked at me and I smiled and asked, 'What's the over/under on tonight's game?' He said, 'Ten.' I said, 'Sounds about right.'"

The final score was 10–0.

"Montreal functioned like a machine," said Mike Marson, who also skated for the Capitals in their maiden trip to the Forum on January 4, 1975. "I remember going into Montreal and one of my first assignments was to shadow Yvon Cournoyer, who was histori-cally renowned as the Roadrunner. In those days, I was considered to be quite quick on my feet so I was supposed to try to contain this gentleman. And I remember we're in the Montreal zone and as the play developed, it was like a military excursion."

Marson was a 19-year-old rookie trying to keep up with Cournoyer, another future Hall of Famer on the Canadiens roster.

"He picked up speed through the neutral zone and I was able to stay with him, but then when we hit the far blue line, he starts going laterally as fast as he was going forward and I was just like 'Wait a minute! Wait a minute! You've got to show me how to do that.' These were the types of things you were dealing when you were up against some of these established pros. They just had tricks up their sleeve that you couldn't even imagine."

The Capitals lost their first 23 meetings with Montreal and were winless through 34 all-time matchups (0–31–3) spanning more than five seasons.

"Montreal, especially going into the Forum," said Ron Lalonde, "the one thing we used to talk about in the dressing room, especially those first couple of years, was, 'Don't score early. Let them sleep, don't get them riled.' And one game we go in there, and about three minutes into the game, Yvon Labre took a slap shot from center, Ken Dryden missed it, and we were ahead 1–0. But that was just kicking over the beehive. We ended up losing 9–3."

What the Capitals lacked in skill against the Canadiens in the 1970s, they tried to make up for in creativity. On January 8, 1977, coach Tom McVie tried an unorthodox goaltending rotation that saw netminders Bernie Wolfe and Ron Low relieve each other every few minutes.

"He said no goaltender should endure for 60 minutes what our goaltenders go through in Montreal," Wolfe recalled in 2016. "And that's why he switched us every five minutes."

McVie ultimately made eight goaltending changes by the end of the night, but the result wasn't much different. The Canadiens beat the Capitals 7–2.

Caps Divisional History

Before the expansion Washington Capitals and Kansas City Scouts made their NHL debuts in the 1974–75 season, the league's 16 teams were neatly divided into a pair of eight-team divisions.

But with two more clubs on board and the number of franchises climbing to 18, the NHL underwent drastic realignment ahead of the '74–75 campaign. For the first time in league history, teams would be split into four divisions, which combined to form two conferences.

When the dust settled, the Capitals found themselves in the Norris Division, which, along with the Adams Division, made up the Prince of Wales Conference. The Clarence Campbell Conference was originally made up of teams in the Patrick and Smythe Divisions.

In addition to the Capitals, the Norris Division included the Detroit Red Wings, Los Angeles Kings, Montreal Canadiens, and Pittsburgh Penguins. The division was literally all over the map.

When the NHL absorbed the Edmonton Oilers, Hartford Whalers, Quebec Nordiques, and Winnipeg Jets from the World Hockey Association in 1979, the league realigned again, this time dividing teams based on geography.

The Capitals moved to the Patrick Division for the start of the 1979–80 season, where natural rivalries were soon established with the Islanders, Rangers, Flyers, and Penguins.

Below is a look at the Capitals' divisional history:

Norris Division (1974–75 to 1978–79): Detroit, Los Angeles, Montreal, Pittsburgh, Washington

Patrick Division (1979–80 to 1992–93): Atlanta Flames (1979–81) NY Islanders, NY Rangers, Philadelphia, Pittsburgh (joined 1981–82), Washington, New Jersey (joined in 1982–83)

Atlantic Division (1993–94 to 1997–98): Florida, New Jersey, NY Islanders, NY Rangers, Philadelphia, Tampa Bay, Washington

Southeast Division (1998–99 to 2012–13): Carolina, Florida, Tampa Bay, Washington, Atlanta (joined in 1999–2000; moved to Winnipeg in 2011–12 and remained in division for two seasons)

Metropolitan Division (2013–14 to present): Carolina, Columbus, New Jersey, NY Islanders, NY Rangers, Philadelphia, Pittsburgh, Washington

The experiment lasted just the one night, but the struggles against Montreal continued for three more years. In all, the Capitals went through five head coaches—Jimmy Anderson (0–4–0), Red Sullivan (0–1–0), Milt Schmidt (0–3–0), McVie (0–15–1), and Dan Belisle (0–8–2)—without ever beating the Canadiens.

But when 26-year-old Gary Green was hired as Washington's sixth bench boss 16 games into the 1979–80 season, he already had the Capitals' next game against the Canadiens marked on his calendar.

"It was my brother's birthday," Green said. "It was February 19, 1980. I phoned him to wish him a happy birthday that morning and I said, 'We're going to beat the Canadiens for the first time tonight.' And he just chuckled and laughed at me because they were still the mighty Montreal Canadiens."

Hours later, Montreal native Robert Picard gave the Capitals a 1–0 lead, Bengt Gustafsson added the eventual game-winning goal, and Mike Gartner sealed the game with an empty-net goal as the Capitals secured a 3–1 win over le bleu, blanc, rouge in Landover.

Wayne Stephenson made 31 saves in the win and later told the *Washington Post* that the Capitals had to beat Montreal, seeing as they had guaranteed it. The game was one of the Capitals' "Guaranteed-Win Nights," meaning that if they had failed for the 35th consecutive time to beat Montreal, fans would have received free tickets to a future home game. The promotion led to a weeknight crowd of 13,551 at the Capital Centre, with many in attendance counting down the game's final ten seconds in unison.

"After the game was over, we all went into the trainer's room," said Paul MacKinnon, then a rookie defenseman. "Mr. Pollin was vacationing somewhere down south, so he wasn't at the game, but I remember he called in after the game because he wanted to talk to each and every player on the phone just to congratulate each of us for getting that monkey off of his back. That win meant a lot to him."

It also meant a lot to Green, who, more than three decades later, still has the original score sheet of the Capitals' first win over Montreal framed and hanging on the wall in his home office in suburban Toronto.

16 First Playoff Appearance

At the time, it was the biggest milestone in Capitals history. But two of the men largely responsible for making it happen weren't around to celebrate.

First-year general manager David Poile was in southern Ontario the night of February 24, 1983, scouting a junior hockey game with Washington's director of player personnel, Jack Button. The Capitals were two time zones away visiting Poile's former employer, the Calgary Flames.

Soon after Poile and Button completed their scouting work, they retreated to their rental car, bound for Toronto, and began fidgeting with the radio stations.

"Because of the time difference," Poile recalled in 2017, "we were trying to listen to the game or at least hear an updated score. We were certainly tracking it. It was an exciting time for all of us."

The game was significant for the Capitals not only because they had a quartet of former Flames in their lineup that night, but because with a 4–2 win in Calgary, the once-hopeless Capitals clinched a Stanley Cup Playoff berth for the first time in team history.

After missing the postseason in each of their first eight years, the revamped Capitals met in Hershey for the start of training camp in September 1982 with one goal in mind.

"We were very confident that we were going to make the playoffs," said Alan Haworth. "There was no doubt in our mind."

Haworth was acquired from the Buffalo Sabres in a draft-day trade in June 1982 and was one of *nine* regulars on the 1982–83 Capitals, playing his first season in Washington.

"Remember that this isn't the team that didn't make the playoffs all those years," Haworth told the *Washington Post* after the win in Calgary. "This is a new hockey team that's a winner."

Other newcomers that season included goaltender Pat Riggin and forward Ken Houston, who were acquired in a draft day trade from Calgary. Rookies Scott Stevens and Milan Novy— Washington's first two selections in the 1982 draft—made the team out of training camp.

Then there was the blockbuster trade that Poile completed with the Montreal Canadiens on September 9, 1982, which brought Brian Engblom, Doug Jarvis, Rod Langway, and Craig Laughlin to Washington, along with the seven Stanley Cup rings between them.

"[The] playoffs was a big thing for us," Engblom said. "That's what we were used to in Montreal, and that's what we were gunning for in Washington. We wanted that playoff spot and as it became a possibility that we could do it, there's a lot of pride in that. You have to take steps and that was a big step for the organization. We really played hard for that."

Despite the optimism heading into the 1982–83 season, it took time for so many fresh faces to adjust to their new surroundings. The Capitals opened the year with three wins in 12 games (3–7–2).

But beginning with a 3–3 tie against Wayne Gretzky and the Edmonton Oilers on November 24, 1982, the Capitals went on a team-record 14-game unbeaten streak (9–0–5). The stretch culminated with a 5–1 win against the New York Islanders on December 23 in Bryan Murray's 100ᵗʰ game behind the Capitals' bench. The win at the Nassau Veterans Memorial Coliseum was the Capitals' first on Long Island after going 0–19–1 in their first 20 visits.

"That whole year, we were reaching milestones within the franchise that had never been achieved before," said Laughlin. "Whether it was most road wins, or longest winning streak, or first playoff berth, you felt that you were a part of something. It was a tightly knit group. We wanted to prove everybody wrong, so we had a burr up our butt to make sure that we got to the playoffs. We wanted to be part of it."

Gould Makes Caps History

Bobby Gould played an even 600 regular season games with the Capitals from 1981 through 1989, but one of his personal NHL highlights came in Washington's first playoff game.

"One of the things that I kind of cherish is you don't get your name too often in the record books," Gould said in 2016. "But I know when I went back many years ago, to see the Caps' new practice facility, they have the history of the team displayed on the walls, and one of the things that is kind of neat is that I was fortunate enough to score the very first playoff goal for the Capitals when we finally made it. It's a feat that nobody else is going to ever accomplish."

The Islanders beat the Capitals 5–2 in Game 1, with Gould scoring both goals in the defeat. Gould scored twice more in Game 2, including the Capitals' first game-winning goal in postseason play, as Washington evened the series at a game apiece with a 4–2 win.

New York took Games 3 and 4 in Landover by scores of 6–2 and 6–3 to close out the best-of-five series. Gould was the Capitals' leading scorer that postseason with five goals in four games.

"Those are the little things that as a player who was a third- and fourth-liner, a checker, it's kind of nice to be able to put your name in the record books."

Washington hit the Christmas break with a 16–9–9 record, just two points out of first place in the Patrick Division.

"I remember the thought process throughout that season," said former Capitals broadcaster Ron Weber. "First there's disbelief that they can keep it up. Then there's 'Hey maybe we can actually do this.' Then it becomes, 'Yes, we're really going to do it.' Just very exciting."

By the time the Capitals embarked on a six-game road trip in mid-February, it wasn't a question of if they would clinch a playoff berth, but just a matter of when.

Fittingly, two of Washington's off-season acquisitions were among the stars in the win in Calgary that secured the playoff berth. Haworth recorded his first career NHL hat trick and Riggin made 26 saves in his first game back in Calgary.

With 17 games still remaining in the regular season, the Capitals already knew they would be playing beyond the first week of April. They'd finish the season with a 39–25–16 record, good enough for third place in the Patrick Division.

"It was significant because whenever you do a first of something it's important," said Mike Gartner, the Capitals' first-round pick in 1979. "Doing it early allowed us to not worry about it—we knew that we were going to the playoffs and we could just focus on being the best team that we could be. We didn't just creep in—we got in pretty solidly into the playoffs and we had a lot of good years after that. But that first time getting in was very special for our franchise."

Bobby Gould—another former Flames player—joined the Capitals midway through the 1981–82 season and would remain with the club through 1988–89.

"At the time, I didn't realize how big of a deal this was," he said of the maiden playoff berth. "We had a little press conference before the playoffs and I didn't realize just how much of an accomplishment it was for the Capitals. It seemed to be the turning point and it certainly helped because the year before they had the big 'Save the Caps' campaign, and with us making the playoffs, all of a sudden we were playing in front of 13,000 people instead of 8,000 or 9,000. So, I didn't realize the importance, but looking back, it was certainly a great achievement for the guys that were there."

The postseason berth was also a long time coming for Dennis Maruk, the former California Seals and Cleveland Barrons center who played 581 regular season games over eight years before skating in the Stanley Cup Playoffs.

"The city was excited, we were excited, the organization was excited because it finally happened," Maruk said. "You want to see it happen earlier than it took, but the biggest thing was that we were able to get there. Then we get there and of course we had to play the [three-time defending Stanley Cup champion] Islanders and they were a powerhouse. It was tough hockey, but I think it was pretty exciting for all the players that we finally made it and had a chance to play for the Stanley Cup for the first time as the Washington Capitals."

The Islanders eliminated the Capitals in four games in the best-of-five Patrick Division semifinal en route to their fourth consecutive Stanley Cup title.

Washington, though, would become a postseason fixture, qualifying for the playoffs in 14 consecutive seasons from 1983 through 1996.

17 The King Is Dead

Joel Ward seemingly became a star overnight in the 2011 Stanley Cup Playoffs. A 30-year-old third-liner with the Nashville Predators at the time, Ward broke out with seven goals and 13 points in 12 games to lead Nashville to the second round for the first time in team history.

It was the type of playoff performance that caught the eye of Capitals general manager George McPhee, whose club was coming off its fourth consecutive Southeast Division title, but another premature postseason exit.

Weeks after Ward's breakthrough, the Capitals signed the free agent to a four-year $12 million deal. According to McPhee, the Capitals were one of 16 teams trying to acquire him. Not bad for a guy who, years earlier, was playing professional roller hockey in Florida and didn't land a full-time gig in the NHL until he was 27.

Despite a shaky first year with the Capitals in 2011–12, complete with a 35-game scoreless drought and a late-season stint as a healthy scratch, Ward ultimately delivered that spring.

The opportunity to do so wasn't guaranteed, as the Capitals didn't secure a playoff berth until their penultimate game of the regular season.

For the first time in the Alex Ovechkin era, the Capitals entered the playoffs as the underdogs, seeded No. 7 in the Eastern Conference and facing the defending Stanley Cup champion Boston Bruins.

Injuries to Tomas Vokoun and Michal Neuvirth forced Washington to turn to their third-string goaltender, rookie Braden Holtby, who had 14 wins in 21 career NHL games. Holtby would be opposed by the reigning Conn Smythe Trophy winner in Tim

Thomas, who had 16 wins in 25 games the previous postseason alone.

Holtby and the Capitals were up to the challenge, though, and the series proved to be a classic. The Capitals and Bruins split the first six games, three of which went to overtime. Bruins rookie Tyler Seguin scored in overtime in Game 6 at Verizon Center, setting the stage for a winner-take-all Game 7 at Boston's TD Garden on April 25, 2012.

"Boston is a hard place to play, and there was a little bit of intimidation going into that," defenseman Karl Alzner recalled five years later. "But it all went back to us wanting to spoil their fun. We wanted to beat them, we wanted to beat the champs, we wanted to beat their fans, we wanted to do it in their building, and we wanted to pound them into the ground while we did it."

"It was a heck of a ride," said Alzner's defensive partner John Carlson. "We needed to have a pretty good push at the end of the year just to get into the playoffs. Going into that series for me, being born up there and having family that are huge Bruins fans, it meant a lot to me personally, too. We played great that series against the defending champs and Game 7 was a big moment for us."

Ward, who was still seeking his first goal of the series, was preparing for his first career Game 7 that afternoon, when he received a text message from his friend and mentor, former NHL goaltender Kevin Weekes.

"He just told me to visualize," Ward said. "I took those words from a guy I've looked up to for many years. It's my first Game 7 experience so I figured I'd listen to someone who's been through it before."

The cliché suggests that all kids who grow up on a backyard rink or playing street hockey have pictured themselves in a starring role in Game 7 in the Stanley Cup Playoffs. In 2012, Ward, a grown man, was doing the same on his way to the rink late that afternoon.

"He told me to do my thing along the boards and go hard to the net. I took it to heart. I tried to visualize as best I could."

Game 7 was another tightly contested, low-scoring affair, with veteran Matt Hendricks opening the scoring for the Capitals in the first and the teenager Seguin answering for Boston in the second. For the fourth time in the series, though, 60 minutes of hockey would not suffice. Overtime would settle the best-of-seven series—the first in NHL history to go the distance with all seven games decided by one goal.

"I was excited for Game 7," said Dale Hunter, the former Capitals captain, who replaced Bruce Boudreau as head coach during the 2011–12 season. "There's nothing better. And I told them [after the third period] there's only one thing better than a Game 7. A Game 7 going to overtime, so have fun with it."

Hunter typically didn't say much to the team between periods, leaving the room primarily to veterans like Hendricks, Mike Knuble, Jason Chimera, and Dennis Wideman. But in a seventh game heading to sudden death, Hunter reminded his players to enjoy the moment.

"He was the best I had ever seen at handling the momentum swings and the intensity of a hockey game," recalled Brooks Laich. "You could tell he was a former player [who] loved it. The tighter and grittier the game got, the more intense but calm he got. He was fine. He was like, 'Yeah! This is hockey! Tie game, Game 7, this is why you play and you have to love it to be here!'"

If anybody knew about the pressure and the potential euphoria of a Game 7 overtime, it was Hunter. Back in Game 7 of the 1988 Patrick Division semifinals, Hunter beat Philadelphia Flyers goalie Ron Hextall in overtime for one of the biggest goals in franchise history.

Twenty-four years later, Ward would join Hunter as Washington's Game 7 overtime heroes. Ward followed the advice he received from Weekes and went hard to the net. It was a blue-collar type of goal in what had been a workmanlike series.

As the first overtime approached the three-minute mark, Bruins forward Benoit Pouliot looked to dump the puck deep into the Capitals' zone to allow for a Boston line change. Pouliot slapped the puck from the neutral zone, but it ricocheted off Knuble just inside the Washington blue line, suddenly providing the Capitals with a chance in transition as Boston changed personnel.

"[Pouliot] was trying to dump it in hard and I was just coming through the pile," Knuble said. "I was heading towards him and it hit me right square in the knees and it kicked out to center ice. We caught everybody in a change, they were assuming the puck was going in and all of a sudden, it's a hard rebound going the other way. And then you come out of the pile and you can't believe that this is where you are on the ice right now, with a two-on-one."

"When it happened, it was a freak play," Ward said. "We were thinking about coming off for a line change at first until he blocked that dump in and we got on our horse, knowing that he was going up the ice. I figured at that stage of the game nobody was going to try to pass it across through a defenseman, so I just tried to trail behind him. I knew he was going to take it to the net."

Knuble broke through the neutral zone and had a clear lane towards Thomas.

"I was carrying that thing right to the crease," he said. "I was going to jam it in one way or another, but Joel was smart—he didn't swing by the net, he was able to pick up the trash."

Knuble's backhand attempt was stopped by Thomas, but Ward followed on the rebound and beat Thomas with a backhand of his own for the biggest goal of his career.

"I was just trying to hide in the weeds and look for a loose puck," he recalled. "When I saw the puck sitting there, I just took a whack at it, and it goes in and it was one of the coolest feelings I had ever had. Just the year that we had, battling and being in and out of the lineup, for it to happen then, it was pretty cool. I don't know too many of those I've had in my lifetime, scoring in Game 7 in overtime."

Play-by-play voice John Walton was in his first season in the NHL and had the call on the Capitals Radio Network:

"The Boston Bruins now turn it over. A two-on-one. Knuble coming with Ward. Knuble with a chance, backhander loose, they score! They score! They score! It's over! Ward on the rebound! Good morning, good afternoon, and good night Boston! The king is dead! There will be a new Stanley Cup champion! The Capitals are still dancing! A rebound off Thomas, and the Capitals have won it in Boston, in Game 7."

As the Capitals emptied the bench and piled on Ward along the boards in the Boston zone, Hendricks went the opposite direction and was the first to embrace Holtby as he approached center ice. Chimera and Roman Hamrlik soon joined them for celebratory hugs and high fives.

Hunter predicted that Washington's "foot soldiers" would emerge as difference makers in Game 7 and that proved prophetic, as bottom-six forwards Hendricks and Ward accounted for the goal scoring. Knuble, who started the play on the winning goal, had been a healthy scratch for the first three games of the series.

"That goal symbolized that whole series," Hendricks said of the overtime winner. "There wasn't anything cute or pretty about that series. It was rough and tough, there were a lot of bruises and beat-up bodies in that seven-game series and that goal was the perfect way to put a stamp on it and move on to the next round. It was great. It was great for Wardo and Knubs, both were tremendous players for us and tremendous people in our room and their ice time had been cut down quite a bit that season as well and for them to get that opportunity and finish that goal in Game 7 was a great feeling."

For Ward, the goal also provided some vindication after signing his free agent deal, but underperforming during the regular season.

"It was huge," he said. "For me personally, I thought I may have lost a little bit of respect from my own teammates just being on the outside so much and I definitely do play for the respect of them. Once you gain the respect from everybody, things seem to go a lot more smoothly. But when you're on the outside a little bit, it's definitely tough. So, for us to get back in the lineup and keep working, we were excited just to be part of it. Listening to Knubs on the bench, it's all about embracing it, staying even-keeled and staying in the moment and it worked out for us."

18 Growing Pains for Early Prospects

Former Capitals defenseman Rick Green knew what he was getting into. As the first overall selection in the 1976 draft, Green joined a Capitals team that won 19 of 160 games in its first two seasons. As the losses continued to pile during Green's rookie season, the No. 1 pick looked on the bright side.

"I really started to hone a lot of my defensive skills because we were spending so much time in our own zone," he said, tongue in cheek, 40 years later. "We had a lot of practice in there. You learn quickly when you're thrown right into the deep end."

Capitals prospects in the mid-1970s weren't just thrown into the deep end; they were thrown in without life vests and surrounded by sharks. With hardly any organizational structure and without the benefit of veterans to show them the ropes, very few of Washington's early draft picks realized their full potential.

"It's really tough to come into an environment and not necessarily have the best supporting cast," said Green, who spent six seasons with the Capitals from 1976 through 1982. "The expectations are there as a No. 1 pick that you're supposed to be way above average, but you do need some help."

In 1974, the expansion Capitals had the first overall pick in the amateur draft after general manager Milt Schmidt won a coin toss over Kansas City Scouts GM Sid Abel.

Washington selected defenseman Greg Joly, who months earlier had led the Western Hockey League's Regina Pats to the Memorial Cup, where he was named Most Valuable Player.

"Joly can do a lot of the same incredible things that [Bobby] Orr does," Schmidt told the *Washington Post*. "He skates extremely well, is intelligent and can either pass or carry the puck out of danger. He's shown signs that he can score like Orr, too."

Orr is the greatest defenseman in NHL history. Joly is arguably one of the game's biggest busts.

Not only was Joly not the best player in the draft, he wasn't even the best player on his junior team. Three picks after the Capitals chose Joly, the New York Islanders took his Regina teammate, future Hall of Famer Clark Gillies, fourth overall.

It was a similar script in Round 2, where the Capitals picked forward Mike Marson at No. 19. Three picks later, the Islanders took future Hall of Famer Bryan Trottier.

Joly played just 98 games across two seasons in Washington, collecting 9 goals, 33 points, and a minus-114 rating. He was eventually traded to Detroit for veteran Bryan Watson.

"Joly had knee surgery that first year," said defenseman Yvon Labre. "That set him back. I don't know that the first year here ever did him any good. It was not good for young guys to be in that [losing] situation."

"He was hurt from the get-go," said forward Ron Lalonde.

Marson played 193 games spread over five seasons with the Capitals, recording 24 goals and 48 points. Besides the pressure of being the second pick on an expansion team, Marson carried additional weight as the second black player in the NHL.

"Mike had difficulty," said goalie Bernie Wolfe. "He was making a lot of money, and the same with Greg Joly. Big-time pressure on both of those guys. And with an expansion team, you're almost set up to fail."

"Our draft choices didn't pan out the way we thought they would and that's the key," head scout Red Sullivan told the *Washington Post* in 1983. "Not a hell of a lot was made available in the expansion draft, so we had to count on the kids, like Joly and Marson, but they didn't work out. In a situation like we were in, we couldn't afford not to have them pan out."

After finishing with the worst record in league history in 1974–75, the Capitals could have picked first overall in the 1975 draft. But Schmidt sent the No. 1 pick to Philadelphia for center Bill Clement. The trade backfired, as Clement lasted just 46 games in Washington before the Capitals dealt him to Atlanta.

Months later, they held onto their 1976 No. 1 pick and selected Green, who had been named the Ontario Hockey Association's best defenseman the previous season.

"I had a great opportunity to play in the NHL, which was my ultimate goal," he said in 2016. "I didn't care at that point where and the Washington Capitals gave me the opportunity.

"But I had to fly quite a bit by myself. There were expectations from a lot people that I had to make the difference. Like any first pick, they're looking for immediate impact. It was a learning experience."

Like Joly two years earlier, Green didn't have too many veterans to follow.

By the time an 18-year-old Scott Stevens made the jump from junior to the NHL in 1982, the Capitals were better prepared to groom young players. As a rookie, Stevens played primarily with veterans Brian Engblom and Rod Langway, whom he credits with teaching him how to handle the rigors of the NHL.

More recently, Alex Ovechkin leaned on veterans like Dainius Zubrus and Viktor Kozlov. Nicklas Backstrom lived with countryman Michael Nylander during his rookie season, and then returned the favor when he hosted Swedish rookie Andre Burakovsky in 2014.

But in the 1970s, because the Capitals were just finding their footing organizationally, there weren't any similar mentor programs in place.

"Some of us were lucky to be on an expansion team, because we wouldn't have otherwise made it," said Wolfe, who spent four years with the Capitals from 1975 through 1979. "But with these guys, if they were say with the Montreal Canadiens from day one, not only would they have made it, but they would have been superstars."

Tom Rowe was teammates with Green with both the junior London Knights and with the Capitals. He agrees that Green could have been a star with another team.

"If Rick Green had gone to the Islanders or the Flyers, he would have developed and blossomed a lot faster," Rowe said. "I used to see him before games and the stress that he'd go through and the emotions that he'd go through. He was very intense in his own way and he took being drafted No. 1 very seriously. I think it ate at him a little bit because the team could never get over the hump."

19 Saint Nick

Sometimes the best trades are the ones you don't make, as the Capitals can attest.

At the 2006 draft in Vancouver, the Capitals were on the clock and preparing to make the fourth overall selection when the Bruins inquired about swapping first-round picks (Washington's No. 4 pick for Boston's No. 5 pick). The Bruins would tack on a second-round pick for the right to move up one spot in Round 1.

"Who do you want?" general manager George McPhee asked Boston GM Jeff Gorton on the draft floor.

"The Swede," Gorton said.

The Capitals rejected Boston's offer and took center Nicklas Backstrom themselves. It's a good thing they did. Over the next decade, "the Swede" would emerge as one of the top players in Capitals history.

"He's the heartbeat of our team," goaltender Braden Holtby said in 2017.

"Without Nicky Backstrom, the Washington Capitals aren't who they are," said former teammate Matt Hendricks.

Backstrom is an elite playmaker and two-way forward. But he's also one of the game's quietest superstars. He doesn't care for the spotlight and he goes about his business with little fanfare.

In his first 10 seasons in the NHL, Backstrom had the third-most assists and the sixth-most points. But over that same stretch, he had just one All-Star selection and only twice finished in the top 10 in voting for MVP (Backstrom was No. 9 in voting in both 2009–10 and 2016–17).

"I think he likes to be overlooked," said former teammate Troy Brouwer. "He doesn't like to be the guy everyone's talking about."

Long considered the greatest playmaker in Capitals history, Nicklas Backstrom made it official on March 15, 2015, when he passed Michal Pivonka as Washington's all-time assists leader.

It's easy to get overlooked when playing alongside Alex Ovechkin, but that suits Backstrom just fine.

"He's so quiet off the ice," former Capitals head coach Bruce Boudreau said of Backstrom. "He doesn't make waves. He's not a media tycoon. He just comes to play every day."

Backstrom was so quiet and unassuming as a rookie that Boudreau actually forgot to include him in the lineup for his first game behind the Capitals' bench.

Boudreau replaced Glen Hanlon 21 games into the 2007–08 season and only put Backstrom on the fourth line when he realized he was a forward short.

By the end of the game, Backstrom made sure that would never happen again. On his 20th birthday, Backstrom capped off a three-point afternoon with the game-winning goal in overtime. The Capitals beat Philadelphia 4–3 in OT to hand Boudreau his first NHL win.

"I think Nick is the best," Boudreau said in 2017. "I think Nick is in a class by himself…. One of my favorite players I have ever coached. I would have loved to have had him as my teammate."

Those who have played with Backstrom don't take it for granted.

"You find yourself at least once a game turning to the guy next to you on the bench and saying, 'Did you see what he did there?'" defenseman Karl Alzner said in 2016. "He's so patient and poised; he's got great hands, great vision."

"He was one of the most fun players I've ever played with," said Hendricks, teammates with Backstrom from 2010 through 2013. "I learned a lot from him in terms of how to take faceoffs and how to be better on the penalty kill. I prided myself on my work ethic, but Nicky taught me ways to be smart—how to play controlled and how to play smarter."

And he makes it look so easy. Even in his first few years with the Capitals, it all seemed to come so naturally for Backstrom.

Holtby remembers his first training camp in Washington in 2009 and the trainers and coaching staff taking issue with a few pounds Backstrom, then 21, had put on in the wrong places.

"They were concerned with his weight," Holtby recalled in 2017. "So, they made him wear a weighted vest in practice one day to show him that he was carrying too much and it would be better if he trimmed down.

"But then he goes out there with the weighted vest and was by far the best player on the ice. It didn't affect him one bit. And so, he comes off the ice and they were just mad at him and told him to take it off because he was so good that their plan backfired. Didn't exactly prove their point. That's one of my earliest memories of Nick. And it's the same today. He's so smooth and effortless in a league that takes so much effort."

Like any good playmaker, Backstrom makes those around him better, and a case can easily be made that no player has benefited more from Backstrom than Ovechkin. In Backstrom's first 10 seasons, Ovechkin scored 432 goals when they were both in the lineup. Backstrom assisted on nearly half—49.3 percent.

"He always puts his teammates in a great position to bury the puck," said Tom Wilson, Backstrom's locker room stall mate at the Kettler Capitals Iceplex.

"You see it a lot with Ovi—Nicky will suck guys in and then he'll dish it and then Ovi has an amazing vantage point for an open shot."

Perhaps it's fitting that the Capitals had Ovechkin go on stage at the 2006 draft to announce Backstrom as their pick. The two have been linked ever since, with Backstrom, the reserved, play-making center, serving as the ideal running mate to Ovechkin, a natural in the limelight and one of the best goal scorers of his generation.

While Ovechkin delivers thunderous hits, unloads a heavy shot, and scores more than most, Backstrom's skill set is more subtle. He's a smooth skater and can slow the game down. There is a calm to his game as he sees plays develop and considers his options. He is the yin to Ovechkin's yang.

"We have great chemistry," Ovechkin said. "It's been a great honor to play with him, he's a tremendous skill guy and we've been able to grow up together in NHL and have success."

"Ovi is the leader and a great player," Brouwer said in 2015, "but Nicky is the guy that makes the team run."

20 Nicklas Backstrom Time Line

From the time Nicklas Backstrom earned an assist in the first period of his first career NHL game, both the assists and milestones have quietly come in bunches. Below are some of Backstrom's career highlights:

June 24, 2006: The Capitals select Backstrom with the No. 4 pick at the 2006 NHL Draft in Vancouver. Alex Ovechkin announces the pick from the NHL Draft stage.

October 5, 2007: In his NHL debut, Backstrom earns his first career NHL assist on a Michael Nylander power play goal midway through the first period. The Capitals beat the Thrashers 3–1.

November 8, 2007: Backstrom beats Ottawa's Ray Emery for his first career NHL goal. The power play marker stood as the game winner as the Capitals won 4–1 in Ottawa. It was the final win for Capitals head coach Glen Hanlon, who was fired two weeks later.

November 23, 2007: Backstrom celebrated his 20th birthday in style, netting the overtime game winner in Bruce Boudreau's NHL coaching debut. The Capitals beat the Flyers 4–3 in Philadelphia.

April 5, 2008: In the 2007–08 regular season finale, Backstrom earned his 55th assist to establish a new Capitals rookie record.

February 14, 2009: On the same night Mike Green set an NHL record by scoring in his eighth consecutive game—the longest streak by a defenseman—Backstrom picked up his 100th career NHL assist. Backstrom became the quickest Capitals player to hit the century mark, doing so in 138 games.

April 9, 2010: With an assist on Ovechkin's 50th goal of the season, Backstrom earned his 100th point. Backstrom finished the 2009–10 season with career highs of 33 goals and 68 assists. He joined Dennis Maruk as the only Capitals with at least 30 goals and 60 assists in the same season.

April 17, 2010: In Game 2 of the Eastern Conference quarterfinals against Montreal, Backstrom capped off his first playoff hat trick with the game winner just 31 seconds into overtime. Backstrom's hat trick helped the Capitals erase a 4–1 deficit and rally for a 6–5 OT win.

May 17, 2010: The Capitals signed Backstrom, then 22, to a 10-year, $67 million contract.

December 30, 2011: Backstrom scored the 100th goal of his NHL career as the Capitals beat Buffalo 3–1 at Verizon Center.

April 14, 2012: Backstrom scored at 2:56 of double overtime in Game 2 of the 2012 Eastern Conference quarterfinals against Boston. The goal secured a 2–1 win as the Capitals evened their first-round series against the defending-champion Bruins at a game apiece.

October 22, 2014: In his 501st career NHL game, Backstrom earned his 500th point with an assist on a John Carlson power play goal in Edmonton.

December 13, 2014: Backstrom picked up his first career regular season hat trick in a 4–2 win over Tampa Bay.

March 15, 2015: The greatest playmaker in Capitals history made it official as Backstrom broke Michal Pivonka's franchise record with his 419ᵗʰ career assist. The milestone came with Backstrom assisting a power play goal from Carlson in a 2–0 win over Boston.

January 6, 2016: For the first time in his career, Backstrom was selected to play in the NHL All-Star Game.

January 7, 2017: Backstrom became the first Capitals player and the 139ᵗʰ in NHL history to record 500 career assists. Backstrom assisted on T.J. Oshie's goal at 1:38 of the first period in an eventual 1–0 win in Ottawa.

21 Natural-Born Leader

Rod Langway didn't seek a leadership role. Leadership, though, found Rod Langway. Whether in life or on the ice, Langway was a natural in guiding others and taking control.

When he was 13, his mother, Elda, died of lung cancer. Shortly after, his father, Kenneth, moved from the family home in suburban Boston. Langway was one of seven children, but when his two older brothers also moved out, Rod became the de facto head of the household.

"You grow up fast," he told the *Washington Post* in 1993.

Langway looked after his siblings and used athletics as motivation to get through high school, where he starred in football, baseball, and hockey. Langway captained all three varsity teams. As a senior in 1975, he led the Randolph High School hockey team to the Massachusetts state championship and earned a scholarship to the University of New Hampshire.

They stay-at-home defenseman began his pro hockey career after leading the UNH Wildcats to the NCAA Frozen Four his sophomore season. Although he didn't return for his junior year, Langway had already been selected as the team's captain.

"To be captain as a junior, that's unusual in college," Langway said in 2017. "But it was the norm for me. In high school and college, and even when I got to the minors, some of the veterans didn't realize that I was a rookie. I guess my demeanor and how I handled myself around the veterans, I could take control of what was going on."

Four years into his NHL career, a 24-year-old Langway was traded to the Capitals from the Montreal Canadiens. The Capitals immediately named him captain despite his never having played for them.

The sixth captain in team history, Langway was the first to lead Washington to the playoffs. He went on to wear the "C" for 11 seasons, with the Capitals reaching the postseason every year. He remains the longest-tenured captain in team history.

"Once he was named captain," said former teammate Craig Laughlin, "it really set into place the blossoming of hockey here. He was 'the guy.' He was the guy without the helmet, the big, tough defenseman. When he got the captaincy, it turned the whole image of this team and this franchise. Everybody all of a sudden liked the way that we played but it was largely because of what he brought from Montreal. He was the man that put us on the map and carried us."

The Capitals were the NHL's most improved team in 1982–83, winning 14 more games than the previous season. All four players Capitals general manager David Poile acquired in the 1982 trade with the Canadiens contributed to the turnaround, but none had a bigger impact than Langway—the spiritual and vocal leader who was consistently among Washington's top performers.

"How can you not win when your best players are also your hardest workers?" Poile told *Sports Illustrated* in 1983. "The other guys see that and wonder, 'How can we not try?'"

Langway won the Norris Trophy as the NHL's top defenseman in each of his first two years in Washington, but it was his leadership and his ability to handle personalities that most impressed his teammates.

"He had a really good grip on that team," said goaltender Bob Mason, who calls Langway the best captain he played with in his 12-year pro career.

"He ran that locker room and we'd follow his lead. He'd get on guys, he'd tell you to wake up, and he'd point out certain guys in the room—and not just the lower-end guys. If someone needed a jolt, he'd let you know.

"He controlled that room as soon as we sat down and untied our skates and relaxed for the intermission. Rod was nonstop chatter. If someone wasn't going, he'd say, 'Hey wake the bleep up.' He'd give it to you. But you knew that he wasn't giving it to

Check's in the Mail

Leaders look out for their teammates, and Langway did that late in the 1990–91 season in a personal example from defenseman Ken Sabourin. Sabourin was acquired by the Capitals midway through the year in a trade with the Calgary Flames. His contract, which followed him to Washington, entitled Sabourin to a bonus if he finished among the leaders on his team in plus/minus rating at season's end. Langway was aware of Sabourin's potential bonus and made a deal with the 24-year-old late in the season.

"Rod knew about the bonus," Sabourin said, "so in one of our last games of the season, whenever he was taking a shift and the play started to go up ice, he'd come to the bench and let me go on. And then if the play was going the other way and coming back towards our end, he'd call for me to come off. He was protecting me because at that stage of my career the bonus was a big deal for me. Rod always did things like that."

Aided by a plus-9 rating he built in Calgary, Sabourin finished the 1990–91 season plus-15—tops among players who finished the year with Washington.

you because he didn't like you. He was giving it to you because he knew that you had more to give."

The son of a Navy man who served 21 years, Langway also showed his leadership in international competition, captaining Team USA at the Canada Cup in 1981, 1984, and 1987 and at the 1982 World Hockey Championships.

"He expected full commitment from all of the players," said Larry Murphy, Langway's occasional defensive partner in Washington from 1983 through 1989. "He was a hard-nosed player and did what he had to do in order to win. When you have that, you have a real effective captain. That's what we had."

Even in his 30s, Langway led by example both on and off the ice. Known for being one of the last NHL players to compete without a helmet, Langway didn't shy away from physicality or battles atop the crease.

"He was solid as a rock," said John Druce, teammates with Langway from 1988 through 1992.

"He'd work his butt off, and I never saw a guy sweat so much. When he would train and ride the bike before or after practice, there would be puddles beside that bike. That was leadership. If our captain is doing that, we better fall in line and be able to keep up with that and work as hard."

Druce was 22 during his rookie season, but nearly 30 years later, he still remembers Langway taking him under his wing, despite his frequent trips to and from the American Hockey League.

"I remember when I joined the team as a young kid," Druce said, "he'd take me out for lunch after practice and invite me to go out with the guys because maybe it wasn't something I'd necessarily be comfortable to ask to be part of. Those are the types of things that leaders do."

22 The Captaincy

Rod Langway may have the longest tenure as Capitals captain, but 13 other players have also worn the "C" in a Washington sweater. The captains have ranged in age and experience, but all appreciated the status and responsibilities that came with being a leader in the NHL.

Below is a look at the 14 captains in Capitals history:

Doug Mohns (1974–75): Mohns was the elder statesman on the expansion Capitals, a 40-year-old defenseman in his 22nd NHL season. General manager Milt Schmidt had coached Mohns for seven seasons in Boston and thought his experience would be valuable on a young team in Washington.

The Capitals purchased Mohns' contract from the Atlanta Flames in June 1974 and, midway through the inaugural season, named him the first captain in team history. Some of Mohns' younger teammates had fun at his expense, as he was among the first players in the NHL to wear a toupee. As a result, Mohns never took his helmet off during the national anthem, choosing instead to salute.

Bill Clement (1975–76): After posting a miserable 8–67–5 record during their expansion season, the Capitals had earned the right to pick first overall in the 1975 draft. Unfortunately, the Capitals traded the No. 1 pick to the two-time defending Stanley Cup champion Flyers for Philadelphia' first-round pick, defenseman Don McLean, and center Bill Clement.

Clement was chosen to replace the retiring Mohns as the Capitals captain, but Clement's time in Washington was brief.

Forty-six games into the season, he was traded to Atlanta for forward Gerry Meehan.

Yvon Labre (1976–78): Labre wasn't especially big—listed at 5'11", 190 pounds—but the hard-nosed defenseman was one of the few members of the early Capitals teams who stood up to tougher players around the league. Labre led the Capitals in penalty minutes in each of their first two seasons before injuries took their toll.

"He fought everybody in the league and most of the time he was on his own in that regard," said goalie Bernie Wolfe. "We didn't have tough guys. We had some older players and some others who weren't fighters. It's hard to develop a team when you have to find people to fill those roles. Yvon took on that role and even though he wasn't the most qualified, he was the first to step in."

Guy Charron (1978–79): Charron was the Capitals' best offensive player in the late 1970s, leading the club in scoring in each of his first two seasons (1976–77 and 1977–78) and representing Washington at the 1977 NHL All-Star Game.

Charron embraced the opportunity to captain the Capitals but was disappointed that his tenure was so brief. After one season, management decided that Ryan Walter would take over the captaincy.

"It meant a lot," Charron said of wearing the "C" during the 1978–79 season. "It was an honor and a privilege to have that. But the year that they decided to make the changes and they gave it to Ryan—it's difficult taking away the captaincy of an individual still on the team. It's very difficult to ask an individual to step down because it tells you, 'Okay, you can't fulfill that role any longer.' There's always a time and place to do that. I've been part of organizations where you feel that changes should be made, but you don't just go to a player and say, 'You know what, we need to make changes now and we're going to give your captaincy to someone else.' I was hurt by it."

Ryan Walter (1979–82): Walter was 21 when he replaced Charron as Washington's captain, becoming the youngest player in NHL history to sport the "C."

"I was ready for it in the sense that I loved the Capitals, I had strong team values, and I would protect my teammates," he said. "All of those pieces were in place to become a captain. But I was young in the area of leadership and I probably made some mistakes in that regard early on. We were still struggling to string together a lot of wins and I think that increased the pressure on the leadership."

Walter was traded to Montreal in 1982 as part of the six-player deal that brought Langway, Brian Engblom, Doug Jarvis, and Craig Laughlin to Washington.

Rod Langway (1982–93): Widely viewed as the best captain in team history, Langway led the Capitals to the playoffs in each of his 11 seasons with the club.

"His work ethic on the ice was the best," said Alan Haworth, teammates with Langway from 1982 through 1987. "Every game, it was the same thing. Rod brought that work ethic to the team where we could accomplish more just by following his lead and putting in the work like he did. We worked hard and had a team where nobody would let up. It started with Rod and everyone followed."

Kevin Hatcher (1993–94): Despite Langway's status as one of the best players in team history, he was used sparingly during the first half of the 1992–93 season. With injuries mounting and his role diminishing, Langway passed the captaincy to Hatcher—a fixture in the lineup.

"That's a little bit hard," Hatcher told the *Washington Post* of taking over the captaincy. "Roddy's taught me a lot about leadership."

Hatcher led all NHL blue-liners with 34 goals during the 1992–93 season—still a Capitals franchise record for a defenseman—but he managed just 16 goals and 40 points in his only full season as captain in 1993–94. The Capitals traded Hatcher to the Dallas Stars for Mark Tinordi just before the lockout-shortened 1995 season.

Dale Hunter (1995–99): Hunter was a leader throughout his 12 seasons in Washington and a natural choice to take over the captaincy in 1995. Three years later, a 37-year-old Hunter played all 82 regular season games and 21 more in the playoffs en route to becoming the first captain to lead the Capitals to the Stanley Cup Final.

"He was a special guy," said head coach Ron Wilson. "He'd fight anybody and he took on all comers. I remember he had a real back-and-forth going with [Flyers center] Eric Lindros in his prime. He always played Eric very rough and mean. That's just the way Dale was. I think he did some things that he couldn't even believe he was doing himself, but that's the way Dale played the game. And he showed all the players on the team that he was willing to do anything in order to win the game."

Adam Oates (1999–2001): The Capitals introduced Oates as their ninth captain at a press conference in front of the White House on September 2, 1999. Oates had been teammates with some of the best captains in league history in Steve Yzerman, Ray Bourque, and Dale Hunter, but this marked the first time in his career that he would wear the "C."

"To have the opportunity to be the captain of an NHL team is something that's very special to me," Oates said. "I'll always cherish it."

The gig didn't last long for Oates, who demanded a trade two years later and was stripped of the captaincy before the 2001–02 campaign. He was eventually dealt to Philadelphia on March 19, 2002.

Brendan Witt (2001–02): Once Oates was stripped of the captaincy in 2001, the Capitals held a team vote to determine his successor. The vote produced a tie between Brendan Witt and Steve Konowalchuk. For the first time in team history, the Capitals went with co-captains in 2001–02.

"I was really honored because you never know what your peers are saying," Witt told the Capitals' official website in 2012. "I thought it was such a great honor to even have that on my jersey. I had it [in junior hockey] in Seattle, but I think having it on an NHL level is a whole different responsibility. You get voted by your peers and it was just a great honor to wear it for a season. I still have my jersey with the 'C' on it and I'll never forget that."

Steve Konowalchuk (2001–04): Konowalchuk was the first piece to move during the Capitals' 2003–04 fire sale, but not before he spent parts of three seasons as captain.

"When I look back," Konowalchuk said in 2017, "I was an average hockey player who had to work hard every day. So to earn the respect of the organization and from my teammates and to get that honor is probably one of the more proud things that I accomplished in my career. I had to work my butt off just to survive in the NHL, so to be able to establish that role with an NHL team, I'm pretty proud of it."

Konowalchuk was traded to Colorado six games into the 2003–04 season, but the Capitals did not select another captain for the rest of the season. Instead, Washington went with six alternating captains. Witt, Peter Bondra, and Sergei Gonchar wore A's for home games with Robert Lang, Jaromir Jagr, and Mike Grier doing so for road games. Ironically, all six alternating captains would also be traded by the end of the year.

Jeff Halpern (2005–06): As if playing for his hometown team wasn't enough of a thrill for Jeff Halpern, the Potomac, Maryland, native would follow two of his favorite players in Langway and Hunter when he was named team captain in September 2005.

"I always looked up to those guys," Halpern said. "I was able to have Dale Hunter to talk to my first year when he had a [player development] job in the organization. Just being able to talk to him after games and after practices, it was an invaluable experience. And to play with Adam Oates and Steve Konowalchuk, there was a lot to learn. Hopefully, I took advantage of that."

Chris Clark (2006–09): After Halpern signed a free-agent deal with Dallas in 2006, the Capitals offered the captaincy to a 20-year-old Alex Ovechkin. Ovechkin was entering his second season, but declined the offer because he didn't believe his command of English was strong enough. So the Capitals selected another American as their new captain, veteran Chris Clark.

"He's a leader in the mold of Dale Hunter," general manager George McPhee said at the time. "He's a quiet man off the ice and cantankerous on it. Leadership is not a sometimes thing, it's an all-the-time thing, and Chris has the all-the-time leadership that all teams covet."

Clark enjoyed his best season while sporting the "C" with career highs of 30 goals and 54 points in 2006–07, playing primarily with Ovechkin on the top line. Injuries limited Clark to just 50 games combined over the next two seasons, though, and he was eventually traded to Columbus in December 2009.

Alex Ovechkin (2010–present): There was some thought after Clark was traded that the Capitals would go the rest of the 2009–10 season without a captain. But a week after the deal, Ovechkin was introduced as the team's 14th captain, with little fanfare.

Ben Raby

As the Capitals prepared to host the Montreal Canadiens on January 5, 2010, Ovechkin came out for the pregame warmup with the "C" stitched on his jersey. That's how many fans and media learned of the change. An official release from the team soon followed.

"I had talked to a lot of [players], and they said Alex is the only choice," then–head coach Bruce Boudreau said. "He's our leader, he's our guy. What shows he was ready was when I talked to him [about the captaincy] he said he would accept the responsibility but 'only if my teammates want it.' He was already thinking about the team instead of himself, which is what captains do."

The Capitals won 17 of their first 18 games after Ovechkin was named captain, highlighted by a team-record 14-game winning streak. They won the Presidents' Trophy that season, but were ultimately upset in the first round against Montreal. Premature playoff exits would become a theme throughout Ovechkin's captaincy.

23 Workaholic Caps Break on Through

A year removed from reaching the Stanley Cup Playoffs for the first time in franchise history, the 1983–84 Capitals were out to prove that they had staying power.

A season-opening seven-game losing streak—another franchise first—raised a few eyebrows, but by midseason, the youngest team in the NHL was developing into a legitimate Stanley Cup contender.

Beginning with a 7–1 win at the Spectrum in Philadelphia on January 8, 1984, the Capitals went on a 16–1–1 run, suffering just one defeat over a 42-day span. Within that stretch, the Capitals enjoyed their first 10-game winning streak and matched a franchise record with a 14-game unbeaten streak (13–0–1).

Fittingly, minutes before every game during the streak, Capitals players cued up a boom box in the dressing room and played the team's unofficial theme song—"Break on Through," by The Doors.

"Davey Christian always pushed the play button," Craig Laughlin told the Capitals' official website in 2010. "[Rod Langway] would say five minutes before warmup, 'Okay boys, we're ready,' and you couldn't talk for the next five minutes because The Doors' song was on."

Reminded of the pregame routine decades later, defenseman Larry Murphy thought back to teammate Gaeten Duchesne's insistence that the song be played throughout the streak.

"Gaeten was so superstitious and he was the guy who would make sure that everything was set the same for the next game," Murphy said. "So he'd get that going on the old radio in the dressing room. He made sure of it. A lot of guys would forget about something like that, but it would set him off if it wasn't done the same way and that song wasn't played."

While the Capitals may have been loose heading into their games, the 1983–84 model hardly goofed around between whistles.

"We were starting to get an identity as a really hardworking team," said Mike Gartner, Washington's leading scorer that season with 40 goals and 85 points in 80 games.

"The tagline at the time was the 'Workaholic Capitals.' The marketing department always loved to have a little marketing slogan and that seemed to work really well because that's how we were establishing ourselves as far as our identity—a really hardworking, strong defensive team."

Washington's 10-game winning streak began with a home-and-home series sweep of the Toronto Maple Leafs, including an 8–0 win at Maple Leaf Gardens on January 28.

Pat Riggin made 22 saves to record the first of his three shutouts over the course of the winning streak. Riggin played every minute during the streak and was twice named the NHL's Player of the Week over that stretch.

Along the way, Riggin set a franchise record that still stands today with a shutout streak of 203 minutes and 52 seconds. This came just weeks after Riggin, who was 0–8–1 in early January, had been assigned to the American Hockey League's Hershey Bears for a conditioning stint.

Riggin was recalled and thrown back into the lineup when a back injury sidelined starter Al Jensen.

"I wasn't playing very well," Riggin recalled in 2017, "but I got called back up when Al was hurt, so they were kind of stuck with me for that little stretch. But I jumped back in and got on a roll."

Wins over the New Jersey Devils and Montreal Canadiens extended the streak to four games, setting the stage for a 9–2 win over the eventual Stanley Cup champion Edmonton Oilers at a sold-out Capital Centre on February 5. Wayne Gretzky missed the game with a shoulder injury, but the Oilers were still the NHL's best.

"We were just on a roll," Laughlin said in 2010. "I remember looking over at [Oilers Mark] Messier and [Glenn] Anderson and Randy Gregg and all these great players and I thought, 'Wow, we've arrived.'

"It was a little bit of an eye-opener for our team because we were young, we were sort of up-and-coming, and nobody really gave us any credit. But when we waxed them, all of a sudden, we knew where we stood."

Three nights later, the Capitals beat the Calgary Flames 6–1 for their sixth consecutive win.

"Their defense is solid," Calgary coach "Badger" Bob Johnson told the *Washington Times* after the game, "their goalie is hot right now and their forwards are working. What else is there in the game?"

The streak hit double digits after wins over Philadelphia, Minnesota, Los Angeles, and St. Louis. The Capitals beat the Blues 4–2 on February 18 for their 10th consecutive win, as the once 0–7–0 club moved into a first-place tie in the Patrick Division.

"We had a great team concept," said Doug Jarvis, Washington's third-line center who sealed the win in St. Louis with an empty-net goal in his 700th career NHL game.

"The chemistry was really good within our group, headed up by [general manager] David Poile and [head coach] Bryan Murray. They got the group assembled and they got us playing the way they felt we could have success. Everybody came together, we were on the same page, and we got a lot accomplished."

The streak ended with a 4–3 overtime loss to the Winnipeg Jets on February 19. Doug Smail scored the game-winning goal after Murphy and Riggin misplayed a puck that had been lobbed into the Washington zone.

The 10-game winning streak would remain a franchise high until the 2009–10 Capitals won 14 consecutive games at the peak of their Presidents' Trophy campaign.

"Winning 10 in a row—we were on a roll," Langway said. "If we were down a goal or two, we knew Mike and Bobby [Carpenter] had the green light. We had the shutouts, we had great goaltending, and we had the best defensive-style players in the league, and that's a major reason we went on the streak."

Soon after the streak ended, Poile met with his players in the dressing room.

"He brought in a box of tapes," Laughlin told the *Washington Post* in 2010. "He had a tape for everybody so we could actually listen to [The Doors] in our car. He had them made and every player got one. I would swear it's still down in my basement in an old box of memorabilia. I still have the tape of The Doors. Every time I hear that song, I think of those days.

"It represented what we were trying to achieve during that stretch there."

Catapulted by their winning streak, the 1983–84 Capitals went 29–7–2 down the stretch to secure the first 100-point season in team history. At 48–27–5 (101 points), the Capitals finished in second place in the Patrick Division and had the fifth-best record in the NHL.

"One of the things, I don't want to say kind of amazed me, but I kind of bought into it was that this team played for the team," said forward Greg Adams. "I don't know if it was Poile or the people he brought in or if it was Bryan Murray or a combination of the solid people that we had—the Mike Gartners, the Bengt Gustafssons, the Dave Christians—but you put them together, we were a team. During that 10-game run, we used to play five-minute segments and it was like, 'Okay, no shots on goal for the next five minutes.' We used to go 15 minutes without a shot on goal against us. That's what I remember about it—just the pride in how we won those games."

The Capitals went on to sweep the Flyers in the best-of-five Patrick Division semifinals for the first playoff series win in team history. The accolades continued to pour in at year's end.

Murray became the first Capitals bench boss to win the Jack Adams Award as Coach of the Year, Langway earned his second consecutive Norris Trophy as the league's best defenseman, and Jarvis won the Selke Trophy as the best defensive forward.

And after the Capitals led the league with the fewest goals against during the regular season, Riggin and Jensen received the Jennings Trophy.

The Capitals had, in fact, broken through.

24 Maryland Native Makes the Capitals

Capitals season ticket holders Mel and Gloria Halpern of Potomac, Maryland, put plenty of miles on their Dodge Caravan. Every weekend, it seemed, they were driving somewhere out of state to see their son Jeff play hockey. Summer tournaments made it a yearlong venture.

One year, when Jeff was attending boarding school in New Hampshire, Mel drove 20 hours round trip to bring Jeff back to Washington to play one of his scheduled games for the Little Capitals. After the game, they drove 10 hours back to Concord, New Hampshire, before Mel did one more 10-hour drive back home. The Dodge Caravan was given that weekend off, with Mel driving a rental car instead.

"When he returned it," Jeff Halpern said, "they couldn't believe how many miles were on there."

All the miles and time spent away from home were done to provide Jeff the opportunity to pursue his goal of playing professional hockey.

The dream began innocently enough when hockey fans Mel and Gloria brought their children, Jeff and Jennifer, to the local rink. Jeff was three when he skated for the first time at the Lake Forest Mall in Gaithersburg in 1979.

"I remember the Caps either held a practice there or they had a couple of players at the rink," Jeff said, "and being exposed to the hockey guys just got me interested."

The interest never wavered. As a four-year-old, Jeff was registered at the Wheaton Hockey Club, and by the time he was nine, he was skating with 10- and 11-year-olds with the Little Capitals—an elite travel team that played against top programs from the United States and Canada.

Halpern later played on a summer team based out of Connecticut; went to St. Paul's School in New Hampshire; spent a year paying junior hockey in Stratford, Ontario; and eventually earned a four-year scholarship to Princeton University.

But at the age of 23, Halpern returned home. In the end, after years of travel to pursue a hockey career, he didn't have to go too far to realize his childhood dream.

When the Capitals opened the 1999–2000 season, Halpern was in the lineup. The kid who had once cheered on Mike Gartner while attending games with his parents at the old Capital Centre in Landover was now the one wearing No. 11 for Washington. Not only would Halpern become the first hockey player raised in Maryland to reach the NHL, but he would do so with his home-town team.

"To walk into a locker room with guys like Olie Kolzig, Calle Johansson, Sergei Gonchar, and Adam Oates, these were guys that two years earlier I was going crazy for on their run to the [1998] Stanley Cup Final," Halpern said. "To join them in that room, it was a different feeling. The saving grace is that when the puck dropped, it felt like hockey."

Halpern signed with the Capitals after his senior season at Princeton the previous spring. The Detroit Red Wings also pursued Halpern, but he felt he had the best chance to play in Washington.

Centers Dale Hunter, Joe Juneau, Michal Pivonka, and Benoit Gratton had all moved on in the months leading into the 1999–2000 season, and Halpern saw an opportunity to make the team as a fourth-line center.

He built his confidence over the summer at the Piney Orchard Ice Rink—where he used to skate with the Little Capitals—playing three-on-three and four-on-four shinny games with his future Washington teammates.

"The closest bonds to this day were from that summer," he said. "It was a good introduction and orientation for me to be on the ice with those guys and to see where I fit in. It was the best thing for my hockey career. I played without fear and without knowing anything."

An undrafted college free agent from a nontraditional market, Halpern made his NHL debut on October 2, 1999, as the Capitals opened their 26th season in Florida.

Jeff Halpern became the first Maryland native to play for the Capitals when he made his NHL debut on October 2, 1999. Halpern went on to play 507 games with the Capitals, recording 91 goals and 230 points across seven seasons.

"I remember that first game, [majority owner] Ted Leonsis put $1,000 up on the board for the game-winning goal. I had no idea that even existed," he said of the old ritual of putting money up on the board.

"I don't think I had ever seen that much cash before in my life. Most people would be nervous thinking about their first game, and all I'm thinking about is how great it would be the get the game winner and get the $1,000. That was an introduction to pro hockey."

One after week after Washington's season-opening loss against the Panthers (the $1,000 prize went unclaimed), the Capitals hosted the Los Angeles Kings in their home opener.

Mel and Gloria were in their usual seats at the MCI Center, watching their son play at the highest level without having to give the odometer a workout.

"My dad was able to walk over from work; my mom would hop on the Metro and meet him downtown," Halpern said of his rookie

Captain Halpern

Playing for his hometown team was surreal on its own for Halpern. But doing so as the team's captain during the 2005–06 season made for an even more memorable experience.

"To this day, if I look back on my career, it's one of the proudest things," Halpern said in 2017. "To play in the NHL is a dream come true, but to be captain for an NHL team was something very special for me. I was very proud to be a captain. I followed guys before me like Adam Oates, Brendan Witt, and Steve Konowalchuk. I had always been around good leaders and wanted to take pieces from those guys and I took a lot of pride in it."

Halpern said that he and the other veterans made it a point to be inclusive that season and to mentor the team's younger players.

"We wanted to make sure that everyone felt part of the team," he said. "We got better as a team as the year went along, and it wasn't just the youth. I think it was that the guys enjoyed playing together. As a captain, I was proud of what we were able to build there."

season. "I knew where their seats were—they were right across from the bench. You could almost have eye contact with them at some points in the game."

"I have to pinch myself," Mel Halpern told the *Washington Post* in 2000. "I mean, how lucky can you get? We've been Caps fans since before Jeff was born. Having him play for them now is like winning the lottery."

Although Halpern lived with a number of teammates in an apartment complex near the team's Piney Orchard practice facility, he was never too far from his friends and family.

"I remember on days off being able to come home and crash on the couch, and they're parents so they're throwing food at you just like as a kid. That first year, they were a huge part of everything. For my whole career, really, but especially that first year. The group of friends that I have to this day were all hockey teammates of mine that I met growing up; it was fun to have those guys around."

As a rookie, Halpern had 18 goals and 29 points in 79 games and led the Capitals with a plus-21 rating. He played primarily with Steve Konowalchuk and Ulf Dahlen during his first year under head coach Ron Wilson.

"When we first picked him up, I thought a lot about him right off the bat," Wilson said. "There weren't any players coming from a place like Princeton at that time, but Halpy did it, and you've got to give him a lot of credit. He was so good for us as a player, not a Peter Bondra type, but he worked both ends of the ice really well. He was great defensively, and you could always count on him to work his butt off, that was really important in that Halpy gave everything he had to our team."

Halpern spent the first six seasons of his NHL career with the Capitals before returning to Washington for the 2011–12 season. He ultimately played 14 NHL seasons with seven teams, finishing with 152 goals and 373 points in 976 career games.

25 Druce on the Loose

Former Capitals forward John Druce played 531 career NHL games spread over 10 seasons, but most discussions about his career begin and end with his five-week run from the 1990 Stanley Cup Playoffs.

The two-way forward emerged as an unlikely star that spring with 14 goals and 17 points in 15 games as the Capitals reached the Wales Conference Final for the first time in team history. For perspective, Druce had eight goals and 11 points in 45 games during the 1989–90 regular season.

"Every year you go into the playoffs and you're looking for somebody to perform above their potential or come out of nowhere, and that's exactly what happened," said general manager David Poile. "When you have a story like that, you're going to have success. It was a terrific time in our history and they weren't fluky goals. It was just like, 'Wow.'"

The surprising part to Druce's playoff run is how poorly his season began. The Capitals held training camp in Europe in September 1989, beginning in Karlstad, Sweden. When the Capitals landed, and checked into their hotel, players were told not to lie down or sleep in order to acclimate to the time zone difference. Apparently, the memo didn't reach Druce, who was rooming with rookie goaltender Byron Dafoe.

"The first instinct was to go back to the room and have a nap," Druce said. "So I'm trying to call down for a wake-up call, trying to set the alarm to make sure we're ready for practice [that first afternoon], and of course, neither of them worked out too well. There must have been a language barrier or something. So I overslept and

I was late to my first practice of the season. It wasn't a good feeling at all, and it wasn't a good start to the year."

The episode set the tone for a poor preseason for Druce, who, after finishing the previous season with Washington, began the 1989–90 campaign with the American Hockey League's Baltimore Skipjacks. It was a step back for the Capitals' second-round pick (40th overall) from the 1985 draft, but in retrospect, the assignment to Baltimore may have contributed to Druce's late-season surge.

Longtime Capitals assistant coach Terry Murray was beginning his second season as Skipjacks head coach and named Druce his team captain that fall. Having earned Murray's trust, Druce had 15 goals and 31 points in 26 games before earning a recall to Washington in mid-December.

Weeks later, Murray and Druce were reunited in the NHL when Terry replaced his brother Bryan as Capitals head coach.

"Terry came in and had some confidence in me after giving me that leadership role in Baltimore," Druce said. "I think maybe in the back of his mind, he knew my personality and my work ethic. But what I think was a huge contributor to the decision to put me in there [in the playoffs] is that I was actually playing pretty well down the stretch.

"I remember late in the season we were in Philadelphia, and I had been feeling pretty good at practice and I had been sniping at practice. So, we went to Philadelphia and I scored a goal that game, and what I didn't know, but what I heard afterward, is that [Terry] had predicted or told someone in the media that day that I was going to score that game. He believed in me."

Druce scored twice in the final three games of the regular season, securing his spot in the lineup for the start of the playoffs.

The Capitals went on to beat the New Jersey Devils in six games in their first-round series, with Dino Ciccarelli leading the way with a league-high eight goals. Druce chipped in with three goals, including two game winners. He also fought Devils defenseman Ken Daneyko in Game 1.

"I scored three goals in the series, but [the fight] really stood out to the team and to Dale Hunter," Druce said. "After the series, Dale said to me, 'You know Drucer, one of the biggest reasons guys committed and were willing to put it out there was because they saw you fight Daneyko.' I didn't realize that it had a big impression on the rest of the team, but that's what Dale expressed to me. At the time, I was just doing whatever I had to do. Terry saw that too—that willingness to do whatever it took."

That's why, when Ciccarelli suffered a knee injury in Game 1 of Washington's second-round series against the New York Rangers, Murray called on Druce to fill the void. It led to one of the best individual performances in a single postseason series in NHL history.

Elevated to top-line duty with Hunter and Geoff Courtnall, Druce scored *nine* goals in five games as the Capitals eliminated the Rangers and won the Patrick Division Final for the first time.

"I was just working hard," he said. "I was going to the net and getting garbage goals. I was scoring a lot from my ass, to be honest."

Druce scored in all five games against New York, highlighted by a hat trick in a 6–3 win in Game 2 at Madison Square Garden.

"It was my first NHL hat trick, and I remember the next day we're back in Washington, stretching in the locker [room], and [goaltender] Mike Liut comes up to me and says, 'Well, Drucer, you scored three last game, the problem here is that now they're going to expect it again.' So, I said, 'Well, let's see what happens.' And then I went out and had a four-point night—two [goals] and two [assists] the next game."

A phenomenon was quickly born, with posters reading DRUCE ON THE LOOSE filling the Capital Centre, where sellout crowds of 18,130 showered him with chants of "Druuuuuuce!" Then 24 years old, Druce had spent the previous two seasons jockeying between the AHL and NHL. He was suddenly the subject of features on *Hockey Night in Canada* and in *Sports Illustrated* and the *Sporting News*.

"When you have a whole building chanting 'Druce,' it's pretty amazing," he said. "I was never a superstar so for that to happen was pretty amazing. Once the playoffs were over, I was reading some of my fan mail and I got a letter from somebody in New York saying that if I left the rink alone that I was dead. It's a good thing I read it later. I don't know if it would have bothered me or not but at the time I thought, 'I can't believe someone took the time to write this.'"

"That was just something special," said forward Kelly Miller. "The way Johnny got hot there and the way the puck went in for him was like nothing I'd ever seen. Here's a guy that was honestly just trying like heck just to make it and to solidify a spot in the lineup on a regular basis and then all of a sudden, he just took off. He could not be stopped in terms of the puck going in the net for him. Obviously, we fed off of that."

Miller remembers Druce as a likeable teammate who didn't let his postseason success get to his head. He was a blue-collar player who kept to himself for the most part.

"He was a young guy trying to really establish himself," Miller said. "He was acting as such. The best way to describe John was very humble, very quiet, and very appreciative of the fact that pucks were going into the net. I think it was probably as much of a surprise for him as it was a surprise for his teammates, but it was a pleasant surprise. We enjoyed every minute of it and we enjoyed celebrating with him. His success just made the whole experience that much more unique."

Druce scored twice more in Game 4 in Landover, which culminated with captain Rod Langway scoring in overtime in a 4–3 win.

"That was an incredible run for him, and it couldn't happen to a nicer kid," Langway said. "He fell into a pile of shit [early in the season] and then he made this happen. He was playing fourth line, he was sitting in the stands, they were talking about sending him to the minors, and then all of a sudden, he goes on this roll and he becomes a superstar. He had all the skills, and when he went on the run, it wasn't something that we were counting on. It just happened. That's the best way to put it. It just happened."

The Capitals eliminated the Rangers with a 2–1 overtime win in Game 5. Fittingly, Druce had the series-clinching goal, redirecting a feed from Courtnall atop the crease to beat goalie John Vanbiesbrouck. A celebratory mob ensued behind the Rangers' 'net.

"As it went in, I was at the end boards and when I turned around, it was just freaking mayhem. I was elated. I remember getting interviewed after the game and I was like a kid in a candy shop. I was so excited, and I don't even know if what I said was making sense at the time. It was a pretty big high for all of us. To be the one get the goal to end that series, I felt pretty lucky and I felt pretty privileged to be playing with Washington and then to have that opportunity in that environment."

Druce scored twice more in the Wales Conference Final, but the Capitals were swept by the Boston Bruins in four games.

A year later, Druce had career highs across the board with 22 goals and 58 points in 80 games, but he could never come close to replicating the playoff success from 1990. In 18 postseason games in 1991 and 1992, Druce was limited to two goals and one assist.

He was traded to the Winnipeg Jets five days before the 1992–93 season and ended his career with the Los Angeles Kings and Philadelphia Flyers.

He concedes that it was at times difficult to traverse the league in the 1990s when all anybody remembered him for was a 15-game stretch from years earlier. It was only in retirement that Druce finally embraced it.

"I wanted to leave a mark in hockey and it's my own calling card," he said. "I remember thinking initially, 'Gosh, I played over 10 years in this league and I did more than just that.' But when looking back at everything, that was my time personally as a player that I got to play at the highest level and show that I could execute. I was very proud of that and I'm very proud that that's what people remember me for. Not many people can say that they've had that opportunity to have that type of success. It was a short period of time in the playoffs, but it got my foot in the door to have a long career."

26 A Brouwer-Play Goal

The 2015 NHL Winter Classic had all the makings of a special afternoon for forward Troy Brouwer. The Capitals were playing his former team, the Chicago Blackhawks, before a national TV audience and the largest crowd to ever watch a hockey game in Washington.

Troy's father, Don, who had suffered a stroke nearly five years earlier and rarely seen his son play since, made the trip from British Columbia and was among the 42,832 in attendance at Nationals Park. Brouwer was in his fourth season with the Capitals, but this marked the first time he'd play in front of his father in D.C.

In 2010, Brouwer won the Stanley Cup with Chicago, just two months after Don's stroke left him comatose for six days. Don's vision was also affected and the mobility on the left side of his body was limited.

"It's always special when I can play in front of my family," Brouwer said the day before the 2015 Classic.

"My parents don't get to travel a ton, so most of the games I play in front of them are in Vancouver. In this [Winter Classic] setting, everything is just amplified. Everything seems to be a little more exciting and memorable."

Even with the added incentive to do well on the NHL's biggest regular season stage, Brouwer could never have predicted just how memorable New Year's Day 2015 would become for him and his family.

But on a perfect sun-splashed afternoon, Brouwer delivered the perfect finish.

With the game tied at 2 late in the third period and the Capitals on the power play, Brouwer fired a shot from the slot that made its way through a maze of players and past Chicago goalie Corey Crawford inside the right post.

It was one of the biggest goals of Brouwer's career, although he never actually saw the puck go in. He didn't have to.

"Heard the noise of the crowd," he said. "Heard the noise of the guys on the ice."

Brouwer was mobbed by teammates Nicklas Backstrom and Mike Green. Alex Ovechkin and Marcus Johansson soon joined the pile.

"We were screaming so hard in the huddle," Green said. "I almost passed out."

"It was kind of like an old Capitals celebration," Backstrom said. "When we were a little bit younger, we used to jump around [like that]. Obviously, lots of emotion."

The scoreboard showed 12.9 seconds remaining and a 3–2 Washington lead. The crowd tossed their seat cushions skyward, not unlike graduates would with their caps.

"It was one of those where you know the time," Brouwer said, "you know the score, and you're just trying to get a puck on net. Thankfully it went in."

Braden Holtby secured the win with a save on Patrick Kane in the final seconds. Eric Fehr and Ovechkin also scored in the Washington triumph, but the day belonged to Brouwer, who enjoyed one last curtain call as the game's first star.

"I've had some good moments in my hockey career," Brouwer said, "but this one, with all the intangibles that played a part in it—my parents being able to come to town, playing my former team, this being the first goal that I score against my former team, and the dramatic fashion at the end of the game of how everything played out is definitely going to be a memorable day, a memorable event."

As the Capitals celebrated the win inside the Nationals' clubhouse, text messages poured in on Brouwer's phone. One was from his father.

"I haven't responded to it yet," he said about an hour after the game. "I figured I'd wait until I got home to share it with him. Knowing how my dad is right now, he probably has a couple of tears."

Hours later, Brouwer reunited with wife, Carmen, two-year-old daughter, Kylie, mother, Kathy, and his father, Don.

"When I got home, he was happy," Brouwer remembered. "He gave me a big hug and said he was proud of me and all the things I've been able to do in my hockey career. It couldn't have worked out any better. It will always be one of those things that I'll always remember."

27 The Swedish Embassy

From 2006 through 2013, the Capitals made nine selections in the first round of the NHL Draft. Five of those first-round picks, or more than half, were used on Swedes (Nicklas Backstrom, Anton Gustafsson, Marcus Johansson, Filip Forsberg, and Andre Burakovsky).

The Capitals' long history of acquiring Swedish players dates back to the late 1970s. At the time, the NHL had grown to 18 teams, while the rival World Hockey Association had eight more. As the demand for players grew, teams in North America started recruiting Europeans to fill out their rosters.

In June 1978, the Capitals joined the fold, signing a pair of Swedes in center Rolf Edberg and defenseman Leif Svensson. They were the first two European-born-and-trained players to skate with the Capitals.

"I always felt bad for Leif and Rolf," said former captain Ryan Walter. "They came over and played hard but in the late 1970s, going into Philadelphia or going into Boston, that wasn't hockey. That was half war. And to come across from a Swedish national team or from a high-level European league and to come into the NHL at that point, that had to be difficult."

Edberg only spent three seasons with the Capitals, while Svensson lasted just two. Neither left a lasting impression with the club, although Edberg finished third on the 1979–80 Capitals with 23 goals in 63 games.

But as the Capitals evolved into a playoff team and a perennial contender in the 1980s, another Swede, Bengt Gustafsson, would develop into one of Washington's best forwards.

Gustafsson wasn't especially big—he was listed at 6'0" and 190 pounds—but he was strong on his skates and difficult to knock off the puck. Although he was a frequent target, the playmaking center didn't shy away from contact.

"He took a beating all the time," said defenseman Greg Theberge. "There was still a stigma attached to the Swedes that you could abuse them and they wouldn't do anything back. So they speared him, slashed him, punched him."

But Gustafsson didn't let it affect his game. He was a 20-goal scorer in each of his first five seasons and recorded a career-high 32 goals and 75 points in 69 games in 1983–84.

"Bengt Gustafsson was a tough son of a bitch," said former teammate Craig Laughlin. "I remember Philly just crushing Bengt. Crushing him. But he fought through it. Guys tried to take him through the boards but he was so goddamn strong. The lower body that Bengt had made him so tough to knock over."

Walter remembers a particular instance during Gustafsson's rookie season in 1979–80 when he was targeted by one of the game's best.

"I'll never forget, we were in Hartford and Gordie Howe was playing with his sons," Walter recalled, "and Bengt ran Marty [Howe] into the corner. So, the next shift Gordie comes out and he's literally chasing Bengt around the ice. It's like, here's dad trying to take care of his son. And I just remember Bengt looking over his shoulder the whole shift, getting chased after by a 52-year-old."

"Where Gussy excelled," said former head coach Gary Green, "was his absolute agility and skill and his incredible mobility. He was so agile, he could be evasive if he needed to be or he could just bounce off guys."

Nearly 30 years since Gustafsson last played for Washington, his former teammates still recall his tremendous speed and versatility. He could play all three forward positions and was a key cog on both special-team units. His speed and puck-handling skills were also among his greatest strengths.

"He could see the ice so well," said Mike Gartner. "He was an unselfish player. Bryan [Murray] played him late in games to take key faceoffs or close out a game. He'd play last minute of a period. Just a guy you that coaches could trust."

Gustafsson remained a target throughout his career, and despite his ability to brush off most hits, he finally met his match late in the 1985–86 season. With only six games remaining in Washington's record-setting 50-win campaign, Gustafsson suffered a broken leg on a hit from Islanders defenseman Denis Potvin.

"It was just a matter of time until Gusty would get tired of taking that crap," Theberge said.

Gustafsson's season was done, and it would be a year and a half before his next game with the Capitals. Despite coming off a 23-goal, 75-point season in 1985–86, a then-28-year-old Gustafsson returned home and spent a year playing in a second-tier Swedish league.

He'd eventually play two more seasons in Washington before putting a bow on his NHL career at the age of 31. He then played 10 more seasons in Europe.

Gustafsson never made an NHL All-Star Game and didn't lead the Capitals in scoring in any of his nine NHL seasons. He wasn't flashy, but he was efficient. According to his former teammates, he was underappreciated by media and fans.

Through the Capitals' first 15 seasons in the NHL, only Gartner had more goals, assists, and points than Gustafsson. Even when the Capitals celebrated their 40th anniversary in 2015, Gustafsson still ranked in the top 10 in all three categories.

"He would go down as one of the best Caps players ever if more people saw him or if he had more longevity," Laughlin said of Gustafsson, who had 196 goals and 555 points in 629 games.

"Just a cerebral Swede—so smart. One of the most talented players I saw in the mid-80s."

Gustafsson moved into coaching soon after his playing career ended in the late 90s in Europe. He ranks among the top coaches in Sweden and won a gold medal as head coach of the men's national team at the 2006 Winter Olympics and at the 2006 World Hockey Championships.

28 See the Capitals on the Road

The day after the Capitals beat the Pittsburgh Penguins in the 2011 Bridgestone Winter Classic from Heinz Field, pride set in for general manager George McPhee as he drove back to Washington with his family.

"The ride home from Pittsburgh," McPhee said, "there were Caps fans all the way back. At the toll booths, at the gas stations, at the restaurants—it was really remarkable."

Announced attendance at the 2011 Winter Classic was 68,111 with the Capitals selling out their allotment of 20,000 tickets. The NHL estimated that another 7,000 to 10,000 Capitals fans bought tickets on the secondary market. That's about 30,000 Capitals fans taking in a road game. Not bad for a club that was averaging 13,931 fans at *home* games just four years earlier.

"It felt like a seminal moment for this franchise," McPhee said. "When you heard the crowd yell 'Red' and yell 'O' during the national anthem, you realized how many people are there. [Defenseman] John Erskine mentioned that it kind of startled him on the bench, so I'm sure the others experienced that too and were thinking, 'Boy, we have a lot of people here tonight.'"

While Capitals fans were well represented on New Year's Day 2011, the Winter Classic in Pittsburgh was just one example of a fan base that has travelled well throughout the Alex Ovechkin era.

With six Metropolitan Division rivals located within a four-and-a-half-hour drive from Verizon Center, Capitals fans are well situated to "Rock the Red" on the road. Capitals fans can also pick up an Amtrak/Acela train from Union Station (minutes from Verizon Center) for trips to Philadelphia and New York.

Fans can always create their own travel itineraries to see the Capitals on the road, but it may be worth checking with the experts first.

Independent from the team, the Caps Road Crew (capsroadcrew. com) is a fan-initiated organization that has coordinated Capitals road trips since the 2000–2001 season. Soon after the NHL schedule comes out, the Caps Road Crew posts its travel itinerary for the upcoming season on its website. The Caps Road Crew will offer about 10 games a season, plus an annual trip to the see the American Hockey League's Hershey Bears.

Fans looking to see the Capitals on the road can buy their tickets directly through the CRC if it is one of the games on their itinerary. Depending on the venue, the CRC often gets a block of tickets in the lower bowl at a reduced group rate, with the savings passed on to Capitals fans. The CRC also provides bus transportation for games within a five-hour drive.

Below are some of the top venues to catch the Capitals on the road:

Raleigh, NC: PNC Arena is just over a four-hour commute from Verizon Center, and it's a relatively easy drive down the I-95 without any tolls along the way. The distance is short enough for a return trip right after the game, but should you indulge in a few adult beverages, or simply prefer to enjoy the evening on Tobacco

Road, overnight lodging in Raleigh-Durham is relatively inexpensive compared with some other NHL markets.

The Hurricanes have struggled to fill PNC Arena in recent seasons (they finished last in home attendance in 2015–16 and 2016–17), meaning tickets are not only among the most affordable in the NHL, but they are also readily available. According to vividseats.com, the Hurricanes had the third-lowest median ticket price in the NHL in 2016–17.

Parking is plentiful outside the arena, where the pregame tailgating experience is worth an early arrival. Backyard Bistro is a popular pregame and postgame establishment within walking distance of PNC Arena, complete with local barbeque favorites and a full-service bar.

New York: Madison Square Garden has undergone multiple renovations since it first opened in 1968, but the "World's Most Famous Arena" remains a historic venue that ought to be on every sports fan's bucket list.

Rangers tickets, though, are both in demand and among the priciest in the NHL, so Capitals fans looking to take in a game at MSG are advised to bring their wallets. On the plus side, the Garden is a short walk from both Penn Station and the Port Authority Bus Terminal.

Capitals fans looking for less-expensive alternatives in and around the Big Apple can see the Capitals play either the New York Islanders at Barclays Center or the New Jersey Devils at Prudential Center.

The Islanders moved to Brooklyn in 2015, but crowds have been small and good seats are often readily available on game days. Capitals fans driving from the Beltway can reach Prudential Center in Newark in less than four hours.

Montreal: Alex Ovechkin once said of Bell Centre in Montreal: "You don't have to drink Red Bull before playing here." The energy on a game day in Montreal is palpable, and the atmosphere at Bell Centre is among hockey's best.

The arena itself is sprinkled with history from the club's 24 Stanley Cup banners hanging from the rafters to the bronze statues just outside the building of legends Howie Morenz, Maurice Richard, Jean Beliveau, and Guy LaFleur.

The building oozes hockey history, and fans making a trip to Montreal may appreciate a Bell Centre tour. English-language tours are available on non-event dates.

Tickets in Montreal are not cheap, but Capitals fans in the United States could potentially take advantage of a favorable exchange rate. The Canadiens consistently sell out the 21,288-seat Bell Centre, but tickets can be found on the secondary market online, or from scalpers outside the arena, who are hardly discreet.

A Bell Centre hot dog or smoked meat sandwich is a must.

Honorable Mention:

Chicago: Home to one of the best pregame national anthems in all of sports and a raucous in-game atmosphere to boot. The Blackhawks led the NHL in attendance for the ninth straight season in 2016–17.

Nashville: Music City offers Capitals fans a little hockey with a side of country music and southern hospitality. With the Predators approaching their 20th-anniversary season, the 2016–17 campaign marked the first time in franchise history that all 41 home games were sellouts at Bridgestone Arena.

Pittsburgh: PPG Paints Arena is about a four-hour drive from Washington, D.C., providing a relatively easy commute for Capitals fans looking to catch one of the game's best rivalries from the "House That Sid Built."

Toronto: The NHL's most expensive tickets can be found at Toronto's Air Canada Centre. Not unlike Montreal, there is a buzz in the city on a game day, particularly if the Maple Leafs are home on a Saturday for *Hockey Night in Canada*. Fans taking in a game in Toronto can also spend a few hours at the Hockey Hall of Fame, which is walking distance from the ACC.

29 Tommy McVie

Tom McVie was an old-school head coach.

Back in the 1970s, even Don Cherry accused McVie of running his team like it was 1948. In retrospect, though, others believe that McVie may have actually been ahead of his time.

A stickler for conditioning and fitness testing, McVie was hired by the Capitals in December 1975, becoming their fourth head coach in less than two seasons. At the time of his hiring, the Capitals had 11 wins in 116 games.

The second-year Capitals were 3–28–5 and in the midst of a then-record 25-game winless drought when the club fired general manager and head coach Milt Schmidt after a 6–0 loss to the Montreal Canadiens on December 29, 1975.

Max McNabb replaced Schmidt as GM, while McVie took over behind the bench.

"I remember [team president] Peter O'Malley introduced us to Tommy," said goaltender Bernie Wolfe, "and Tommy's very first words were, 'Boys, this country club is now officially closed.' So, you knew things were going to be different. Before, we'd lose 6–0 and Milt would say, 'Good effort boys, nothing tomorrow.' Tommy wasn't having any of that."

A career minor leaguer as a player, McVie came to Washington after two and a half seasons as head coach of the International Hockey League's Dayton Gems. He made his NHL coaching debut on New Year's Eve 1975 and was welcomed with a 4–0 loss in Detroit.

It was the first of 11 consecutive defeats to begin his NHL career as Washington dropped to 3–39–5.

"It was," McVie told the *Washington Post*, "like trying to win the bleeping Kentucky Derby with a bleeping mule.

"It was hell. I probably should have had six nervous breakdowns while I was there, but I was too dumb to realize it."

The talent pool was thin, but if the results weren't going to change, McVie was keen on changing how this hapless group went about its business.

"He came in and he made guys accountable," said Gordie Smith, who played for five coaches in as many seasons in Washington. "For the guys who maybe partied a little too much, well guess what? He made you come in and go to work. With Tommy McVie, if you didn't hustle, if you didn't work, then you didn't play."

Soon after McVie took over, he instituted two-a-day practices on non–game days.

"His motto was, 'Hard work gets it done,'" said Ron Lalonde. "If we weren't that good, we were at least going to be the hardest-working team."

McVie realized quickly that he too had a lot of work ahead of him.

"The Capitals had nothing but a bunch of rejects from other teams," McVie told *Sports Illustrated* in 1984. "I went to the first practice, and guys were smoking cigarettes and drinking coffee in the locker room and wandering in late. I was in good shape and all pumped up to finally be in the NHL, so during the drills I was skating around like Rocket Richard, and they were looking at me like, 'This guy's nuts.'"

McVie also raised a few eyebrows by revamping the old-fashioned morning skate. Gone were the days of coming out in track pants with a stick and gloves and taking a few leisurely laps to work up a sweat.

"With McVie, it was like a practice," Lalonde said. "We were doing drills, we were doing wind sprints and the visiting team would come into Washington and they'd see us in the morning out there in full gear and they'd be looking at us like, 'What's going on?!'"

Even Wolfe, the Capitals' backup goaltender at the time, had to skate in his full gear during wind sprints and fitness tests.

"We were becoming the talk of the NHL," Wolfe said, "not because of our play on the ice, but because during our morning skates, Tommy was making us do push-ups. Guys from the other teams would stick around to see this. It was entertaining to them."

McVie gave the Capitals a businesslike attitude, and in the end the team earned some credibility as their play on the ice eventually improved.

"They thought I was a maniac, but I'm not crazy," McVie told *Sports Illustrated*. "When you're playing the Montreal Canadiens and there's not one guy on your roster who could make their team, you have to work harder than they do."

In his first full season as an NHL head coach, McVie led the 1976–77 Capitals to a 24–42–14 record and a fourth-place finish in the Norris Division. Washington missed the playoffs, but its 24 wins were five more than its first two seasons combined.

McVie was runner-up for the Jack Adams Award as NHL Coach of the Year, finishing behind Montreal's Scotty Bowman.

Along the way, McVie also reformed the attitude in and around the Capitals' dressing room. It was a workplace, he made clear, not a playground.

"The first year, we had a community room down beside the Caps' and Bullets' dressing rooms," said Lalonde. "There was a pool table in there, a fridge, some Ping Pong, all kinds of things. But the first year, we had more guys injured hanging out in there than we had in the dressing room playing. And before games, we'd be in the dressing room, getting ready to play, trying to get up for the game and talking strategy and all we'd hear was laughing and whatnot going on next door. So Tommy put an end to that right away. Injured players weren't allowed anywhere near the dressing room, which was a step in the right direction."

The pregame distractions were replaced by a McVie staple. With the aid of a friend who worked at a local radio station, McVie put together a collection of cassette tapes with marching music. The music was the last thing the Capitals heard in the dressing room before taking the ice.

"I remember before games," said defenseman Robert Picard, "we always listened to military songs—Army, Navy, and Air Force music before every game to get us going. The first time I heard it, I didn't know what the music was for. You know, coming from Canada, I didn't know what they were. [Bryan] Bugsy Watson was sitting next to me and he just said, 'Get used to it.'"

Lalonde believes the music had an effect.

"When you went on the ice, you were ready to go," Lalonde said. "It got your adrenaline going. I don't think some of the older guys—Bryan Watson or Ace Bailey—thought it was all that necessary. But [McVie] had some interesting ideas and in my view, some of them worked."

One of those ideas was to launch tennis balls at his goaltenders from a semiautomatic Lob-ster machine in the days leading up to training camp.

McVie told the *Washington Post* that he wanted his goaltenders to be spared the "total shock when the puck starts coming at them the first day. This way they're acclimated and toughened up. They're not facing pucks while they're nursing aching muscles."

The Capitals regressed in McVie's second full season, as Washington missed the playoffs again in 1977–78 with a 17–49–14 record. It came as a tremendous surprise, though, when McVie was fired two days before the 1978–79 season opener in Los Angeles and replaced by Dan Belisle.

"That was my first NHL job and my soul belonged to it," McVie told the *Washington Post* in 1991. "The Washington Capitals were more important to me at that particular time than my family. To have the rug pulled out like that was really like a death in the family."

McVie went 49–122–33 during his two and a half seasons with the club.

"I asked them, 'Please tell me why I was fired so I won't do it again,' but I never got an explanation. You'd almost think I'd embezzled their money."

Four decades later, McVie's firing remains a mystery, and the men who were behind the decision have passed away.

"For as long as I've been in the business in hockey," said former captain Guy Charron, "there are always some things that happen and you always wonder and you never find out the real reason. It was weird for that to happen during training camp. I really don't know what caused it, but it was a very unusual situation."

Hours after McVie was let go, a group of Capitals, including Tom Rowe, Gordie Lane, Bill Riley, and Rick Green, went to his home.

"We all felt terrible that he got fired," said Rowe, who had 13 goals and 21 points in 63 games as a rookie in 1977–78. "We wound up at his house for about two, two and a half hours, and he had us on the floor laughing. He was such a funny guy. He didn't want us feeling sorry for him. He thanked us for playing as hard as we did for him and we thanked him for helping us become established players in the NHL."

Four months after the Capitals fired McVie, he was hired as a midseason replacement by the Winnipeg Jets of the World Hockey Association. The Jets went on to beat Wayne Gretzky and the Edmonton Oilers for the WHA championship—the Avco Cup—that spring.

30 Could Pat Quinn Have Coached the Capitals?

There is no denying that Bruce Boudreau was the right man for the job when he took over as Capitals head coach in November 2007. Less than six months after he was promoted from the American Hockey League's Hershey Bears, Boudreau received the Jack Adams Award as the NHL's Coach of the Year.

Boudreau would become one of the most successful head coaches in team history, leading the Capitals to four consecutive Southeast Division titles, two Eastern Conference regular season titles, and a Presidents' Trophy for the NHL's best overall record in 2009–10.

But what if the Capitals had gone a different direction? What if, after introducing Boudreau as the interim head coach on November 22, 2007, the Capitals eventually brought in someone else to take over on a full-time basis?

General manager George McPhee was confident that Boudreau would succeed in the NHL, but the Capitals had a backup plan on standby.

"I did talk to one other person," McPhee revealed in 2017, "and that was Pat Quinn."

While Boudreau did not have any prior NHL coaching experience, Quinn had more than most. When discussions first took place that fall, Quinn was the fourth-winningest coach in league history, behind only Scotty Bowman, Al Arbour, and Dick Irvin.

"Pat was a great coach and manager," Capitals president Dick Patrick said in 2017, "and he'd had a lot of impact on George throughout his career. George really admired him. So it was something that was under consideration at the time."

Quinn, who was inducted into the Hockey Hall of Fame in 2016, was among McPhee's most important mentors and someone he viewed as a father figure. So significant was the bond that George and his wife, Leah, gave their eldest son, Graham, the middle name Quinn in tribute.

"Pat had an impact on a lot of people's lives," McPhee told The Fan 590 in 2014, "and for me, when he called, it was like your father calling."

McPhee's working relationship with Quinn went back to the early 1990s. At the time, Quinn wore many different hats with the Vancouver Canucks, where he served as president, general manager, and head coach. Soon after McPhee earned his law degree from Rutgers University in 1992, Quinn hired him as the Canucks' vice president and director of hockey operations.

They worked together for five seasons in Vancouver, highlighted by a trip to the 1994 Stanley Cup Final.

In June 1997, McPhee was hired as Capitals GM, and a year later he was back in the Stanley Cup Final with Washington. Although he watched his team by himself from the GM's box for much of the postseason, McPhee invited Quinn to join him for the Final. Quinn had been fired in Vancouver early in the 1997–98 season.

"I was proud to ask Pat and [his wife] Sandra to come down," McPhee said. "They were there for the Finals, and I was just trying to pay him back somehow. It actually helped him, I think, because

Cherry a Finalist to Become Capitals Coach

The Capitals were only in their eighth season, but they were already hiring their eighth head coach. In November 1981, owner Abe Pollin narrowed his search to two finalists—Bryan Murray and Don Cherry.

Murray was 38 at the time and had no prior NHL experience. He was coaching the Capitals' minor league affiliate in Hershey, but was not a well-known commodity. The other finalist was among the NHL's most recognizable coaches in the late 1970s—the always dapper Don Cherry, who never met a custom-made suit he didn't like.

Cherry had six years of NHL coaching experience, including five with the Boston Bruins and one with the Colorado Rockies. The 1976 Jack Adams Award winner wasn't actively pursuing the Washington vacancy, but team president Peter O'Malley persuaded him to fly to Washington to interview with Pollin.

They met for two hours, but Cherry and Pollin had one philosophical difference. The outspoken Cherry wanted control. Pollin wouldn't give it to him.

After clashing with Bruins GM Harry Sinden in Boston and with Rockies GM Ray Miron during his brief stay in Denver, Cherry would only come to Washington if he were named both head coach and GM.

"Don Cherry is a very fine gentleman and I was very impressed with him," Pollin told the *Washington Post*. "He wanted sort of a Billy Martin–type condition here, where he would be in total control. I was concerned about it for the Washington Capitals at this time. And told him so."

So the Capitals hired Bryan Murray, who *Washington Post* columnist Ken Denlinger wrote, "may as well have been Eddie Murray or Bill Murray for all the impact it made."

"I go with what my heart tells me and what my gut tells me," Pollin said at the time. "My gut tells me that Bryan Murray's the guy that's gonna bring the Capitals out of their doldrums."

Pollin wasn't wrong. Murray would emerge as the winningest and longest-tenured coach in team history. He led the Capitals to the playoffs in each of his seven full seasons behind the bench and was named Coach of the Year in 1984.

Cherry never coached in the NHL again, but he'd become one of the game's most colorful television analysts for his work with CBC's *Hockey Night in Canada*.

his profile was out there and then Toronto ended up hiring him and it was a really good move for both Pat and the Maple Leafs."

Quinn was named Maple Leafs head coach before the 1998–99 season and held the position until he was fired on April 20, 2006.

When the Capitals relieved Glen Hanlon in November 2007, Quinn was still out of work and eyeing a return to the NHL. While a move to Washington wasn't entirely out of the question for Quinn, it became clear within a few weeks that the "interim" Boudreau wasn't going anywhere.

"I told Pat that I thought Bruce was a heck of a coach and if he gets the team going, we're going to let him keep going," McPhee said. "So I called Pat a few weeks later after I saw how the team had responded and told him that Bruce was going to be our permanent head coach."

After taking over a 6–14–1 club on Thanksgiving, Boudreau led the Capitals to a 7–5–3 record in his first 15 games. By Christmas, Boudreau was told to settle in. On December 26, 2007, the Capitals officially announced that they were removing the interim tag from Boudreau's job title.

"We just thought it was about time that we let the players know," McPhee said at the time. "There was something about it that seemed to look and feel right."

While Boudreau remained in Washington for four years, Quinn would return to the NHL for one more season, guiding the rebuilding Edmonton Oilers to a 27–47–8 record in 2009–10. He died in November 2014.

"Of all the blessings that I've had in the game of hockey," McPhee said, "and all of the good things, he was number one; to be able to work with that man."

31 Barry Trotz First Meets the Capitals

Soon after Barry Trotz was hired as the Washington Capitals' 17th head coach, the walls of his new office at Kettler Capitals Iceplex had already been sprinkled with reminders of just how far he had advanced in his hockey career.

On one wall hung a framed photo commemorating his 1,000[th] career game coaching the Nashville Predators. On another wall rested an 8-by-11-inch memorial to Jack Button.

Button spent 17 years with the Capitals as director of player personnel and recruitment from 1979 through 1996. In 1982, he invited a 20-year-old Trotz to his first professional training camp with the American Hockey League's Hershey Bears.

Trotz still remembers finding Button in the stands one day after practice and the awkward introduction to pro hockey that followed.

"I walked up and said, 'Mr. Button, I'm Barry Trotz.' And he sort of snapped back, 'I know who the hell you are! I invited you.'"

Trotz thanked Button and first-year general manager David Poile for the training camp invite and insisted that the Capitals would have a hard time cutting him. Button didn't think it would be that tough.

"'The only reason that you're here is that you might be a good minor league leader or coach someday,'" Trotz can still recall Button telling him. "And at 20 years old, that's probably not what I wanted to hear. But at the same time, I'd say he was pretty accurate."

Within days, Trotz was released. The 5'8" defenseman, who never appeared in a minor league preseason game, let alone an

NHL regular-season contest, saw his professional playing career end before it even took off.

What Trotz could not have predicted at the time was how big of an impact Button, Poile, and the entire Capitals organization would have on his life years later.

"Definitely didn't burn any bridges," Trotz said of his training camp cameo. "I left graciously, I went back home; I later went back to school and I played at the University of Manitoba for Wayne Fleming, who really was a big influence and later got me into coaching."

When a series of back injuries forced Trotz to stop playing altogether at the age of 22, Fleming offered Trotz a volunteer position as an assistant coach with the Manitoba Bisons.

"He was the guy who kept sliding me pamphlets for coaching schools and encouraging me to go to Roger Neilson's coaching clinics," Trotz said. "He talked about the game with me, and he was a great influence as far as getting me into coaching and thinking the game from that perspective."

Thirty years later, Trotz also kept a 5-by-7-inch photo of Fleming in his office, well aware that if not for Fleming's encouragement and the support of his junior coach Bryan Murray, the transition behind the bench in his early 20s might not have gone as smoothly as it did.

Trotz played for Murray with the Western Hockey League's Regina Pats during the 1979–80 season. Murray would later become both the winningest and the longest-tenured head coach in Capitals history.

"You have to rely on people in the business," Trotz said. "When I first started coaching, Bryan and Wayne were pretty influential on my thought process. I also kept asking questions and I was very fortunate to be around some great people who had those experiences."

Within five years of Trotz's training camp invite with the Capitals, he had become the head coach at the University of Manitoba. That's when Button reached out to him about scouting for the Capitals.

Over the course of the next three seasons—from 1987 through 1990—Trotz went from a part-time scout to a full-time scout to the Capitals' head of scouting in western Canada. It was during that time that Trotz discovered goalies Olie Kolzig and Byron Dafoe.

The Capitals drafted both Kolzig and Dafoe in 1989, with Kolzig going on to win more than 300 games with the franchise.

"It was different," Trotz said of his experience scouting. "I learned a lot about the game, I enjoyed it, and I actually thought I was heading in that direction."

But a funny thing happened in June 1990 as Trotz and his wife, Kim, were preparing to buy their first home in Vancouver, British Columbia, where Trotz was stationed as the Capitals' head western scout.

"Jack asked me if I'd consider coming to Baltimore as an assistant coach [with the AHL's Baltimore Skipjacks] and do some pro scouting for the organization," Trotz said. "I still had a little bit of the coaching bug, so I called the bank because we were about to close the deal on this house, and I told them that our plans had changed. I thought it was a great opportunity."

Trotz would ultimately spend seven years with the Capitals' top minor league affiliate, first as an assistant coach for nearly two full seasons and then as the head coach for five years.

As players came and went, as the uniform colors changed and even as the farm club moved from Baltimore to Portland, Maine, Trotz remained the constant.

During the 1993–94 season, Trotz led the Portland Pirates to a Calder Cup championship and was named the AHL's Coach of the Year. Two years later, Trotz again directed Portland to the

AHL finals before falling to the Rochester Americans in a seven-game series.

Among those Trotz coached in the AHL were future Capitals players Jason Allison, Jim Carey, Sergei Gonchar, Steve Konowalchuk, and Richard Zednik.

According to Trotz, it was during that time that he truly embraced the entire package that comes with coaching professional athletes. For the first time in his coaching career, Trotz worked with players with considerably different backgrounds—some of whom spoke little English.

"When you first start coaching, you think it's all Xs and Os, and yes, there is the tactical side to it, but coaching is also about managing people, managing egos and managing situations," he said. "And you're trying to do it all in a manner where there's discipline, accountability, and compassion."

In addition to his head coaching responsibilities, Trotz was also the Pirates' director of hockey operations, responsible for rounding out his AHL roster with minor league free agents.

"I've been working in the game for 30 years now as a part-time scout, a full-time scout, a head scout, an assistant coach, a head coach, and a director of hockey operations," Trotz said in 2014, "but I've been going to 'Hockey University' for 30 years, where every experience is different."

The time spent in the AHL, he said, was a crash course in dealing with personalities, contracts, travel itineraries, practice schedules, assembling a staff, and perhaps most important, creating a family atmosphere despite players constantly shuffling in and out.

Trotz points to his time in the Capitals' minor league system in the 1990s as a turning point in his career, as he discovered how to build, motivate, and get the most out of a championship team.

"Building a hockey team is like building a house," he said. "You need all kinds of craftsmen to build a good house, but everyone needs a strong foundation, and then you build it from there. So, to build a good team, you need all kinds of individuals—skilled guys, tough guys, guys with specialties like faceoffs, so as a coach you just want them to play to their potential and you want to put them in the best possible position to succeed."

Soon after the 1996–97 season—Trotz's seventh campaign with the Capitals' top minor league affiliate—Poile was named the general manager of the expansion Nashville Predators after a 14-year stint in the same position with Washington.

Once Poile was hired in Nashville, he reached out to Trotz, 35 at the time, and offered him his first career NHL head coaching job.

The move went against the conventional wisdom, which suggested that an experienced NHL leader would be best suited to handle the inevitable challenges with a startup franchise.

"I was the third employee with the team," Trotz said, "so I did everything from scouting and evaluating players, to ordering carpets, to helping build our facility, to figuring out where everyone was going to park, to helping build the staff.

"It was a big endeavor, but in my mind, the goal was just not to embarrass myself and keep the job for one year."

Ultimately, Trotz kept the job for much longer, working in Nashville for nearly 17 years, coaching the Predators for the first 1,196 games in club history and developing a team with a reputation for its hard work and disciplined play. His 557 career wins with the Predators are the third most by any coach with a single franchise.

"The big advantage for me in Nashville was that even when we'd have some rough patches, like a five-game losing streak, David had my back," Trotz said. "We'd have closed-door meetings with the team and he'd say, 'The solution is in this room. Let's get it fixed.' And we became a better organization as a result of it.

"For a small-market, low-budget team, we had great success and we wouldn't have had that success if any time there was a road block we panicked and made changes. The attitude was we can outwork a problem, we can handle adversity."

Trotz also relied heavily on his assistant coaches in the NHL, notably Brent Peterson, Paul Gardner, Peter Horachek, Mitch Korn, and Lane Lambert.

Korn and Lambert followed Trotz to Washington in 2014. "When family moves, you go with family," said Korn, who first met Trotz at a Roger Nielsen coaching clinic in the late 1980s.

"Getting a strong staff helps you grow and lets you learn the game even more," Trotz said.

"When you're a young coach, you probably think you know everything. I've been doing this for 30 years and I've yet to know everything. You keep evolving. As a young coach, maybe you listen less, you think, 'It's my way or the highway,' but as an older coach you listen more. Maybe I talk more, but I listen more, too. You have to."

Having spent nearly two decades as an NHL head coach, Trotz can't help but appreciate working again with the organization that gave him his first taste of the professional game more than 30 years ago.

"Everything I have today is from the game of hockey," Trotz said, "and everything I have is from Jack Button taking a chance on me and David Poile listening to the people he trusted."

32 Dale Hunter Trade

Goaltender Bob Mason spent the first four years of his pro career in the Capitals organization, but his decision not to return to Washington after the 1987 season was the catalyst for one of the biggest trades in team history.

Less than two months after allowing the game-winning goal in the infamous Easter Epic in Landover—a quadruple-overtime loss to the New York Islanders in Game 7 of their first-round series—Mason told general manager David Poile on the morning of the 1987 NHL Draft that he was going to sign a free-agent deal with the Chicago Blackhawks.

The Capitals suddenly needed a goaltender. The Quebec Nordiques were willing to part with one of theirs.

By coincidence, Poile and Nordiques GM Maurice Filion had spoken throughout the 1986–87 season about a possible deal involving Quebec center Dale Hunter.

Trade discussions cooled off during the year, but talks quickly resumed at the 1987 draft in Detroit, where the Capitals had a growing shopping list.

"We could move a goaltender," Filion told Poile on the draft floor.

From there, a trade that would dramatically shape both franchises for the next decade took shape.

Poile and Filion negotiated a deal that would send Hunter and goaltender Clint Malarchuk to Washington with forwards Gaetan Duchesne and Alan Haworth heading to Quebec, along with the Capitals' first-round pick (15th overall).

With the Islanders on the clock with the 13th overall pick, and Washington's turn fast approaching, Poile pulled the trigger. Hunter and Malarchuk were Washington Capitals.

"Dale was coming off of a broken leg" that limited him to 46 games the year before, Poile recalled in 2017. "And I think if you were to ask Maurice Filion in Quebec, they really had their doubts if Dale would come back or come back to his old abilities after the injury. So there was certainly some risk involved in the trade on our side."

Hunter spent the first seven years of his NHL career in Quebec, where he recorded 140 goals and 458 points in 516 games. He also racked up 1,545 penalty minutes while sporting the fleur-de-lis, building a reputation as one of the game's biggest agitators and clutch performers.

"Pound for pound, one of the toughest players I played with and against," said former Capitals defenseman Robert Picard, who played with Hunter for parts of two seasons with the Nordiques. "He had the biggest heart of a hockey player that I've seen."

"We knew we were getting a warrior when Dale arrived," said Kelly Miller, the only Capitals player who was teammates with Hunter throughout his 12-year tenure in Washington.

"Dale gave us something that we didn't have down the middle," said Lou Franceschetti. "We got a guy [who] would go through the wall. We got a guy [who] was an instigator [who] more or less would do anything to win. He'd spear your eyes out if he had to, just to win a playoff game. And he pretty much showed that in Game 7 against the Flyers that first year."

Hunter's overtime game-winning goal in Game 7 of the Capitals' 1988 first-round series against Philadelphia will forever be a signature moment both from Hunter's career and in Capitals franchise history.

A year after blowing a 3–1 series lead and falling in the fourth overtime in Game 7 against the Islanders, the Capitals rallied from a 3–1 series deficit and a 3–0 hole in Game 7 to beat the Flyers. Hunter had two goals and an assist in the 5–4 OT win.

"You knew what kind of player Dale was," said Mike Gartner. "He was a hard-nosed guy. So, as he's coming in, you're assuming he'll add that dimension to the team, which he did, but I found the surprising thing with Dale is that he was a very skilled player at the same time. He may not be remembered as a skilled hockey player, but he was more skilled than I think anybody really realized until you actually played with him."

Longtime Capitals captain Rod Langway was patrolling the Montreal Canadiens' blue line in the early 1980s when he was first introduced to Hunter, then a pesky forward in Quebec.

"I knew we were going to have a lot more [battles] with Philly with Hunts on our team, and sure enough we did," Langway said. "But as captain of the team, it helped me out because of his leadership. He was a true pro, an old-school hockey player. We lost some skill with Alan Haworth, but I didn't realize how good Dale was with his passing ability and clutch goals every year. Hunts could play the dirty game and he could play the skill game."

Hunter and Malarchuk were welcome additions in Washington, but the off-season dealing of Duchesne and Haworth hit hard for one of Haworth's frequent linemates in Greg Adams. Along with Craig Laughlin, Adams and Haworth often made up Washington's third line under head coach Bryan Murray.

"From a selfish point of view, I was extremely disappointed to lose Alan," Adams said. "Just a wonderful guy and a wonderful friend and teammate, and also a linemate who helped me so much. But having said that, Dale Hunter was the biggest prick in the league."

Adams wasn't exactly a saint himself, having led all Capitals forwards in penalty minutes in the two years before Hunter's arrival. Adams embraced his role as a pest who could chip in

Dale Hunter is the only player in NHL history with 300 career goals, 1,000 points, and 3,000 penalty minutes. "You have to get on the score sheet somehow," he used to say. "Gotta let them know you played."

offensively—he had career highs of 18 goals and 56 points in 1985–86—but he knew that there was always room for more feistiness.

"We had a little bit of it, but you could never have too much of that," said Adams. "I probably played that role and I'm a third- or fourth-liner. So, if you get that further up the food chain, on the first or second line, with that kind of intensity and mentality, it really does impact the team. There's a certain sense that even though I'm intense and play like a prick, it influences the team a little bit but maybe it doesn't influence all the guys. But if one of your best players, if one your top one or two players has that atti-tude, it drags everyone up. Not just half the team or two-thirds of the guys—it brings *everyone* up. Dale could do that."

Capitals "Absolutely" Would Have Drafted Sakic

Although Haworth and Duschesne didn't last long in Quebec, the first-round pick proved to be the key to the deal for the Nordiques.

Thanks to the No. 15 pick that the Nordiques obtained from the Capitals, Quebec selected a center named Joe Sakic from the Western Hockey League. Sakic would enjoy a Hall of Fame career with the franchise, eventually captaining the Colorado Avalanche to the Stanley Cup in 1996 and 2001.

Sakic retired in 2009 with 625 goals and 1,641 points spread across 20 seasons. In 2017, he was named one of the NHL's 100 Greatest Players as part of the league's centennial anniversary.

But just because the Nordiques drafted Sakic with a pick that originally belonged to Washington, would the Capitals have necessarily done the same? Poile barely hesitates.

"Absolutely," he said in 2017. "We had him rated at that same spot. If we kept the pick, we would have drafted him."

Still, Poile has no regrets.

"It was absolutely the right thing for Washington to do at the time. [Dale] Hunter got us back up and running when we were a little wobbly there. He was a fantastic player, a fantastic presence, he knew how to win, and he helped us win some playoff rounds."

While Hunter emerged as a leader in Washington over a dozen seasons, Haworth played just one year in Quebec while Duchesne spent two seasons with the Nordiques.

The Capitals reached the playoffs in each of Hunter's first nine years in Washington, and later advanced to the Stanley Cup Final for the first time in 1998, with Hunter serving as captain.

The Nordiques, on the other hand, missed the playoffs five straight years after the Hunter trade and didn't win another playoff series until 1996, when they had already relocated and become the Colorado Avalanche.

"Not taking anything away from Gaeten or Alan, but I think that was a mistake of a trade for Quebec," said Picard, who played with Hunter in Quebec from 1985 through 1987. "My biggest thing is that Dale was the catalyst on the team and when things were not going on a given night, he'd find a way to get something done that would change the game's characteristic and momentum and try to put it on our side. In the playoffs, he was as hard of a competitor as you'd ever find. To me, that's probably one of the centerpieces that made the difference in getting the Capitals from where they were to where they went."

33 Holtby Emerges as Fourth-Round Gem

The name Darrell Baumgartner may not resonate with too many Capitals fans, but those around the organization are well aware of the impact he's made for Washington.

Baumgartner is a former elementary school educator in Regina, Saskatchewan, who worked as a part-time regional scout for the Capitals during the 2007–08 Western Hockey League season.

That's when Baumgartner first introduced Capitals management to an 18-year-old goalie on the Saskatoon Blades named Braden Holtby.

"He really liked Braden a lot," said Capitals assistant General manager Ross Mahoney.

"He was putting in some really positive reports on Braden, so he really went to bat for him as far as putting his name out there, and he always had really positive things to say about him. I know in his reports, he always had some comments like, 'This player would be a real solid pick for the Capitals.'"

While Baumgartner saw tremendous potential in Holtby, the rest of the scouting community wasn't sold. After missing the playoffs in back-to-back seasons as the Blades' No. 1 goalie, Holtby was rated No. 4 among North American goaltenders in Central Scouting's final rankings ahead of the 2008 NHL Draft. Throw in international goaltending prospects as well, and Holtby was a projected mid-round pick.

"In junior hockey," Holtby said in 2016, "there is way more talk than there needs to be about where you're going to go in the draft with rankings and all that, so you obviously pay attention to them. But come draft time, yeah, we were probably expecting to go a little higher than I did."

Holtby attended the 2008 NHL Draft in Ottawa with his parents, his sister, his grandparents, and his agent, David Kaye. It proved to be an exercise in patience as Holtby watched *nine* goalies get picked before him.

"The first and second rounds, I wasn't too stressed out when I didn't go," Holtby said. "It was one of those things where I was told I may go there but I never really believed it, I just didn't see that—but there were a lot of goalies that went right before me [late in the third round], so that was kind of the weird part."

Holtby admits that being omitted from Hockey Canada's Under-20 Program of Excellence summer camp in the weeks leading up to the draft may have hurt his stock as well. But regardless of what the rankings suggested, the Capitals were quietly keeping an eye on him.

"We actually had him rated really high as far as all the goalies went," Mahoney said in 2016. "In all honesty, he wasn't the tenth goalie on our draft board. We had Braden ranked much higher—there may have been one goalie that went ahead of him that we had also ranked ahead of him, but other than that, we really had him pegged high—certainly higher than most other goalies that were drafted ahead of him."

And so, it was an easy decision for the Capitals when they announced Holtby's name early in the fourth round with the 93rd overall pick.

"We didn't have a third-round pick that draft," Mahoney recalled. "We went from 58th to 93rd and quite honestly, had we had a third-round pick, we probably would have taken Braden in the third round."

Throughout the draft process, Holtby didn't care which team called his name, but the Capitals, he said, proved to be a pleasant surprise.

"I had talked to the Capitals a couple of times at the combine," he said. "I knew that they were interested, but they were pretty honest at the start that they didn't think they would draft me because of their draft position."

Two years before Holtby's draft year, the Capitals stocked up on high-end goaltending prospects when they selected Semyon Varlamov [22nd overall] and Michal Neuvirth [34th overall] in 2006.

"Seeing what they already had, they weren't going for goalies high and they didn't think that I'd be there in the [later rounds]. There were a few teams I was pretty sure I was going to—there were three or four of them—and lo and behold it comes around and [former Capitals goaltending coach] Dave Prior said to me that when I was there in the fourth they just felt that they had to take me, because they were going for the best player on the board in their mind, and that's what they did."

While Holtby was the third goalie the Capitals selected in as many drafts, he was never bothered by the potential hurdles in beating out the organization's other goaltending prospects.

"That really didn't come into mind," he said. "If anything, I was actually extremely happy to go there because they didn't have a long-term goalie in place. Most teams, 75 percent of teams, have a guy that's there for a long time, or going to be there for a long time. So you're looking if there's an opportunity where you can turn some heads and with the Capitals, there was that chance. So there was that chance and things worked out."

In retrospect, the Capitals' drafting Holtby seems like a no-brainer. While Holtby was the tenth goalie taken in the 2008 NHL Draft, he entered the 2017 off-season with more NHL wins and shutouts than the nine goalies taken ahead of him *combined*.

He has emerged as one of the best goalies in the world, winning the Vezina Trophy in 2016, and representing Canada on the international stage at the 2016 World Cup of Hockey in Toronto.

"I knew from a pretty young age that I was never going to be that highly sought-after prospect. I was never one of those goaltenders where goaltending came extremely easy to me at a young age, so I knew I'd have to get there through work and proving people wrong and proving that I can just win games."

And as Holtby emerged as on the NHL's top goalies and arguably the Most Valuable Player on a Stanley Cup contender, Mahoney and the rest of the Capitals management team have remained thankful for the job Darrell Baumgartner and the scouting staff did in identifying an under-the-radar goaltending prospect.

"Darrell was a former goalie himself, and he was really positive about Braden and his ability," Mahoney said of Baumgartner, who has since been hired as a full-time scout with the Capitals.

"Darrell has to get a lot of credit for identifying Braden and going to bat for him. I think his being a former goalie, he took a real keen interest in the goaltenders. The scouting staff all liked him, but Darrell especially deserves a lot of credit for that one."

34 Veterans Bellows and Tikkanen Join '98 Capitals

Brian Bellows had 1,001 regular season games on his NHL resume, but an odd feeling set in for the veteran of 15 pro seasons as he prepared for his next one. He was nervous.

Bellows had spent much of the 1997–98 campaign playing in Germany, recording 32 points in 31 games for the first-division Berlin Capitals (no affiliation). During downtime between games in Europe, Bellows searched for finance jobs as he pursued his business degree and pondered life after hockey. A late-season offer from the Washington Capitals, though, had him back in the NHL for one more shot at the Stanley Cup.

On March 28, 1998, at GM Place in Vancouver, Bellows made his Capitals debut, facing a Canucks team that had cut him at training camp the previous fall. As he dressed for his first NHL game in nearly a year, Bellows knew that he was also playing for his professional future. His soon-to-be linemate, veteran Adam Oates, lightened the mood.

"Just before I was about to step out on the ice in Vancouver," Bellows recalled, "Oates came up to me and said, 'Hey kid! Don't hurt yourself out there!' It just kind of broke the tension. It was sarcastic and funny at the same time. It probably did me some good."

Later that night in his NHL return, Bellows could not have looked more comfortable. The 33-year-old scored twice on the power play, including the game winner, as the Capitals beat the Canucks 3–2.

Bellows proved to be a terrific late-season spark for the Capitals, who went 8–1–2 after his debut and secured home-ice advantage in the first round of the Stanley Cup Playoffs. Bellows had six goals and nine points over the 11-game stretch, playing primarily with Oates and Joe Juneau.

"I knew Brian pretty well," said Ron Wilson, Washington's head coach at the time, who had played with Bellows with the Minnesota North Stars in the 1980s and later coached him with the Anaheim Mighty Ducks.

"I had a really good experience with him in Anaheim and I thought he'd be perfect for our team—we needed somebody to play in front of the net on the power play, and Brian did a perfect job. He filled the bill perfectly. He was everything a coach could have wanted at that time."

The Capitals signed Bellows on March 21, with general manager George McPhee taking advantage of a loophole in the league's rules. The rules stated that any player returning to the NHL from Europe had to clear waivers before playing. There was also a rule stating that any player claimed off waivers (by another team) after the trade deadline would not be eligible for the playoffs. With this in mind, the Capitals waited three days for the March 24 trade deadline to pass before putting Bellows through waivers on March 25.

If any of the 25 other teams had claimed Bellows off waivers at that point, he wouldn't have been eligible for their playoff roster. Since the Capitals originally signed him on March 21, though, he was able to play for Washington in the postseason.

"I remember getting a call from [Flyers general manager] Bob Clarke right away and then having a discussion with [Rangers GM] Glen Sather a little while after that," McPhee told the Capitals' official website in 2014. "Bob Clarke said, 'You shouldn't be allowed to do that,' and he told me why I shouldn't be allowed to do it. And Glen Sather was the opposite. He said, 'Hey, that was a really smart move.'"

The Capitals signed Bellows for $50,000 for the final 11 games of the regular season plus the playoffs. It wound up as a steal for Washington, as Bellows emerged as a key cog during the Capitals' run to the Stanley Cup Final.

"I felt we needed a right winger, a right shot," McPhee said. "Sometimes it falls into your lap. His agent [Brian Lawton] had called and said, 'This guy might be available; his season is over in Europe.' And that was the key; his season was over.... Ronnie [Wilson] had him in Anaheim, and we talked about it. He said, 'I think this could work and if you want to do it, I'll play him. This guy has probably got enough left in the tank to do this.' So we did it."

McPhee was fairly conservative in his first season in Washington, relying heavily on the roster he absorbed from his predecessor David Poile. But with the Capitals fighting for playoff positioning down the stretch, McPhee acquired a pair of veterans in Bellows and Esa Tikkanen. Between them, Bellows and Tikkanen had 1,926 regular season games and 287 playoff games on their resumes.

The Capitals landed Tikkanen, a five-time Stanley Cup champion, from the Florida Panthers on March 9, 1998, for minor leaguer Dwayne Hay and future considerations.

"They were two totally different personalities, but they both brought a lot of experience," said goaltender Olie Kolzig. "Esa brought his five Stanley Cup rings that he carried around in his shaving kit. They were just unique individuals. You look at Esa Tikkanen, he played in those glory days with the Oilers and he told stories and just had a sense of calm before big games because he's been there and done that. I think that rubbed off on a lot of us. BB was the same way. He was a gamer. He came through in big situations. He was a guy that could have fun, but he also let you know that he was the veteran."

Both Bellows, a Stanley Cup winner with the Montreal Canadiens in 1993, and Tikkanen were instrumental in leading the 1997–98 Capitals to the Stanley Cup Final for the first time in franchise history.

"Their experience was very valuable," Wilson said. "It got played up in the news a lot because they had won Stanley Cups, but it was really important to our team. Even though we had veterans, we didn't have anybody with any kind of [Stanley Cup] experience at all on that team. Those two guys really led the way. They were excellent."

In Washington's first-round series win over the Boston Bruins, Bellows opened the scoring in the first period in Game 1 (an eventual 3–1 Capitals victory) and later scored the series-clinching goal in Game 6, with the Capitals winning 3–2 in double overtime at the Fleet Center.

Bellows blasted a slap shot past Byron Dafoe from 50 feet out as the Capitals celebrated their first series win in four years. Two rounds later, Bellows assisted on Juneau's overtime series clincher in Game 6 of the Eastern Conference Final against the Buffalo Sabres.

Bellows finished fourth on the Capitals in playoff scoring with seven goals and 13 points in 21 games, while Tikkanen chipped in with three goals and six points.

Although Tikkanen may be best remembered in Washington for the goal he didn't score—missing an open net in Game 2 of the Stanley Cup Final after deking Red Wings goalie Chris Osgood—his defensive play was among the reasons the Capitals were able to reach the finals in the first place.

"He was a good hockey player," McPhee told the Capitals' official website in 2014. "He shadowed [Jason] Allison in the Boston series and [Alexei] Yashin in the Ottawa series. He could do that really well and drive people crazy. But when he got the puck on his stick, he was really good, too. Good defensively, good offensively. He was a heck of a player for a little while. It helped us get to the Stanley Cup Final. I thought it was what put us over the top, to have a good veteran guy who had won a lot of Cups who we could get a lot of ice time out of and who we could use in so many different ways: power play, penalty kill, shadow, defensive play, faceoffs, five-on-five. It was a really good move for the club."

While Tikkanen returned to the New York Rangers for the 1998–99 season, Bellows re-signed for one more season with Washington.

The 1998 playoff run will always hold special memories for Bellows, highlighted by the birth of his son, Kieffer, in the middle of the Stanley Cup Final.

After the Capitals dropped Game 1 in Detroit, Bellows flew home to Minnesota. Then–Capitals owner Abe Pollin provided Bellows with his private plane.

"The Stanley Cup playoffs are a game," Pollin explained to the *Washington Post*. "A game. Having a baby is life. We all want to win, of course, but it's a game. Life comes first."

One day later, Bellows' wife Tracy was induced and seven-pound Kieffer Bellows was born healthy.

"It was pretty interesting the way it played out," Bellows said. "We went on that [playoff] streak and then it was like, 'Oh god, what are we going to do?' And thank god that my wife was healthy enough to be induced at the right time."

Bellows returned to Detroit that night and was back in the Capitals' lineup the next day for Game 2 at Joe Louis Arena.

"I think [in] Game 2 I was going on adrenaline," he said. "That was the game that in my mind we really needed to win. We had our chances, but we just didn't do it."

Bellows only played one more season in Washington, retiring after the 1998–99 campaign. Years later, though, he again crossed paths with McPhee after the New York Islanders selected Kieffer in the first round of the 2016 draft.

McPhee had been working with the Islanders during the 2015–16 season before being named GM of the expansion Golden Knights in Las Vegas.

"Kind of an odd story is the fact that George McPhee was advising the Islanders and he was partially behind my son being drafted 18 years later, which is kind of wild. When you look at the connection, and George and I, our sons played together the year before, and when they say hockey and sports can be a small world, it really is."

35 Roger That

The late Roger Crozier wore many different hats during his time with the Capitals. He just didn't wear any of them for very long.

Crozier was an NHL goaltender for 14 seasons, appearing in more than 500 games with three different teams. After lengthy tenures with the Detroit Red Wings and Buffalo Sabres, Crozier's playing career culminated with a three-game stint with the Capitals in 1977.

He retired that off-season due in part to his ongoing battle with pancreatitis, but he remained with the organization as an assistant general manager and goaltending consultant.

When Capitals owner Abe Pollin fired head coach Gary Green and GM Max McNabb on November 5, 1981, Crozier was named an interim replacement for both jobs. Washington was on an 11-game losing streak and had a 1–12–0 record at the time. Crozier coached just one game before Bryan Murray took over full time, but he held the GM post for 10 months.

Crozier remains the answer to a longstanding Capitals trivia question, as he is the only man in team history to have served as a player, head coach, and general manager.

And while his time as GM may have been brief, Crozier made a series of moves that would have a lasting impact.

Twenty days after being named acting GM, Crozier acquired Bobby Gould and Randy Holt from the Calgary Flames. The former went on to play 600 games with the Capitals over eight seasons.

At the 1982 draft in Montreal, Crozier acquired goaltender Pat Riggin and forward Ken Houston in another trade with Calgary. He also landed forward Alan Haworth in a deal with Buffalo.

Crozier then made the executive decision to select defenseman Scott Stevens with the fifth overall pick in the draft, despite some Capitals scouts pushing him to take forward Rich Sutter. Crozier later chose forward Milan Novy, a 30-year-old Czechoslovakian, in the third round.

The next season, Gould, Holt, Riggin, Houston, Haworth, Stevens, and Novy were all key cogs as the 1982–83 Capitals clinched the first playoff berth in team history. Crozier, though, wasn't part of the celebrations.

On August 27, 1982, just three days after Pollin declared that the Capitals would remain in Washington after a successful Save the Caps campaign, Crozier was fired.

In a prepared statement, Pollin said, "We appreciate the job Roger did for the organization, and for stepping in on an interim basis during a difficult time."

The Capitals announced Crozier's firing on a Friday afternoon at 4:00 PM.

"I helped build a helluva hockey club for them," Crozier said at the time. "I believe we have done enough good things that the team is going to win. We made all the moves we could.

"The new guy has a solid foundation to build on. This is going to be a really exciting and competitive hockey club. It would be a real shame if a new guy comes in and tries to unravel this thing because we are in pretty good shape right now."

David Poile, then 33, was hired on August 30, 1982. Discussions between the Capitals and Poile, at the time the assistant GM in Calgary, began weeks before Crozier was let go.

Poile was barely 10 days into the job when he pulled off a blockbuster trade and acquired Brian Engblom, Doug Jarvis, Rod Langway, and Craig Laughlin from Montreal, but Crozier wasn't wrong in suggesting that the moves he made helped provide a strong nucleus for years to come.

Crozier was 40 when the Capitals relieved him of his duties, but it marked the end of his hockey career. In 1983, he moved to Wilmington, Delaware, and began working with MBNA Bank.

Although Crozier died in 1996 after a battle with cancer, he is still fondly remembered around the NHL and continues to hold a number of rare distinctions.

In addition to being the only member of the Capitals organization to have served as a player, coach, and GM, Crozier was the last goalie to start all of his team's games during the regular season.

Crozier started all 70 games for Detroit in 1964–65 and captured the Calder Trophy as Rookie of the Year. The next season, Crozier became the first Conn Smythe Trophy winner as playoff MVP to come from the losing team in the Stanley Cup Final.

36 The Goal

Alex Ovechkin has scored more than 500 career NHL goals, but few remain as memorable as goal number 32 from his rookie season. To some, it's simply known as "The Goal"—a play that saw Ovechkin carry the puck through the neutral zone and drive to the net before being tripped up by Phoenix Coyotes defenseman Paul Mara.

It was then—while sliding on his back—that Ovechkin maintained control of the puck and connected on a no-look, over-the-shoulder, one-handed swat to beat Coyotes goalie Brian Boucher in a 6–1 win.

Those in Arizona for the January 16, 2006, matinee still have fond memories of what many, including Ovechkin himself, describe as the best goal of his career.

"We couldn't believe exactly how it went in," Brooks Laich said in 2016. "He was kind of like a tumbleweed and dust and all of a sudden, the puck was in the net and we're like, 'How did that happen?'"

Capitals defenseman Brendan Witt, who assisted on the goal, was most impressed with Ovechkin's stick-to-itiveness on a play that appeared dead in a game the Capitals led 5–1.

"It was an early glimpse of Ovi showing his magic," Witt said. "Ninety percent of players give up on that play, but he showed that amazing raw talent that you started to see as he became his own type of player with a special identity."

Chris Clark, a teammate of Ovechkin's for parts of five seasons was also on the ice for The Goal, trailing the play in the neutral zone as Ovechkin cut to the Coyotes' net.

"At first, you're like, 'No, he didn't try to do that for real,'" Clark recalled. "Just having the wherewithal to finish it on his back and sweep the puck towards the net was unbelievable…. You look at the replays and you can tell that he's basically in control while sliding on his back. He has that unique gift to stay focused and to contort his body and sweep it the right way."

The in-house replays couldn't come fast enough for the 14,110 in attendance at then–Glendale Arena. Players and coaches on both benches also stared upward, waiting for second look of the goal to appear on the scoreboard.

"It was the longest five or six seconds in the world waiting for it to come on the jumbotron," said Brian Willsie, Ovechkin's first NHL roommate.

"I was beside Matt Pettinger on the bench, kind of looking at each other [like], 'Did that really happen?' And then everyone saw [the replay] together and there was this collective gasp. Everyone was so captivated, just staring at the screen."

In video clips and highlights of the goal on YouTube, the collective gasp of the crowd watching the replays on the jumbotron is clearly audible in the background of the broadcast.

"At first, the whole building went quiet," Laich said, "and it was weird because you could really feel the announcement of a superstar. That moment, it was against Wayne Gretzky's team, who was the best player the game had ever seen, and all of a sudden, a young guy that was really, really good makes a play that really announced his superstardom like, 'I'm here and I'm the next generation of the league.' You could feel it in the building clear as day.'"

Gretzky was coaching the Coyotes at the time, and he was also left dumbfounded after seeing the goal both live and then again on the jumbotron.

Even Ovechkin himself needed a second look.

"I didn't see the puck go in because I was on my back," he said. "But I see [teammate Boyd Gordon] and [Witt] come to me and start to celebrate so I have to go and see what happened, how I did it. It was pretty amazing and pretty cool."

Even before social media had really taken off, Ovechkin's goal quickly went viral.

"He really got not just the hockey world's attention," said Witt, "but the whole sports environment's attention with that goal. It was on ESPN forever, it was in the top plays of the year. It was great."

"It's probably the biggest goal," Ovechkin said. "Obviously lucky, but I'll take it. For that moment, it was unbelievable time. My dream was come true—I play in the NHL, I did that kind of special goal and Gretzky was there."

For Ovechkin's older teammates, it was just another shake-your-head moment from a memorable freshman campaign that saw Ovechkin finish with 52 goals and win the Calder Trophy as Rookie of the Year.

"When he got the puck, there was always a buzz in the crowd," said then–Capitals captain Jeff Halpern. "Even in visiting arenas, fans recognized how electrifying he was and when people got in his way, he just bulldozed them over. It was special to see him go through the league and showcase his talents."

The Capitals would finish in last place in the Southeast Division during the 2005–06 season, but veterans understood that what they witnessed in Arizona on that January afternoon was one of many early signs that brighter days were ahead.

"As that season progressed," said Clark, "Alex gave us that little edge that we needed to win some games down the stretch. And to see him progress, and to see [opposing] defensemen, they just kept backing up because they didn't want to get beat at the blue line, it was fascinating to see."

Unlike many first-year players who may hit a rookie wall by midseason, Ovechkin's game took off. The Goal in Arizona was his fifth tally in two games and part of an incredible month that saw

him earn both NHL Rookie of the Month and Offensive Player of
the Month honors.

"You were starting to see him become his own type of player
with his own identity," Witt said. "It's those dog days of the year
that really hit the young guys but he just seemed to thrive on it.
Each game, he was showing something new, he was coming up
with something different and it was great for us older guys, because
he was an energizing person."

37 Olie the Goalie

Before Olie Kolzig started breaking franchise records, the feisty
goalie often broke his sticks.

"He had a problem with his temper," said head coach Ron
Wilson.

"If I wasn't happy," Kolzig explained, "I'd break my stick on
the crossbar or across someone's legs."

Weeks before Kolzig became Washington's starting goalie in
October 1997, he broke three sticks on the crossbar after allowing
a goal to teammate Joe Reekie in a scrimmage.

"The only reason he didn't break a fourth is because he didn't
have any left in his rack," said former teammate Bill Ranford.

"I thought it was the funniest thing," said Jeff Halpern. "He
always had a thing going with Joe Reekie. If you shot high on Olie
in practice, like near the collarbone or the neck, he came running
out of the net, it didn't matter who you were."

Kolzig didn't have much patience. The Capitals, though,
showed plenty of patience in Kolzig. After selecting him in the
first round of the 1989 draft—on a recommendation from their

head western scout Barry Trotz—the Capitals waited *eight* years for Kolzig to finally solidify the No. 1 job in Washington.

"That wouldn't happen in today's game," said Kolzig, who went 14–36–8 in his first 71 NHL appearances. "Organizations don't wait that long for guys to live up to their potential."

Kolzig made the Capitals as a 19-year-old rookie but played poorly in his first two appearances and returned to his junior team. His second NHL start was an 8–4 loss in Toronto on *Hockey Night in Canada*.

"That can be unnerving for a younger player," said former teammate Alan May. "He got spanked. It was a chaotic night. He wasn't ready to be in the NHL yet—not emotionally or mentally. He wasn't there."

Kolzig spent the next few years toiling in the minors. In 1991–92, he was 5–17–2 with a 4.17 goals-against average with the American Hockey League's Baltimore Skipjacks. That led to a stint with the ECHL's Hampton Roads Admirals. The NHL didn't exactly seem around the corner.

Despite backstopping Hampton Roads to the 1992 Kelly Cup, the Capitals loaned Kolzig to the Buffalo Sabres' AHL affiliate in Rochester for the 1992–93 season.

"I went to Rochester thinking that my time with Washington was done," he said. "I went with a bit of a chip on my shoulder trying to impress the Buffalo staff, hoping I might latch on to them."

Working with then–Sabres goaltending coach Mitch Korn, Kolzig had a strong year in Rochester. He led the Americans to the Calder Cup Final and earned a nickname that followed him for the rest of his career.

"I didn't like getting pulled and I wore my emotions on my sleeve," he said, "so I may have had a few temper tantrums on the bench or gotten into a few fisticuffs with some guys. So, one day I came to the rink for a game in November and there was a fan in the stands and he had a sign that read NOBODY BEATS GODZILLA. It had me in my full goalie garb breathing fire out of my mask. So the guys in the room had fun with it, and the nickname stuck. Then they shortened it to 'Zilla."

The Godzilla name took off and it appeared that Kolzig was ready to do the same. His best season in the minors came in 1993–94, when he returned to the Capitals' AHL affiliate and led the Portland Pirates to the Calder Cup title. Kolzig was named playoff MVP.

When the Capitals traded starting goalie Don Beaupre before the lockout-shortened 1994–95 season, Kolzig seemed well positioned to emerge as Washington's No. 1.

Instead, he went 2–8–2 and was passed on the depth chart by 20-year-old rookie Jim Carey. A year later, Carey won the Vezina Trophy with Kolzig serving as the backup.

It wasn't until the 1997–98 season that Kolzig had another chance to emerge as the full-time No. 1. Kolzig battled the veteran Ranford for the starter's job in training camp and although Ranford got the nod on opening night in Toronto, it didn't last long. A groin injury kept Ranford from going out for the start of the second period.

Kolzig came in and took over as the starter while Ranford rehabbed over the next few weeks. Kolzig, though, held on to the gig…for the next decade.

"The opportunity came and finally after the previous five or six years, I took advantage of it," Kolzig said. "The funny thing is that for that first game, Toronto had not been kind to me over the course of my NHL career. I had a few pastings in that building. So I went in and we had a 4–0 lead, and it's a bad way to think, but I went there thinking, 'Okay, don't blow this lead.'"

The Capitals won 4–1.

"I overcame some of my demons that night and I think it just freed me up."

Kolzig broke through in 1997–98. He posted a 33–18–10 record, made his first NHL All-Star Game, and represented Germany at the 1998 Nagano Olympics. He later tied an NHL record with four postseason shutouts while leading Washington to the Stanley Cup Final for the first time.

"It was good to see him finally have his day in the sun and have it all click in," said Capitals forward Kelly Miller. "It felt good to watch from a distance as this young kid figured it out. To see him have his moment was kind of cool."

Olie Kolzig's breakthrough 1997–98 season saw him play in his first NHL All-Star Game and represent Germany at the Olympics. He also led the Capitals to the 1998 Stanley Cup Final with a then-record four shutouts in a single postseason.

Kolzig credits goaltending coach Dave Prior for helping him turn his career around that season. Kolzig and Prior briefly worked together at the 1996 World Cup of Hockey and first-year general manager George McPhee recruited Prior to join the Capitals in 1997.

"I had to get my emotions under control and channel them the right way," Kolzig said. "When Dave Prior came around, that's when everything fell into place."

With a new head coach, a new goaltending coach, and a new GM, plus an upcoming move to a new downtown arena, Kolzig had a newfound confidence and attitude.

He learned to keep his cool. There were fewer tantrums. Not as many doors were slammed. And the hockey stick companies were suddenly receiving less business.

"There were points in time where I really felt for him," said defenseman Todd Krygier, who played with Kolzig in both the AHL and NHL. "You knew this guy was an unbelievable, fantastic goaltender. You wanted to see it happen for him, but early on he had to struggle through some frustrations. He had to earn every bit of it."

Olie's Resume

Along the way to becoming the winningest goalie in Capitals history, Kolzig racked up plenty of personal accolades. Below is a sampling:

Kelly Cup Champion (ECHL): 1992
Calder Cup Champion (AHL): 1994
Jack A. Butterfield Trophy (AHL Playoff MVP): 1994
Two-time Olympian (Germany): 1998 and 2006
Two-time NHL All-Star: 1998 and 2000
NHL First-Team All-Star: 2000
Vezina Trophy: 2000
King Clancy Memorial Trophy: 2006
ECHL Hall of Fame inductee: 2010
Most wins in Capitals history: (301)

"A big part of it is taking advantage of the opportunity," Wilson said. "It all lined up where he was finally emotionally and physically prepared. He grasped a hold of it."

And he didn't let go.

From 1997 through 2004, only Hall of Famers Martin Brodeur and Ed Belfour won more games than Kolzig.

In 1999–2000, he set franchise records across the board with 41 wins in 73 games. At season's end, he was named a First Team All-Star and won the Vezina Trophy as the NHL's top goalie.

"To see him in the net in that Vezina form," said Halpern, "it was a reassuring feeling. He was so big and quick. He was like a sumo wrestler in net. There was nothing to shoot at. And everything was so quick."

By the turn of the century it was apparent that the patience the Capitals exercised in Kolzig and the time he spent in the minors were worth it.

Along with Peter Bondra, Kolzig was among the most popular players on the team and one of the more recognizable D.C. athletes.

'Olie was our captain," Halpern said. "Other guys had the 'C,' but Olie was basically our captain. He was a guy that you wanted to play on the same team with, and as a goalie behind you, you wanted to do anything for him."

That's why, Halpern said in 2017, one of the most disheartening defeats of his career was Game 1 of the 2000 Eastern Conference quarterfinals. The Capitals lost 7–0 to Pittsburgh at the MCI Center. The Penguins eventually won the series in five games.

"We left Olie out to dry that first game," Halpern said. "We never recovered. We had the best goalie in the league and couldn't get out of the first round."

As the Capitals transitioned from a veteran-laden club to a rebuilding one after the 2005 lockout, Kolzig remained among the few holdovers. In March 2008, he became the 23rd goalie in NHL history with 300 career wins and the fifth to do so with one team.

After 19 years with the Capitals organization, Kolzig signed a free-agent deal with Tampa Bay in 2008 and retired one year later. Although Kolzig settled in Florida after his playing career, he has worked with the Capitals in player development and as a goaltending coach.

Kolzig remains the most recent Capitals player to wear No. 37, and many Capitals fans have clamored for the number to be raised to the Verizon Center rafters.

"I think for any individual to have their number retired, that's the ultimate compliment other than the Hall of Fame," he said. "But that's not a decision for me to make. I was just honored to wear that number for the amount of years I was in Washington. And if one day it happens, it will be one of the happiest days of my career."

38 The Stanley Can

No matter if it was against Buffalo, Toronto, or Vancouver, Jim Anderson couldn't get that elusive win. Red Sullivan tried in Chicago, Kansas City, and St. Louis, but also to no avail.

The first two head coaches for the expansion Capitals during a forgettable 1974–75 season and not a single road win between them.

Anderson went 0-for-28 on the road, with eight defeats coming by at least six goals. Sullivan lost all seven of his road games, including three by six or more goals.

On December 14, 1974, the Capitals lost 12–1 in Boston under Anderson. Three months and one day later, they lost 12–1 in Pittsburgh under Sullivan.

That was the final road game for Sullivan, who resigned after two more home defeats dropped his overall record to 2–16–0.

Capitals general manager Milt Schmidt took over behind the bench, with the former Bruins captain, coach, and GM returning to the Boston Garden on March 22, 1975. The Bruins welcomed Schmidt back to Beantown with an 8–2 win. Washington's road losing streak hit 36.

The Capitals were now three coaches into the season and still searching for road win No. 1.

After falling 5–0 at home the next night to the Atlanta Flames, the Capitals embarked on a two-game California road trip. With only four road games remaining, including one final visit to the Montreal Forum, the Capitals faced the real possibility of going oh-for-the-road in their maiden season.

A 5–1 loss to the Los Angeles Kings at the Great Western Forum on March 26 brought the road losing skid to 37. It was also Washington's NHL-record 17th consecutive defeat overall.

"It was a long year, that first year," said Ron Lalonde. "There were things we experienced that I don't think any other NHL team has ever had to go through."

Finally, on March 28, 1975, the Capitals had their opportunity at the Oakland Coliseum. Facing a California Golden Seals team that the Capitals had beaten at home in November, Washington took an early 2–0 lead.

Doug Mohns and Ron Anderson scored in the first 4:12 before Oakland rallied to tie the score 3–3. Nelson Pyatt, acquired from the Detroit Red Wings a month earlier, restored the Capitals' lead at 6:31 of the third period, netting the eventual game-winning goal in a 5–3 Capitals triumph.

"The Washington Capitals won a road hockey game tonight. Honest," read the lede of Ken Denlinger's game story in the *Washington Post*.

The 17-game losing streak and the 37-game road losing streak were both snapped. They remain NHL records more than four decades later.

"It's like winning the Stanley Cup," Schmidt told the *Oakland Tribune*.

For some Capitals players, winning that first road game was in fact cause for a Stanley Cup–like celebration.

"Let's face it, that was one of the longest seasons of my life," Yvon Labre told Sports Talk 570 in Washington in 2013. "Tommy Williams had gotten this little trash can out of the dressing room, and he had a bunch of guys sign it. Him a couple of other guys [brought it out] on the Oakland rink, and were skating around with it. They called it the Stanley Can."

Depending on whom you ask from that team, there are different recollections as to who exactly initiated the Stanley Cup celebration. But everyone took part, hoisting the trash can above their heads and parading it around the ice, as if it were, you know, an actual trophy.

"I know Nelson Pyatt, who we traded for, he was a pretty quiet guy but he had a couple of goals that night," said Lalonde, "and I think he was the one who kind of spearheaded it. It's hard to know whose idea it was, but we all quickly joined in because we had all felt the frustration of going 37 consecutive games without a win on the road. There had been a few close ones, but there were also a lot of lopsided ones too."

Ron Low made 17 saves in the win in Oakland, as the Capitals *improved* to 7–64–5 on the season.

"You started to really feel like you might never win another hockey game," Low told NHL.com in 2008. "You started to think, 'Maybe it's just not possible.' It felt like forever. That's why there was so much jubilation in our room that night when we broke it."

The story of the Capitals' first road win, and the celebration that followed, will forever have a place in team history, but few hockey fans actually saw or heard it unfold live.

Only 3,933 fans were in attendance that night in Oakland, and with the game taking place three time zones away, the Capitals didn't secure the win until the early hours of the morning back in Washington.

"By the time we got into the dressing room," Lalonde said, "and came up with the idea of raising the garbage can—an old plastic green garbage can, and walking around with it—by the time we got back out on the ice, there was nobody left in the arena other than a handful of ushers and people cleaning up. So it kind of went unnoticed besides internally in our room, but we all signed the garbage can and when we went back the next season, our names were still on that garbage can in the visiting team's dressing room. That was quite an event."

It was also the only road win of the Capitals' inaugural campaign. The Capitals lost in Detroit and in Montreal during the final week of the regular season to finish the road portion of their 1974–75 itinerary with a 1–39–0 record.

39 Easter Epic

It remains the longest Game 7 in NHL history and one of the Capitals' most gut-wrenching defeats. To many hockey fans, it is simply known as the Easter Epic.

Game 7 of the 1987 Patrick Division semifinals between the Capitals and the New York Islanders began on April 18, at 7:40 PM. It ended six hours and 18 minutes later—just before 2:00 AM on

Easter Sunday, April 19—when New York's Pat LaFontaine scored the game-winning goal in the fourth overtime.

Capitals goalie Bob Mason collapsed in his crease as the Islanders mobbed LaFontaine before a subdued crowd at the Capital Centre in Landover, Maryland.

To help paint the picture of the Easter Epic, we spoke to several former Capitals players, plus general manager David Poile.

Prelude

The Capitals and Islanders were meeting in the postseason for the fifth time in as many years. New York had won three of the previous four series, but the Capitals built a three-games-to-one lead in 1987.

It just so happened that 1987 was the first year since the NHL expanded the first round from a best-of-five series to a best-of-seven. That opened the door for the Islanders to rally and again eliminate the Capitals.

Larry Murphy (Defenseman): Trying to get by the Islanders, in the early 80s, they were the dominant force in the National Hockey League. Even when the Oilers started winning the Cup in the mid-80s, the Islanders were still the toughest team in the East.

Lou Franceschetti (Forward): You've got to learn how to lose before you can learn how to win. And we did a lot of losing against them.

David Poile (General Manager): We caught them when they were one of the best teams in the league.

Mike Gartner (Forward): To be honest, I think it got a little discouraging. The way the playoffs were set up back then was intradivision play early on, so we'd be a team that was in the top five in the entire league, and they'd be in the top five in the entire league and we'd always be playing them in the first round.

Regulation

Gartner gave the Capitals a 1–0 lead late in the first period of Game 7, before New York's Patrick Flatley and Capitals forward Grant Martin traded goals in the second. Martin's goal was the biggest of his NHL career. It was also the only goal of his NHL career.

Martin was recalled from AHL Binghamton the morning of Game 7 with veteran Alan Haworth out with a knee injury. Martin played 44 regular season games with Hartford and Washington, but never scored. The Easter Epic was his only playoff game.

The Capitals led 2–1 and were outshooting the Islanders 25–10 after two periods. With just over five minutes remaining in the third, New York's Bryan Trottier beat Mason with a soft backhander to tie the score 2–2. Mason later revealed that he had a broken rivet on his skate. The rivet attaches the skate boot to the blade.

Poile: It wasn't a great shot. But when he went to make the save on Trottier's backhand, his skate stuck to the ice because the blade was loose.

Bob Mason (Goalie): I remember shuffling to my left and my ankle buckled. There was nothing there—nothing to support the ankle. [Equipment manager] Doug Shearer came out on the ice, but he couldn't fix it there. So I played the last five minutes of the third period with a broken skate.

Poile: When you talk about stuff like that, that seems to be more than your normal bad luck.

Mason: I guess they didn't want to throw [backup] Pete [Peeters] in for the final five minutes of regulation in Game 7 in a tie game. So I just had to hold on. I don't even know how I did it. We couldn't fix it until the intermission.

Poile: I came down after regulation, before the overtime. I was just hanging around near the dressing room and I saw Doug Shearer working on Mason's skate. You're holding your breath when overtime starts.

Overtime

Both teams had quality scoring chances in regulation and plenty of opportunities to win the game in overtime. The Capitals outshot the Islanders 75–57, but Islanders goalie Kelly Hrudey made a career-high 73 saves. That doesn't even include the close calls from Capitals forward Mike Ridley and defenseman Greg Smith, who were both denied by the goalpost. More than three decades later, the Capitals are still haunted by the chances they missed.

Bob Gould (Forward): The thing I remember more than anything is that we had 75 shots on net. That sticks out in my mind—75 shots and we could still only score two goals.

Franceschetti: How do you expect to win a series when we have those chances and can't finish? Gartner and Ridley, they had a 2-on-0 breakaway in Game 7, but couldn't beat Hrudey.

Rod Langway (Defenseman): Both teams could have won it in the first overtime. There were so many posts. Greg Smith didn't play that often, but we were on empty and he took a shot from just outside the blue line. It went over Hrudey's shoulder and hit the net square, but it hit the top post and fell right back. But both sides, nobody had any energy.

Franceschetti: I still ask myself, "Why couldn't I stay on my skates on a breakaway in the third overtime?" I had a breakaway if I had stayed on my skates. Mind you, if that's today, I probably would have had a penalty shot.

[Islanders defenseman] Tomas Johnson would have gotten nailed [for tripping]. I got taken out at the blue line trying to chase the puck.

The Capitals and Islanders played 68 minutes and 47 seconds' worth of overtime. Neither team had a power play opportunity.

Poile: I remember Mike Gartner, it just seemed like he was getting dragged down left and right every shift and Andy Van Hellemond, who was the referee, never called one penalty.

Greg Adams (Forward): It was the Wild West out there.

Kelly Miller (Forward): It was kind of like rugby or football out there. They were letting everything go. It was just a matter of who was going to score the goal. But you're just trying to survive.

Gartner: One of the things that stands out is just how everyone felt. There wasn't a whole lot said during the intermissions. Guys were getting new gloves or trying to dry their gloves or change their equipment. Everything was soaking wet.

Mason: I was exhausted. I think I lost 10 or 12 pounds. I was just drained. You keep pushing through the game and while you're playing, you don't realize how tired you are. When it's over, it hits you.

Murphy: We were basically riding four D, which was a huge torture test. You just mustered up everything you could do.

Adams: Larry Murphy, he pruned up. He played so much that he pruned up like he was in a sauna or a bathtub. His skin was all crinkled. Christ, I think he lost 13 or 14 pounds that game.

Murphy: You definitely weren't 100 percent. When the puck drops at the start of the game, the tank is at 100 percent. I don't know how you measure where you are by the sixth or seventh period. You're pretty much digging deeper than you've ever had to dig before in your life.

Adams: You look at a marathon runner at the end of a race and they start to get delirious. Every one of us, on both teams, had to feel like that a bit. How do you prep to play that much?

Gartner: Everybody was starting to cramp up and they were passing out potassium pills to get some potassium back in your system. Everybody was dehydrated.

Adams: We played seven games in 14 days, plus travel back and forth. And then you're playing a seventh period in Game 7? You're pretty wasted.

The Goal

For the first time in 44 years, a postseason game needed quadruple overtime. Eight minutes and 47 seconds into the seventh period, the Islanders won it.

With the Capitals caught scrambling in their own end, Islanders defenseman Gord Dineen skated out from behind the Washington net and fired a shot from the left faceoff circle. The shot was blocked by Capitals defenseman Kevin Hatcher, but it ricocheted right to LaFontaine in the high slot.

LaFontaine spun around and fired a slap shot from 54 feet out. The shot made its way through a maze of bodies and past Mason to give New York the 3–2 win.

Mason: Dineen was circling the net and just throwing something towards the slot. Hatcher goes down for a block, it hits his stick and scoots out towards the blue line.

Langway: I remember Lafontaine starting to go to the bench for a change and then somebody yelled at him to keep the puck in, so he just turned and fired it.

Mason: I'm sitting there pretty deep in my net and I didn't see the puck. I heard a clank, and I heard the crowd, and you knew it was over.

Gartner: It was disheartening losing that way. You kind of knew it was going to be one of those types of goals. I remember guys saying on the bench, just get the puck on the net, you never know, you just never know. And it was that type of goal.

The Aftermath

LaFontaine's goal sent the Islanders to the Patrick Division finals, where they'd eventually fall in seven games against Philadelphia.

For the Capitals, a franchise still seeking its first Stanley Cup title more than three decades later, the Easter Epic and the blown 3–1 series lead against New York remain among the biggest "What Ifs" in team history.

Craig Laughlin (Forward): It was a morgue in the locker room after the game. The guys couldn't speak. I remember [head coach] Bryan Murray just standing there and he was just dumbfounded. He didn't have anything to say. There was nothing that could be said.

Adams: We're talking seven periods of hockey, seventh game, you beat the shit out of each other every period for seven games. By the end of that game you're just so freaking exhausted.

Gould: Quite often I just sit back and ask myself, "What if I had scored?" What a difference it would have made. It might have been the big step that the Capitals were waiting to take.

Miller: Certainly, we had our chances. But it was a great game and I feel very proud to have been a part of something like that. I just wish I had been on the other end of it.

Franceschetti: You take your equipment off, you sit in your stall, you think about what could have been, what should have been.

Poile: I've watched the game just once. We outplayed them by such a wide margin in terms of scoring chances, shots, and territory and all of that and they still beat us.

Gould: To this day, I have not watched the game and I don't know if I'll ever watch because I might watch it and start saying, "I should have done this," or 'What if we had done that?" It certainly was a historic game. But I always ask myself, "What if?"

40 Deadline Blockbuster

David Poile has never shied away from making a big trade, but few of his in-season moves rival the deal the former Capitals general manager pulled off just before the trade deadline on March 7, 1989.

With the Capitals two points out of first place in the Patrick Division, Poile traded Mike Gartner and Larry Murphy to the Minnesota North Stars for Dino Ciccarelli and Bob Rouse.

It remains one of only two trades in NHL history that involved at least three future Hall of Famers.

"It was a 3:00 PM trade deadline and we got traded right at three," Gartner said. "We were in Montreal, we were in a day early for a game the next night, and we had gone on the ice for a practice at the Forum and just before the practice started, Larry and I were skating and [assistant coach] Terry Murray came up to us and said, '[Head coach] Bryan [Murray] wants to see you in the dressing room.' We knew it was trade deadline so we were pretty sure we got traded, and we did."

The trade was especially difficult to stomach for Gartner, the Capitals' first-round pick in 1979, who spent the first 10 seasons of his NHL career in Washington. At the time of the trade, he was the club's all-time leader in games played (758), goals (397), assists (392), and points (789).

"I felt like I was kind of spinning for the rest for the year," Gartner said. "Looking back on it, any player that gets traded, that first time you get traded is a real shock. I had been there almost 10 years, I had been drafted there, my kids were born in Maryland, and I had been part of that organization and then to get traded, it was real tough."

In an odd twist, Gartner actually broke the story himself among the Washington, D.C., media, thanks to a relationship he had at the time with WTOP Radio.

"I had my own radio show with WTOP; it ran three minutes, Monday through Friday, four times a day," Gartner told NHL.com in 2008. "I hadn't phoned in my radio show for the day, so when I got the news I was traded, I figured WTOP had been good to me for the last couple of seasons, it was the third season I had the radio show, so I figured that I would give them an exclusive on my feelings on the trade.

"So I phoned them up and did one last show on my thoughts on being traded just 15 minutes after it happened. I got a hold of the news director and I asked him if they wanted me to come on and answer a few questions. It was a little different format but we still had it as the final *Mike Gartner Show*, so it worked out pretty good and they were pretty good about it. I don't know if I was a professional radio person—my first reaction was that I obviously was a little shocked at what happened, and I did my best to say my feelings at the time. It was really more or less thanking them for what they had done for me in Washington, all the friends I had made and all the people I got to know."

The Capitals had the NHL's fifth-best record when the deal was made, but with just eight wins in their previous 21 games, Poile felt that his club was trending in the wrong direction. Poile also looked at the big picture—his team had reached the playoffs the prior six seasons, but had yet to advance beyond the second round.

"We just needed to make a change," Poile said in 2017. "I liked Mike Gartner and how he played, and I liked Larry Murphy. Those guys were great players, but it just seemed at the time that we needed a change. Ciccarelli was the key. We were looking for that catalyst, that energy and that emotion. The team we didn't feel was playing up to its potential, so we wanted to shake things up."

Just as Gartner was Washington's all-time scoring leader, Ciccarelli left Minnesota as the North Stars' franchise leader with 332 goals and 651 points in 601 games. Both were gifted goal scorers, but they went about their business differently. Gartner was among the game's fastest skaters and often scored off the rush; Ciccarelli played a more physical game and was no stranger to scoring from atop the crease.

"What David did was I guess he just wanted a different look on that right side," said forward Lou Franceschetti. "He wanted someone a little feistier than Mike was at that time. But you're going for two different styles of players. You're going from a guy with a lot of wheels to a guy who's just going to go up and down and get you goals within three or four feet of the net and cause havoc and get under people's skin. He's a similar player to what Dale Hunter was, and I guess after being there for 10 years, they felt that Mike wasn't that type of player. Mike is a Hall of Famer;

Dino is a Hall of Famer—they're just different types of Hall of Famers."

Captain Rod Langway wasn't privy to the trade in advance, but he also recognized that the move was done to give the Capitals a fresh identity.

"The way it sounded to me, was we were just getting more players like Hunts," Langway said. "Dino was feisty. He would take your eye out in a heartbeat. Everywhere he went, he had to fight to gain position. I guess that's what the organization wanted. We knew we had to go through Philly and the Islanders and the way everyone played back then, you had to have some meanness and dirtiness to the game. Mike was not a dirty player, but boy he could score goals. Dino was the same thing—he was naturally a goal scorer. You look at Mike—he was like the Roadrunner—and then you've got Dino, who was more of a turtle. But he's going to get there too, and he'll have someone bleeding when he gets there."

Gartner left the Montreal Forum soon after he was traded, quickly packing his belongings and leaving the premises before his teammates had completed their practice. He was blindsided by the trade and felt that he had unfinished business with the only franchise he had known.

"Certainly, as a team we had team playoff shortcomings," Gartner said. "But one of the things that I didn't appreciate is that there were reports coming out after I got traded that I couldn't perform in the playoffs, and I never felt that was very fair and I really didn't appreciate it. When you look statistically, it wasn't something that was accurate."

Gartner was the only player who skated in all 47 of Washington's playoff games from 1983 through 1988. His 16 goals and 43 post-season points were also franchise highs when he was traded.

"It was also something that kind of left a bad taste in my mouth for quite some time," he said of the playoff criticism. "It wasn't until time kind of takes care of those things and you realize there's no sense in dragging that around for too much longer and so we didn't. We have since, over the last number of years, actually had a very good relationship with the organization, but it was tough at that time."

The trade had an immediate impact for the Capitals, who went 9–3–0 to close out the 1988–89 season and clinch their first Patrick Division title in team history. Ciccarelli had 12 goals and 15 points in 11 games.

A year later, Ciccarelli led the 1989–90 Capitals in scoring with 41 goals and 79 points in 80 games. Gartner, meanwhile, moved again at the 1990 trade deadline, dealt this time from Minnesota to the New York Rangers. Less than two months later, the Capitals advanced to the Wales Conference Final for the first time in franchise history after a second-round series win over Gartner and the Rangers.

"It was tough," Gartner said. "I think I played every single shift against Rod and this was back when you could clutch and grab and hold and everything, and Rod kind of just smothered me in that series. I had kind of gotten past [the trade from Washington] by that time, but it would have been nice obviously to be part of the Capitals when they did make that move past the second round."

While Gartner lasted one year in Minnesota, the North Stars traded Murphy to the Pittsburgh Penguins in December 1990. Five months later, Murphy and the Penguins happened to beat the North Stars in the 1991 Stanley Cup Final. It was the first of four championship rings Murphy earned in eight years, a stretch that culminated with the Detroit Red Wings sweeping the Capitals in 1998.

Rouse played 130 games with the Capitals before he was traded to the Toronto Maple Leafs in January 1991, in a deal that brought Al Iafrate to Washington.

Of all the players involved in the March 1989 trade, Ciccarelli had the longest tenure with his new team, recording 112 goals and

209 points in 223 games with Washington. The Capitals traded Ciccarelli to Detroit in June 1992 for Kevin Miller.

All four players in the Capitals–North Stars trade went on to play more than 1,000 career NHL games, with Gartner (2001), Murphy (2004), and Ciccarelli (2010) all earning enshrinement in the Hockey Hall of Fame.

The four-player deal remains among the biggest in Capitals history.

41 Attend Practice at the Kettler Capitals Iceplex

Fans interested in seeing their favorite Capitals players up close—but not looking to break the bank for front-row seats along the glass—may be best served by attending a practice or morning skate at the Kettler Capitals Iceplex.

The Kettler Capitals Iceplex is located in Arlington, Virginia, and has served as club's primary training facility since opening in November 2006. The 137,000-square-foot facility includes two NHL-size ice rinks, a pro shop, a Capitals team store, and a snack bar. It is also the home base for the club's administrative offices.

There is ample parking for those driving—KCI is located on the roof of an eight-floor parking garage—and the facility is Metro accessible via the Ballston Metro Station along the Orange Line.

While the Capitals' practice schedule varies day to day, most on-ice sessions begin at either 10:30 AM or 11:30 AM. They don't usually go much beyond 60 minutes.

From rookie camp in early September right on through to the early rounds of the Stanley Cup Playoffs, all of the Capitals' on-ice sessions at KCI are free and open to the public. Depending on the day, fans can often stand right up along the glass—ideal for taking pictures—as the Capitals go through their drills and practice reps.

Weekends and school holidays tend to bring out big crowds, with the facility providing seating for up to 1,200 fans. Those fans whose schedules permit a late-morning weekday getaway to KCI will likely have the best access to players and may be able to secure some autographs or photos.

It doesn't hurt to have a sign (or a cute kid) that may catch a player's attention. Players are often drawn to signs with a birthday or a hometown reference (for those who have travelled a great distance to be there).

From the Capitals' perspective, KCI has been the ideal team headquarters. Prior to the 2006–07 season, the Capitals spent 15 years practicing out of the Piney Orchard Ice Arena in Odenton, Maryland.

This made more sense when the team played at the Capital Centre in Landover and the team flew out of BWI Airport in Baltimore. There was an even a time when both the Capitals and their American Hockey League affiliate, the Baltimore Skipjacks, practiced out of Piney Orchard.

But without an affiliate in Baltimore, and with their home games now in downtown Washington, D.C., it was practical for the Capitals to move their headquarters inside the Capital Beltway when their lease at Piney Orchard expired. Enter the $42.8 million KCI, which was funded by Arlington County through the sale of bonds and has been leased long-term to the team.

The 20,000-square-foot training center for the Capitals features a state-of-the-art weight and fitness room, athletic-training and medical facilities, as well as a theatre-style classroom and a high-tech video room.

There is no question that the amenities provided to players have come a long way. Back when the Capitals practiced in Mount

Vernon in the 1980s, players changed in trailers and took turns riding the one exercise bike.

For the growing number of community and rec-league hockey players in northern Virginia, KCI has served as a central hub. An estimated 12,000 hours of ice time is used at KCI by youth, high school, and college hockey teams.

Members of the Washington Little Capitals, a top tier-1 program, also train and play at KCI.

KCI is the first indoor ice rink inside the Beltway in Virginia and just the second facility of its kind anywhere inside the Beltway. (Fort DuPont Ice Rink in D.C. is the other.)

For more information, including schedules and ice rental, visit kettlercapitalsiceplex.com.

42 Joel Ward's Unlikely Journey

Days before Joel Ward skated in his 500th career NHL game in March 2015, the Capitals winger had a few folks he wanted to thank.

Without the benefit of any notes, Ward went nearly four minutes, uninterrupted, thanking so many people who played a role in his hockey life that the monologue had the feel of an acceptance speech at the Academy Awards. But standing in the middle of the Capitals' dressing room, without an orchestra to play him off the stage, Ward couldn't help himself.

"I'm very appreciative of all the help I've had," he said after listing a half dozen junior and amateur teams he played for in Canada. "I've had a lot of friends and a lot of [neighborhood] parents that helped me along the way with a lot of [car] rides. I'd like to thank a lot of people from all those organizations that I played with.

"I don't take it for granted at all. I appreciate where I came from and, my story, I guess you can say. My journey getting to the NHL was a very long one."

The son of two immigrants from Barbados, Ward's journey was also an unlikely one. He grew up modestly in the working-class neighborhood of Scarborough, Ontario, just east of Toronto, playing street hockey with his two older brothers and with neighborhood kids, including future NHL goaltender Kevin Weekes.

Ward's father Randall, an auto mechanic who never played hockey himself, was drawn to the game soon after he moved to Canada as a teenager. Years later, he enrolled his sons in the local house leagues and occasionally took them to games at Maple Leaf Gardens—"our Disney World," as Joel later described it.

Randall predicted that Joel would someday reach the NHL, but the Ward patriarch never saw the day. In December 1994, while attending one of Joel's youth games, Randall suffered a stroke in the stands. From the players' bench, Joel could see a commotion around his father. Two days later, Randall died from a blood clot in his brain. Joel was 14, left to chase a dream without his father in the picture.

"That's why everyone's support means so much to me," he said. "It could have gone one direction, but hockey saved me and the people in minor hockey and the parents were a big part of that."

Joel's mother Cecilia worked two nursing jobs—one during the day and one overnight—to ensure that the bills were paid and that her boys could continue playing hockey. Others chipped in along the way.

"When I was a teenager, my captain was a friend named Brian Friedman," Ward recalled, "and his dad ended up purchasing two hockey sticks at a time because we couldn't really afford it. Little things like that really helped along the way. I appreciated [it] and my mother did, as well."

Ward went on to play four years with the Ontario Hockey League's Owen Sound Attack. But he was hit with a harsh reality in June 1999 when he and his family drove nine hours to attend the NHL Draft at the Fleet Center in Boston, only to return home without hearing his name called.

Years later, there were tryouts with the Detroit Red Wings and Atlanta Thrashers, but ultimately no job offers. So Ward enrolled at the University of Prince Edward Island, where he played varsity hockey for four years and earned a degree in sociology. He was 24 when he graduated, having never played a shift of professional hockey at any level.

"My goal coming out of college was to get to the American League," he said. "I figured if I get to the American League, anything is possible. But I wanted to get there as quick as I could because I knew my age, in the hockey world, wasn't working in my favor. But I was hungry to get after it. I had a few good years at PEI. It was a big responsibility with the school part, so it was a good challenge for myself and it kept me pretty hungry and humbled and I really appreciated that."

Ward's pro career began in the unlikeliest of ways when he was discovered at a roller hockey tournament in Florida. That led to tryouts with the ECHL's Florida Everblades and with the AHL's Houston Aeros. Houston ultimately paved the way for a career in the NHL. The Aeros were affiliated with the Minnesota Wild and coached by former NHL bench boss Kevin Constantine, whom Ward credits with teaching him the details and intricacies of the pro game.

Houston was home for three years, with 11 NHL games sprinkled in with the Wild. But three months shy of his 28th birthday and with only the 11 NHL games on his resume, Ward's hockey journey was at a crossroads when he sought full-time work with the Nashville Predators in September 2008.

"I really thought it was a do-or-die kind of moment in my career," he said of his first training camp in Nashville.

That's when Ward first met future Capitals head coach Barry Trotz, who was beginning his 10th season with the Predators.

"I remember Joel came to camp," Trotz said, "and all the amateur scouts were telling me how good the young prospects were. But maybe this is where amateur scouts and coaches differ because I saw the detail and maturity in Joel's game. He could handle a lot more than most of the kids."

After four years of junior hockey, four years of Canadian college, and three years in the minors, Ward finally became a bona fide NHLer during the 2008–09 season.

"I'll never forget that feeling when coach Trotz told me, 'You can get a place,'" Ward recalled. "I think those words, next to hearing that I graduated from school, were probably some of the biggest words I ever heard. It was a sense of relief that all of those years of hard work paid off."

Forever grateful to those who helped him along the way, Ward made it a point to give back to the community when he settled in Nashville. He joined the Big Brothers Big Sisters of America and was partnered with an at-risk 12-year-old boy named Malik Johnson.

Like Ward, Johnson had lost his father at a young age. He had a troubled upbringing, with academic challenges and discipline issues. For three years when the Predators were home, though, Ward met Johnson multiple times a week, whether it was playing basketball, grabbing dinner, or bringing him to a game or practice. He worked with Johnson on his homework and preached the need to do well in school.

They remained in touch when Ward signed with the Capitals in 2011, and saw each other when Ward's schedule allowed for it. They also kept in touch over phone and email.

Ward had plenty of incentive to keep tabs on his Little Brother. It was Ward who financed Johnson's tuition at Lighthouse Christian School, one of the top private schools in Tennessee.

"You just can't pick up and leave somebody behind like that," Ward told the *Tennessean* in 2015.

In 2016, Johnson became the first member of his family to graduate from high school. That same month, Ward competed in the Stanley Cup Final with the San Jose Sharks, with more than 500 career NHL games on his resume and the unlikeliest of journeys.

"One of those guys you can't help but support," said Jason Chimera, teammates with Ward for four years in Washington. "On the ice, he's as quality a player as anyone, but off the ice, he's an even better person."

43 Stevens Checks In

Like the bone-crunching hits he would deliver throughout his Hall of Fame career, Scott Stevens caught everyone's attention at his first NHL training camp in 1982.

"He was just rocking everybody," said Mike Gartner. "He was playing with such passion and reckless abandon."

The Capitals selected Stevens with the fifth overall pick in the 1982 draft, despite some Washington scouts urging general manager Roger Crozier to take forward Rich Sutter.

Crozier liked Stevens, an 18-year-old defenseman who had helped lead the Ontario Hockey League's Kitchener Rangers to a Memorial Cup title the previous spring.

But by the time the Capitals reported to training camp in September, Crozier was out of a job—fired in late August and replaced by first-time GM David Poile.

"At the training camp that we had in Hershey, I was a little hesitant to keep 18- and 19-year-olds," Poile said. "But this kid just wouldn't be denied."

The Capitals' options with Stevens were limited because as an 18-year-old, he could not be sent to the American Hockey League. Stevens was either going to begin the year as the youngest player in Washington or he would return for a second season in Kitchener.

In his first season in the OHL, Stevens led all rookie defensemen in scoring with 42 points in 68 games while racking up 158 penalty minutes. He was also an OHL all-star.

"I went [to camp] with the mindset that I wasn't going back to junior," Stevens told the Capitals' official website in 2007. "I just wanted to play in the NHL. That was my goal ever since I was growing up. Every time [you get to] the next step, it's a faster pace and in the NHL, I was finally at the level where I wanted to be. I went in there playing physical and fighting."

That was evident from day one. Despite having no pro experience, Stevens played with an edge and was impossible to miss.

"One of my more vivid memories," Poile said, "is him fighting [Philadelphia Flyers prospect] Dave Brown in training camp. And as an 18-year-old, it was like, 'Wow. This is unbelievable.' He didn't give us any choice but to put him on the team."

"It was a big decision for the organization," said Rod Langway. "But I remember playing a game against Philly in Hershey and he nearly broke a player's legs with a hip check. The whole bench was looking at each other, like we couldn't believe it, like, 'Who is this kid?' He won the position by himself. He deserved to play his rookie season, there's no question."

Stevens went on to play 1,635 career games over 22 seasons without ever skating in the minors. He made the Capitals' opening night roster on October 6, 1982, and scored in his NHL debut on his first career shot as the Capitals beat the New York Rangers 5–4 at Madison Square Garden.

"He's thrown three of the best checks I've seen in a couple of years," head coach Bryan Murray told *The Hockey News* in October 1982. "We've taken him aside and talked with him about position and using his partner, and he's responded well. There's no doubt in my mind that he can step right in."

Besides Stevens, Langway and Brian Engblom were also fresh faces on the Washington blue line in 1982, having been acquired from the Montreal Canadiens just days before the start of training camp. While a pair of veteran defensemen came in, only one blue-liner in Rick Green went to Montreal. That meant that the already slim chance Stevens had of making the Capitals out of camp was made even tougher with one fewer roster spot open for competition. Stevens, though, saw things differently.

"When Langway and Engblom came from Montreal," he said in 2017, "everyone probably thought that my chances of making the team weren't as good, but actually, it probably helped me be able to slide in there and make the team with those guys being on the back end. It just made us that much better and solidified the team. So, I think that helped me."

Stevens was the fourth defenseman the Capitals selected with a top-five pick, but the first who had reliable veterans to lean on. Greg Joly (No. 1 pick, 1974), Green (No. 1 pick, 1976), and Robert Picard (No. 3 pick, 1977) had no such luxury.

"The good news for Scott was that we had made the trade to get Langway and Engblom, two experienced defensemen," Poile said. "And while Scott could hold his own, I think that just enhanced his chances the way our team was set up. Bryan Murray basically put him with Brian Engblom from day one and Brian was a great partner and mentor during that first season."

Engblom only spent one full season with the Capitals before being traded to the Los Angeles Kings for Larry Murphy in October 1984, but it was long enough to make a big impact on a teenaged Stevens.

"Brian was outstanding to me," Stevens said. "He had a lot of knowledge—he knew all of the players in the league and he'd take time before every game and sit down with me and let me know everybody's tendencies, what guys did well. He let me know the guys that have speed, which guys shoot the puck, which guys were shifty one-on-one, so it was very nice to play with him and have a partner that kind of took me under his wing, which made things easier."

Thanks in part to the guidance he received from Engblom, Stevens made the NHL's All-Rookie Team and was a finalist for the Calder Trophy as Rookie of the Year as the Capitals reached the playoffs for the first time in franchise history.

Stevens played 77 games during his first season, finishing with nine goals and 25 points. He also had 195 penalty minutes while quickly building a reputation as one of the game's hardest hitters and most physical defensemen.

"Somebody would be coming down on me one-on-one and all the sudden this force of nature would come from the left and, 'Boom!' There'd be this giant collision," Engblom told NHL.com in 2016. "He almost took me out a couple times. I'd go, 'What the [heck] was that?' It was Scott laying people out all over the place."

Thanks to some mutual friends in Kitchener, Capitals defenseman Greg Theberge was familiar with Stevens, but nothing prepared him for what Stevens would bring to Washington beginning with his first NHL audition.

"He was another guy [who] helped change the culture and identity of the Washington Capitals," Theberge said. "He's an 18-year-old kid, and I remember sitting on the bench during an exhibition game against the Pittsburgh Penguins and a guy was coming down the neutral zone and in one of Scotty's first shifts, he planted his feet and then all of a sudden he elevates his upper body and torso and just caught the guy in the midsection and flipped him right over his freakin' shoulder. The bench was in awe. We had never seen that type of check before. It was like a football hit. Scotty Stevens brought in that type of identity where you're going to pay the price. There's no more pushing the Washington Capitals around."

Stevens would spend the first eight seasons of his career with the Capitals, recording 98 goals and 429 points in 601 games in a Washington sweater. He represented the Capitals at two All-Star Games (1985 and 1989), was runner-up to Ray Bourque for the 1988 Norris Trophy, and ranks No. 2 in franchise history with 1,628 penalty minutes, behind only Dale Hunter (2,003).

44 Ace Bailey

Exactly four months after the Capitals fell 6–3 to the New York Rangers in the first game in franchise history, they returned to Madison Square Garden on February 9, 1975.

The result was nearly identical in the rematch. This time, the Rangers beat the Capitals 7–3 as Washington completed a five-game road trip with a fifth straight defeat. Four months and 54 games into their inaugural season, the Capitals had a woeful 4–45–5 record.

General manager Milt Schmidt fired Jimmy Anderson, the club's first head coach, shortly after the loss in New York.

One day later, Schmidt completed a deal with the St. Louis Blues, trading Denis Dupere—who three weeks earlier had become the first player to represent the Capitals at the All-Star Game—for Garnet "Ace" Bailey and Stan Gilbertson.

Bailey was 26 when he joined the Capitals, but he had already played in more than 350 games with the Boston Bruins, the Detroit Red Wings, and the Blues.

"Ace is the kind of player you need when you're building a team," said Schmidt, who was part of Boston's management team when Bailey broke into the league with the Bruins in the early 1970s. "He's a good checker, a hardworking digger, and he can play center or the wing, whichever you want."

Bailey also arrived in Washington with some credible postseason experience.

"I remember watching Ace Bailey as a young man, when Boston was playing St. Louis [in the 1972 Stanley Cup Final]," former teammate Mike Marson recalled in 2016, "and I remember when Ace was out there, he was just like a machine. He could do it all. He could skate, he could bump and grind, he knew how to see the ice, and he was one of the guys that if you were an aggressive player at all, you immediately felt an allegiance to his tenaciousness."

Ron Lalonde, who had joined the expansion Capitals a few weeks earlier in a trade from the Pittsburgh Penguins, knew his teammates would enjoy playing alongside Bailey.

"We all looked up to Ace because he was a Stanley Cup winner," Lalonde said.

"He played for the Bruins in '72 and played a pretty key role in that championship and you could tell that he was talented. I'm sure that he was frustrated playing on an expansion team, but he was a good player and he was a heck of a character."

The mounting losses were in fact foreign to Bailey, who had also won an AHL Calder Cup championship as a Bruins prospect with the Hershey Bears in 1968–69.

Playing parts of four seasons with the Capitals, though, Bailey would never sniff the postseason again. In 207 games with Washington, Bailey recorded 43 goals and 114 points. The Capitals won no more than 24 games in any of his four seasons.

But as the losses came, Bailey's good-natured character was among the biggest assets he brought to the team. Even during those trying years, Bailey could always be counted on to lighten the mood.

"It was all about the fun of the game for Ace," said Rick Green, teammates with Bailey from 1976 through 1978. "I don't know how serious he really took it. He just liked everything that went with the game on the ice and even off the ice. He was just going to make sure that everyone around him was going to enjoy the whole experience."

On one particular western road trip, Bailey made sure his teammates got the last laugh, even if it came at the expense of an unassuming head coach in Tom McVie.

"We got out to Vancouver and Tommy was pissed off about something," Lalonde said, "and so he scheduled an early-morning practice out at the Pacific Coliseum, which wasn't very close to where we were staying. So, he puts in *four-in-the-morning* wake-up calls for everybody and then we're waiting outside the hotel and it's freezing cold. And then the bus isn't showing."

With the Capitals out west for an extended road trip, players were provided with detailed travel itineraries to give to their wives and families, complete with flight and hotel information and various phone numbers and contacts.

Among the items on the itinerary was the name and phone number for the Vancouver-based bus company that would be chauffeuring the Capitals to and from the arena.

In the interest of avoiding an early-morning commute and practice, Bailey took it upon himself to call the bus company and cancel the order.

"We knew something was going on" when the bus wasn't showing up, Lalonde said. "But Tommy obviously didn't know. So he's out there, pacing back and forth, wondering what the heck is going on."

"Ace knows what's going on," recalled goaltender Bernie Wolfe, "I'm sure a couple of the older guys knew, but we're all down there and the bus doesn't come. So McVie finally turns to all of us and in this disgruntled voice and just says, 'Nothing today, boys.'"

Thanks to Bailey, the Capitals had the full day off in Vancouver. Moving forward, the Capitals also had a new way of conducting business on the road.

"After that trip," Wolfe said, "there were no longer any phone numbers or names of the bus companies on the itineraries."

The Vancouver bus incident wasn't the only time that the lighthearted Bailey got one past his old-school bench boss. After McVie was named head coach midway through the 1975–76 season, he provided Bailey with a four-inch manual with tips for off-season conditioning.

Bailey made great use of the manual, although not exactly in the manner that McVie had envisioned. According to the *San Francisco Chronicle*, Bailey used the manual to prop up a beer keg in his bar that off-season.

By the time training camp rolled around that fall, though, Bailey beat several teammates in the Capital Mile—the one-mile run McVie instituted on the first day of camp.

"Ace, I can you see used your book this summer," McVie said.

Bailey replied: "Coach, I used it every day."

McVie was a stickler for his players being in top shape, and Bailey's weight was often north of what the coach deemed acceptable. Team-administered weigh-ins became common practice during McVie's reign, and making weight was always an adventure for Bailey.

"They'd weigh him the day after Thanksgiving and he was seven pounds more than some doctors said he should weigh," Wolfe said. "And they'd fine him $700, which was a lot of money back then. But he'd say, 'Hey, I'm in good shape for the shape I'm in.' He was a character."

Hockey's Loss on 9/11

Ace Bailey was beloved by his teammates for his sense of humor and the positive energy he brought to any group he was a part of. His life was taken too soon, though, when he died tragically in 2001.

Bailey was among 60 passengers and crew members killed on United Flight 175 when it crashed into the World Trade Center on September 11, 2001.

Bailey was the Los Angeles Kings' pro scouting director at the time. He was flying from Boston to L.A. to meet with the Kings coaching and management staff before the start of training camp that fall.

According to the 9/11 Commission, Bailey made four phone calls to his wife, Katherine, after the plane was hijacked, but was unable to reach her.

Former Capitals head coach Bruce Boudreau, who was coaching the Manchester Monarchs, the Kings' AHL affiliate, in 2001, was originally scheduled to be on the September 11 flight as well. Boudreau's flight was bumped up a day earlier so that he could attend a staff dinner in Los Angeles.

Bailey also had the option to fly out a day earlier, but, according to Boudreau, Bailey didn't want to hit the Kings with the $750 cost to change flights.

Bailey was 53 years old.

www.acebailey.org

"Ace always had this trouble making the weigh-ins and getting the proper weight," Green said. "He used to try to find ways to dehydrate himself at the time when he was getting called to the scale."

Lalonde recalls Bailey going to extreme measures to make weight.

"We had a steam room and he's in there with a rubber jacket to try [to lose the weight]," Lalonde said. "It was like he thought he was a jockey trying to get under the weight. I don't know how he found out, because it was a random weigh-in, but he always seemed to have a pretty good knowledge of when that was going to happen."

Bailey returned to Boston in the fall of 1978, thanks to a training camp invite from Bruins general manager Harry Sinden. It was a last-ditch attempt to stick around the NHL, but Bailey couldn't make the team out of camp.

As Bailey packed up, he left Sinden a bottle of Scotch and a note thanking him for the opportunity.

"That's the kind of guy he was," Sinden told *USA Today* in 2001.

Bailey went on to sign with the upstart Edmonton Oilers of the World Hockey Association. That's where a 30-year-old Bailey first met a 17-year-old prodigy named Wayne Gretzky. The two were roommates on the road—Bailey in his final professional season, Gretzky in his first.

"Ace may have not been the greatest athlete to play in the NHL, but he taught many players how to be champions, and more importantly, he was a winner as a person," Gretzky said after Bailey died in 2001.

45 Caps Deal Can't-Miss Kid

Four months before the Capitals selected Bobby Carpenter with the No. 3 pick in the 1981 NHL Draft, he was a senior at Peabody High School just outside Boston. He was also a *Sports Illustrated* cover boy.

"He exuded confidence," said former Capitals defenseman Greg Theberge. "He had so much attention and pressure. But he was loaded with confidence."

"He had a swagger and attitude," said Greg Adams, who played with Carpenter for four seasons. "A young kid from Boston. Boston—gotta love the town, but there's some swagger there."

According to *Sports Illustrated,* Carpenter was the "Can't-Miss Kid." A year after the 1980 Miracle on Ice, Carpenter was the future of USA Hockey. The thought of an American phenom playing in the nation's capital appealed to Capitals owner Abe Pollin.

Washington held the fifth pick in the draft, but Pollin told GM Max McNab to make sure the Capitals landed Carpenter.

"We're not drafting a kid from some small town in Canada ahead of an American kid on the cover of *SI,*" Pollin told McNab.

With the Hartford Whalers expected to take Carpenter at No. 4, McNab completed a deal with the Colorado Rockies for the No. 3 pick. The Capitals had their guy.

"You could see the talent right away," said former teammate Wes Jarvis. "You wonder if he ever met the expectations from USA Hockey. But boy, once he got his feet under him, he was a great player. You could see him coming."

At the time, Carpenter was the highest American draft pick and the first to make the jump from high school to the NHL. He joined a young Capitals nucleus that already included Mike Gartner and Ryan Walter, and he impressed as a rookie. During the 1981–82 season, Carpenter ranked No. 4 on the team with 32 goals and 67 points in 80 games.

His breakout season came in 1984–85, when he represented the Capitals at the All-Star Game and had career highs with 53 goals and 95 points in 80 games. Gartner had a career-best 50 goals that season, marking the only time the Capitals have had two 50-goal scorers in the same campaign.

Within two years, though, Carpenter's tenure with the Capitals came to an abrupt end. General manager David Poile sent him home. The decision came after a contentious contract negotiation was followed by Carpenter frequently clashing with head coach Bryan Murray over usage and playing time.

"I think everybody knows that Bryan and I don't get along," Carpenter told the *Washington Times* in 1986. "I think that's pretty obvious, and that's a good reason why I wouldn't mind leaving here."

Even Carpenter's father, a former Boston policeman who worked with the Capitals' scouting staff, often suggested that his son wasn't being put in the best position to succeed.

By November 1986, the Capitals had had enough. They effectively suspended Carpenter, who had an ironman streak of 422 consecutive games played to begin his career.

Poile told Carpenter to stay away from the team and that he'd be notified once a trade was completed.

"I reached my boiling point with the things that were taking place," Poile said in 2017. "I thought that [a trade] would happen in three or four days based on how good of a player he was."

Instead, trade talks stalled. A month after Carpenter's last game, the Capitals hadn't completed a deal.

"I got calls from everybody for the first few days, but when I wasn't able to work out a deal with anybody to my satisfaction, the phone stopped ringing," Poile said. "Now, here we go. I've put myself and the team in a really bad position where I've kicked the guy off the team and I haven't replaced him with anybody."

The Capitals struggled without Carpenter, winning just five of the 17 games they played before a trade was finally made.

"It did not unfold well," Gartner said in 2016. "It just didn't feel like it was handled well. It really didn't. The guys did not feel good about the way Bobby was being treated. It didn't feel great. It was not a good way to treat somebody who had been a pretty big part of your organization and was still very young."

As trade talks slowed, the Capitals considered bringing Carpenter back in late December. It soon became a moot point. On New Year's Day 1987, Poile finalized a trade with Rangers GM Phil Esposito.

Poile sent Carpenter and a second-round draft pick to New York for forwards Kelly Miller, Mike Ridley, and Bob Crawford.

"It felt good to be wanted by the organization," said Miller, who spent 13 seasons with the Capitals. "We were excited to get going and to see if we could prove ourselves and prove that the Rangers made a bad move getting rid of us."

While Carpenter lasted just 28 games in New York before he was traded again, Miller and Ridley grew into key cogs in Washington. Miller played 940 games with the Capitals, third most in team history, while recording 162 goals and 408 points. Ridley played 588 games with the Capitals, and had 218 goals and 547 points.

"The Rangers probably got the best player in the deal," said former Capitals forward Lou Franceschetti, "but he didn't last long in New York. We got two workhorses. Literally workhorses [who] put up 60 points every single year. I don't think I ever played with a harder worker than Kelly Miller."

The Carpenter trade turned into one of the best in Capitals history, but it remains a somewhat sour point given how it unfolded. The turmoil that surrounded Carpenter's relationship with the team left many in the organization with a bad taste.

"That's probably not a highlight for him or for me," Poile said. "With Bobby, there [were] a lot of highs and lows. A 50-goal season, a tough contract negotiation, so it wasn't a perfect situation. It could have been handled better by both of us."

"We became the collateral damage," Adams said of the players on that team. "It's our teammate but it's also our bosses and we were just like, 'What's going on here?' It wasn't comfortable for anyone."

In an odd twist, the Capitals brought Carpenter back to Washington on a one-year deal for the 1992–93 season.

"He eventually reinvented himself as a two-way player during the second half of his career," said team president Dick Patrick. "And one of the easiest negotiations we ever had was when he came back. He was happy and I was happy to see him, and I said, 'Boy, that was easier than last time!' He was laughing. I think he was happy to finish on a better note in Washington."

46 The Feisty George McPhee

Former Capitals forward Kelly Miller has a unique perspective of George McPhee. Miller is the only person to have skated alongside McPhee as an NHL teammate and to have also played for McPhee, the general manager.

Miller and McPhee were teammates with the New York Rangers from March 1985 until Miller was traded to the Capitals on January 1, 1987.

The two were reunited for Miller's final two NHL seasons in Washington when McPhee was hired as GM in June 1997.

Miller wasn't sure how McPhee would fare as a GM, but given the way he played the game, Miller figured he would bring a take-no-prisoners attitude to the District.

"George was not a very big guy, and yet he was probably one of the toughest characters out there on the ice," Miller said in 2016.

Miller was particularly impressed with how the 5'9" McPhee handled himself during the 1986 Patrick Division semifinals when the Rangers faced the Philadelphia Flyers.

"We ended up winning the series, and I give a lot of the credit to George. He was an undersized tough guy and he had to fight all the biggest, toughest guys on Philly's team and he did it tremendously. Without that, without him injecting that fearless, competitive spirit into the rest of the team, I think we would have had a very difficult time winning that series and I give George a lot of credit for doing what he did. Without it, we didn't have a chance to win."

In 115 regular season games with the Rangers and New Jersey Devils, McPhee fought 23 times. He had five more fights in 29 playoff games.

"George as a player in the NHL made his living fighting," said former Capitals head coach Ron Wilson. "In college, at Bowling Green, he was an all-time leading scorer. But when he got to the NHL, he didn't do anything but fight. That was his job. He got very good at it and pound for pound, he could fight with anybody. He was a small guy, but he was really mean and tough."

It was rare to see that side of McPhee, at least publicly, during his 17-year tenure as Capitals GM. Given his small stature and his conservative appearance with neatly pressed suits and glasses, McPhee the GM looked more like a politician than a former player.

But there was one exception as the Capitals prepared for the 1999–2000 season—McPhee's third with the organization—where that old-school feistiness was on full display.

The Capitals were winding down their preseason schedule that fall with a neutral-site game against the Chicago Blackhawks in Columbus. A day before the game, former Toronto Maple Leafs head coach Pat Quinn reached out to Wilson and McPhee to caution them about the Blackhawks.

"The Leafs had faced them the night before," Wilson recalled in 2017, "and Pat warned us that [the Blackhawks] were just looking to start a bunch of brawls."

Because the regular season was approaching, Wilson was hoping to use something close to his opening-night lineup in one of the final dress rehearsals.

"But during the warmup," he said, "we saw all the guys that Chicago had in their lineup and they dressed basically a goon squad. We were looking to ice our best team, so we had a lot of guys that didn't necessarily fight. So George said to me, 'Wils, you've got to change the lineup, we've got to toughen things up in case it comes to that.' So, right off the bat, [Bob] Probert hit somebody and a bunch of stuff happened and it went on all game. There was so much nonsense going on, guys just running around."

The exhibition included five fights, three of which involved Capitals defenseman Trevor Halverson. Halverson was a Capitals first-round pick in 1991, but he journeyed through 10 minor-league teams spread over three leagues before finally making his NHL debut during the 1998–99 season.

Halverson played 17 games for the Capitals that year and was hoping to crack the opening-night lineup in 1999–2000. Instead, after fighting Chicago's Mark Janssens and Nathan Perrott in the first period, Halverson was knocked out cold after one punch from Remi Royer in the third. Halverson never played pro hockey again.

Royer was among the "goons that didn't belong in the game," according to Wilson. The 21-year-old would spend the entire 1999–2000 season with the International Hockey League's Cleveland Lumberjacks, where he finished with three goals and 204 penalty minutes in 57 games.

"So this is all going on and we were pissed," Wilson said. "And I remember George tapped me on the shoulder with about five minutes left in the game and he said, 'Wils, if you want to, you can pull the team off the ice.' And I said, 'No way, George, I'm not going to embarrass them like that. I just told them to turn the cheek on a few incidents. It would be embarrassing for our team to leave now.'"

The Capitals played out the final few minutes and when the forgettable exhibition came to a merciful end, McPhee made his way towards the Blackhawks dressing room. When he arrived, he confronted Chicago head coach Lorne Molleken and a physical altercation ensued.

McPhee landed a punch that left Molleken with a black eye before a few Chicago players came to their coach's defense and brought McPhee down. McPhee wound up with a broken thumb and a torn suit jacket.

"He had to wear a back brace at times," Wilson said, "so the fact that he had gone down there to start this fight, we couldn't believe it. He had a bunch of clothes ripped, and I was like 'What the heck is going on here?' At that point, everyone on our team thought that George was crazy. But at the same time, he went down there by himself and got into a fight, and that also meant a lot to our players that he did that in order to stick up for the team."

The NHL wasn't impressed, though, handing McPhee a one-month suspension without pay and a $20,000 fine. For 30 days, McPhee couldn't attend any Capitals games or practices or communicate with any players or team personnel.

Wilson was also fined $5,000 after he was quoted as saying that he wished he had known McPhee was confronting Molleken because he and his players would have followed suit.

"An executive should not be involved in a physical confrontation," McPhee told the *New York Times* after the suspension was handed down. "I'm sorry for the incident, but I will never regret standing up for the organization or for what I think is right for the league."

Fifteen years later, McPhee was still remorseful in discussing the incident with the Capitals' official website:

"It's not going to change," he said. "But what I did was wrong; I never should have gone down there. I thought that what [the Blackhawks] were doing was really, really bad for the game. And it was. But that doesn't mean that you take matters into your own hands. I shouldn't have done it because I embarrassed the team and their coach. It was the wrong thing to do."

47 King of Capitals Broadcasts

Most Capitals fans are familiar with the broadcast tandem of Joe Beninati and Craig Laughlin. They have been calling games together for CSN Mid-Atlantic for more than 20 years. The versatile Al Koken has also been on a fixture on Capitals broadcasts since 1984, having worked as a host, play-by-play voice, color analyst, and sideline reporter.

While these names are synonymous with Capitals TV coverage, some fans might be surprised to learn that Larry King was once part of the team's TV coverage as well.

Yes, that Larry King.

The legendary broadcaster, who has interviewed nine U.S. presidents over the course of his Hall of Fame career, was once the intermission host on local Capitals broadcasts from 1984 through 1986.

"The fact that we had Larry King legitimized us," said Bill Brown, the executive producer of Capitals broadcasts on Home Team Sports from 1984 through 1996. "That put us on the map. That made people stand up and take notice."

According to Brown, King approached the Capitals in 1984 and offered his services.

"He told them, 'Whatever you need from me, I'd love to be a part of it.'"

Brown thought that King would make for a terrific intermission host. King was occasionally seen at other points in the broadcast, but the second intermission was his baby.

Brown and the HTS production staff set up a makeshift set on the concourse at the Capital Centre, where King would handle his hosting duties with a live audience looking on.

"You'll see during big playoff games today when [the networks] go on the road, they're in the arena, and surrounded by fans. Well, we were doing this in 1984 on the concourse at the Capital Centre. The crowds around Larry King and whatever guest we had were 10 deep. The lights were on, he'd be on a riser stage, and it made Larry feel that he was part of the Capitals experience."

King interviewed other Washington celebrities on the set, including politicians or members of the media. He also interviewed Capitals players on a split screen, with King at his set in the concourse and the player standing outside the Capitals' dressing room.

"Larry loved it," Brown said. "I felt like we had to do something to promote him (King wasn't getting paid much for the gig), and getting him out in the public at the arena was one way to do that. And he came back to me and said, 'I love this. This is fabulous.' It was Larry's idea to be part of the broadcast early on and my idea to put him up on the concourse."

King moved to Los Angeles in 1986 to begin a 25-year run as host of CNN's *Larry King Live*. But those who worked on the Capitals' HTS broadcasts at the time still have great memories of King's early involvement.

"It looked bigger," Brown said of the broadcast. "It looked like a big-time production. It was a happening thing in the Capital Centre to have Larry King there. We gave him the production and he took the product and ran with it."

48 Early Trips to Philadelphia

The distance between Washington and Philadelphia is short, but trips up I-95 in the 1970s were just long enough for the Capitals to feel uneasy. Players' stomachs churned and their minds wandered when the Flyers were on deck. The mood on the bus and in the dressing room was often somber.

"You'd lose the game before you even played," said former Capitals captain Ryan Walter. "The anxiety and the worry of what might happen doesn't allow you to play your best. It's future negative thinking. That's what playing in Philadelphia was all about."

The Capitals' struggles against Philadelphia their first few seasons were not unlike the challenges they faced when opposing the mighty Montreal Canadiens. Simply put, they couldn't win. In 53 combined meetings with the Flyers and Canadiens in the 1970s, the Capitals were 0–46–7.

Road games against the Canadiens at least provided Capitals players the chance to skate at the famous Montreal Forum. Games in Philadelphia didn't quite have the same appeal.

"I remember getting on the bus, and it was so quiet, it was like we were going to a funeral," said Ron Lalonde, a Capitals forward from 1974 through 1979. "The only sound you heard was the knees knocking because you knew what you were in store for, going to Philadelphia."

While the expansion Capitals were just getting their bearings in the NHL, the Flyers were beating up all comers both on the scoreboard and on the ice.

Thanks in part to their brute strength, the Broad Street Bullies won the Stanley Cup in consecutive seasons in 1974 and 1975. Along the way, the Spectrum emerged as one of the most intimidating buildings for any visiting club, let alone a team like the Capitals that won just 20 of their first 160 road games.

"In those days, they started with the early mind games," said Mike Marson, who played 193 games with the Capitals from 1974 through 1978. "You'd go into Philly and they had those strobe lights that go around and around. They were the first team, if I recall, in the National Hockey League to have that kind of pregame light-show setup. You really felt like you were being led into something that was going to be a big problem."

Marson recalls going to Philadelphia as a 19-year-old rookie and recognizing early on that the Capitals didn't have the muscle to stand up to a rough-and-tumble team like the Flyers.

Years later, general manager Milt Schmidt said that with the league trending toward more physical play in the 1970s, he made a point to draft big bodies. The problem, he later said, was that none of his picks liked to fight. When Max McNab replaced Schmidt as GM, he also tried to build a tougher team in Washington.

"That was one of the benchmarks of a player in those days— could you play in Philadelphia?" said Walter, the second overall pick in the 1978 draft.

"The idea of the Flyers having that huge domination over the Capitals was intimidating. There were a couple of bench-clearing brawls that just sort of fueled that fire of, 'Here we go again, we're back in Philadelphia.'"

"You paid the price in Philly," said defenseman Greg Theberge. "I used to take so many slashes and cross-checks and spear jabs from [Bobby] Clarke. You would change your hockey gloves from 12-inch cuffs to 16-inch cuffs for those games."

Not unlike when the Capitals faced the Canadiens in the early years and some veteran players would come up with mysterious ailments or last-minute injuries, the same held true for games in Philadelphia.

"I remember [head coach] Tommy McVie coming up to me the day before we were going to play in Philly," said Tom Rowe, a rookie in 1976–77. "I had just been called up maybe the week before and he said, 'Hey, you're going to play an awful lot tomorrow night in Philadelphia.' And I said, 'Oh, great! You're happy with the way I'm playing?' And he said, 'Hell no! We're going to Philadelphia and nobody else is going to want to play, so you'll get lots of ice time.'"

Even the Capitals goalies didn't care to play in Philadelphia.

"I remember one time," said goalie Bernie Wolfe, "Ronnie [Low] and I went into Philly one night, and they didn't tell us too far in advance who was going to start. So, we went up to [coach] McVie and we asked, 'Who's going to start?' And he looked at both of us and almost apologetically said, 'Ronnie, you'll go.' And I just said 'All right!' quietly pumping my fist. It was like, 'Thank god I don't have to go in tonight.'"

Ironically, it was a terrific goaltending performance that helped the Capitals finally secure their first win against the Flyers on December 21, 1980. After losing their first 12 games in Philadelphia and going winless in 25 games overall against the Flyers, the Capitals got an early Christmas gift with a 6–0 win.

Mike Palmateer was the star of the game with a 44-save shutout. The Flyers outshot the Capitals 21–10 in the first period, but a Dennis Maruk power play goal gave Washington an early 1–0 lead. Yvon Labre also scored for the Capitals and Jean Pronovost had two goals as the Capitals snapped Philadelphia's 16-game home unbeaten streak. The Flyers were also a league-best 23–6–5 entering the game.

"You've got to get psyched up against Philly, the best team in the league, or you can't beat them," Palmateer told the *Washington Post* after the win. "But you can't do it by yourself. The guys played a whale of a game out there."

There were also plenty of fisticuffs, but the Capitals were up to the challenge. The fighting began just 19 seconds into the game with a line brawl sending all five skaters from both teams to the penalty box. That set the tone in a game that would include 344 penalty minutes and 15 game misconducts.

Capitals rookie Archie Henderson—all 6'6", 220 pounds of him—made his NHL debut and had two first-period fights with Flyers tough guy Behn Wilson.

"Probably the best road win I can remember for the franchise while I was playing," Labre told the Capitals' website in 1999. "Archie took it on the chin for the team, but he was more than willing. That was a big highlight for me. After all of those years taking thumpings from the Broad Street Bullies, that we went into their building and thumped them."

49 Snowvechkin

On Super Bowl Sunday 2010, Bruce Boudreau opened the door of his northern Virginia home and walked out to his driveway. He thought he had stepped into a different universe.

"I felt like I was in a movie where there had been a nuclear war and there was nobody left on earth," Boudreau recalled in 2017.

"I walked out and all you could hear was your feet on the snow—every step. But that was it. And then trying to get someone to plow the driveway, it cost $200 to get the driveway plowed. I was still pretty cheap. It was only my [second] year outside the minors. Two hundred bucks—are you kidding?!"

The Washington metropolitan area was buried in more than 20 inches of snow from an early February blizzard that President

Barack Obama dubbed "Snowmaggedon." It remains the biggest snowstorm to hit the District since 1922. Streets were deserted, thousands were without power, and most weekend plans were put on hold.

The Capitals' Super Sunday matinee against the rival Pittsburgh Penguins was not. With the Capitals riding a franchise-record 13-game winning streak and Alex Ovechkin and Sidney Crosby set to meet on national television a week before the Olympics, both the NHL and NBC had plenty of incentive to see the game played as scheduled on Sunday, February 7, at 12:00 PM.

This was also Pittsburgh's first visit to Verizon Center since eliminating the Capitals in Game 7 of the 2009 Eastern Conference semifinals.

"My bet is that if the other team is here, we will be playing," Capitals owner Ted Leonsis wrote on his blog. "This is hockey weather. If we can play, we will."

While the Capitals had the Saturday off after a 5–2 win over the Atlanta Thrashers the night before, the Penguins fell to the Montreal Canadiens that afternoon at the Bell Centre. The Penguins were scheduled to fly into Washington that evening, but with all area airports closed, the team instead flew to Newark, New Jersey, before busing more than five hours to snow-covered D.C.

It was the type of travel usually seen in the minor leagues, complete with a post-midnight pit stop at a highway Burger King. The Penguins did not get in until after 2:00 AM. Less than 10 hours later, they'd face the league-leading Capitals at Verizon Center. One would think that would have been advantage Washington, but Boudreau saw things differently.

"I think it's totally the opposite," he said. "All they had to do was sit on a bus. We had to shovel out our houses. Half the city was without power. I know a lot of the guys had no power. You're digging out cars...and I think that's more taxing than just sitting down."

Despite the unorthodox travel, the Penguins jumped out to a 4–1 second-period lead. Sidney Crosby and Jordan Staal had two goals each for Pittsburgh, while Alex Ovechkin's 40th goal of the season accounted for all of Washington's early scoring.

The Capitals' 13-game winning streak began with a three-goal rally in Florida on January 13—an eventual 5–4 shootout win—and another three-goal comeback would make for a memorable Super Sunday in D.C.

Eric Fehr began the comeback with 2:48 remaining in the second period to pull the Capitals within two at 4–2. Ovechkin scored twice more in the third to tie the score 4–4 and earn his first hat trick of the season. Ovechkin would finish the game with three goals and an assist and a game-high six shots on goal in 25 minutes 36 seconds of ice time.

"You can tell when he's having one of his *days*," Boudreau said of Ovechkin. "Days when I see that his recovery rate is unbelievable. He sits on the bench for 30 seconds and I know he wants to go again."

Years later, Ovechkin's performance that day still resonates with Capitals fans, who refer to it as the "Snowvechkin" game.

"Ovi was crazy," Fehr said. "He was awesome. He took the team, put us on his back, and carried us. That's what we needed tonight. He was wonderful."

The game went to overtime, where Penguins defenseman Brooks Orpik was called for a two-minute minor for high-sticking Alexander Semin.

"He sells it all the time," Orpik said of Semin. "The kid's a baby. I've got zero respect for the kid. If it was a penalty, it was a penalty. I don't know. But the kid does that all game long. It's tough to lose on that."

On the ensuing Washington power play, an Ovechkin one-time attempt hit the goal post, but the puck ricocheted to veteran Mike Knuble, who was able to jam it past Marc-Andre Fleury from atop the crease for the overtime game winner. It was Knuble's 11th goal on what had now become a 14-game winning streak.

The goal also completed a Gordie Howe hat trick for Knuble, who fought Pittsburgh's Craig Adams in the first period after Adams hit Ovechkin along the boards. It was Knuble's fourth fight of his NHL career and his first in more than seven years.

It was all part of a memorable snowy afternoon in D.C., in which the Capitals rallied to beat Pittsburgh 5–4 in OT to extend their winning streak to 14 games—the third longest in NHL history.

The 2009–10 Capitals went on to win the Presidents' Trophy while setting franchise records with 54 wins (since broken) and 121 points. Few of the wins compared to the comeback triumph on Super Sunday against the defending Stanley Cup champion Penguins.

50 Ovechkin's 50-Goal Seasons

As the years pass and legends come and go, there are certain numbers in sports that continue to register with players and fans alike. In hockey, some of those numbers include 300 wins, 500 goals, or 1,000 games.

These benchmarks represent greatness and durability. They were relevant decades ago and in all likelihood, they will still hold great significance decades from now.

As far as single-season milestones, few hold as much weight in hockey circles as 50 goals.

Ninety players in NHL history have scored 50 goals in a season at least once, but only two have hit the mark more often than Alex

Ovechkin. Wayne Gretzky and Mike Bossy share the NHL record with nine 50-goal seasons each, while Ovechkin is the only other player to have reached the feat at least seven times.

Below is a look at each of the seven times Ovechkin hit the half-century mark:

April 13, 2006, at Atlanta Thrashers (Mike Dunham)

Having already been eliminated from playoff contention, the 2005–06 Capitals had little to play for down the stretch, other than job security and pride. For Ovechkin, the final few games of the year were an opportunity to lock up a few personal milestones and pad his resume for the Calder Trophy as Rookie of the Year.

On April 13, just one game after recording the 100th point of his rookie season, Ovechkin beat Atlanta Thrashers goalie Mike Dunham with a one-timer for the 50th goal of his freshman campaign.

"Alex Ovechkin—number 50!" Joe Beninati said on the call on Comcast Sportsnet. "The golden moment in a sparkling rookie year."

Ovechkin became the fourth rookie in NHL history with a 50-goal season, and he joined Teemu Selanne as the only first-year players to record both 50 goals and 100 points.

"I'm happy he got to 50," head coach Glen Hanlon told reporters after the eventual 5–3 defeat in Atlanta. "I would have hated to see him finish at 49 goals. It would have been sad because I know what it has meant to him."

Ovechkin would set Washington rookie records across the board, finishing with 52 goals and 106 points in 81 games. He later beat out Pittsburgh's Sidney Crosby and Calgary's Dion Phaneuf to become the first rookie in Capitals history to win the Calder Trophy.

March 3, 2008, vs. Boston Bruins (Tim Thomas)

Ovechkin recorded a first-period hat trick in an eventual 10–2 rout of the Boston Bruins as he joined Dennis Maruk and Peter Bondra as the only Capitals with multiple 50-goal seasons.

The first of Ovechkin's three goals against Boston came on a breakaway at 6:18 of the first and secured his second career 50-goal campaign. Rookie Nicklas Backstrom found Ovechkin with an outlet pass through the neutral zone before Ovechkin beat Thomas glove side.

"It just happens," Ovechkin told reporters after his fifth career hat trick. "You are going to score lots of games, and some games you aren't. Today, everything just went to the net."

Starting with the authoritative win against Boston, the Capitals finished the year on a 13–3–0 run, clinching a playoff berth on the final day of the regular season.

Ovechkin would finish with a franchise-record and league-high 65 goals on the season. He capped off his third season by winning the Hart Trophy as NHL MVP.

March 19, 2009, at Tampa Bay Lightning (Mike Mckenna)

Ovechkin's 50th goal during the 2008–09 season came in a 5–2 win over the Tampa Bay Lightning, but the milestone is best remembered for the elaborate celebration that followed.

Soon after Ovechkin beat Lightning goalie Mike McKenna with a wrist shot off the rush, he laid his stick down on the ice behind the Tampa Bay goal and acted as though the stick was on fire.

Ovechkin later explained that goalie Jose Theodore came up with the idea and that Backstrom and Mike Green were supposed to join him in hovering over the stick. In the end, neither Backstrom or Green participated in the celebration, leaving Ovechkin to stand over the stick by himself. Many Lightning players and hockey pundits around the world suggested that Ovechkin was showing up the opposition and disrespecting the game.

"They're not laughing with you," commentator Don Cherry said on *Hockey Night in Canada*. "They're laughing at you, Alex. You're a class guy. You can have class. You should be a role model. You don't need to do this. You are above stuff like that, you're the best hockey player playing today, so have a little class and do it right."

April 9, 2010, vs. Atlanta Thrashers (Ondrej Pavelec)

Ovechkin missed a career-high 10 games during the 2009–10 campaign, but still joined Gretzky and Bossy as the only players to record four 50-goal seasons in their first five years in the league.

Ovechkin recorded his 50th goal in the penultimate game of Washington's Presidents' Trophy–winning campaign, netting the eventual game-winning goal in a 5–2 win over the Thrashers.

The goal served as a double milestone, with Backstrom assisting on the play for his 100th point of the season.

"Before the game, we talked about it, we said, 'Hey, let's go. Today is going to be our night,'" Ovechkin told reporters after being named first star of the game.

The duo became the first set of Capitals teammates to record 50 goals and 100 points in the same season. After the game, much of the discussion surrounded who would lay claim to the keepsake puck.

"We're going to split it," Ovechkin said.

April 8, 2014, at St. Louis Blues (Ryan Miller)

Ovechkin was on pace for a 50-goal season in 2012–13, but a lockout-shortened 48-game schedule kept that from happening (Ovechkin led the league with 32 goals in 48 games).

A year later, though, with the benefit of the usual 82-game itinerary, Ovechkin returned to the 50-goal club when he opened the scoring on St. Louis Blues goalie Ryan Miller in an eventual 4–1 Capitals win at Scottrade Center.

"It means a lot," Ovechkin said after becoming the 11th player with at least five 50-goal seasons. "It's a big number and it's going to be in history for my whole life. I'm pretty sure my family happy, the guys happy for me, I appreciate all players who give me opportunities, and coaches, to be in right position and find the right spot."

Ovechkin finished with 51 goals and 79 points in 78 games in 2013–14, capturing his fourth Rocket Richard Trophy as the NHL's leading goal scorer.

March 31, 2015, vs. Carolina Hurricanes (Cam Ward)

Ovechkin's league-leading 50th goal of the 2014–15 season came in a 4–2 win over the Carolina Hurricanes at Verizon Center. It was also the 472nd goal of Ovechkin's NHL career, which tied him with Peter Bondra for the Capitals all-time goal-scoring record.

He also became just the sixth player in NHL history with as many as six 50-goal seasons, joining Hall of Fame members Gretzky, Bossy, Marcel Dionne, Guy LaFleur, and Mario Lemieux.

"That's a tribute to his talent and to his ability to play every game," Capitals coach Barry Trotz said. "It's a hard league to score goals in because the goaltenders are so good.... But that's part of being a great player in any sport—being able to produce all the time, no matter what's thrown at you."

Ovechkin, who matched Bondra's 472 career goals in 206 fewer games, would break the club's all-time goal-scoring record one game later in Montreal.

He finished the 2014–15 season tops in the NHL again, with 53 goals. Only two others player had as many as 40 (Steven Stamkos, 43; Rick Nash, 42).

April 9, 2016, at St. Louis Blues (Anders Nilsson)
Ovechkin hit the 50-goal plateau for the seventh time in his career during the 2015–16 season, but not without a tremendous late-season surge.

With seven games remaining, Ovechkin was sitting at 43 goals, having scored just twice in the previous 12.

But Ovechkin got hot down the stretch, with four goals in the next five games, and entered the penultimate game of the season with a league-best 47 goals on the year.

With the Presidents' Trophy and home-ice advantage throughout the Stanley Cup Playoffs already clinched, there was also the possibility of Ovechkin sitting out the regular season finale—a makeup game from a previously postponed contest against the Anaheim Ducks.

In other words, the Capitals game in St. Louis may have been his final shot at 50 goals. He made it count, recording the 15th hat trick of his NHL career in a 5–1 win over the Blues.

It was another double-milestone night for the Capitals, as Braden Holtby earned his 48th win of the year, tying Martin Brodeur's single-season NHL record.

51 See the Hershey Bears

Few teams in professional sports boast the history of the American Hockey League's Hershey Bears. The Capitals' top minor league affiliate since 2005, the Bears celebrated their 80th anniversary during the 2017–18 season. They have won a league-high 11 Calder Cup championships and they remain the AHL's longest continuously operating team still playing in its original city.

Hershey has a rich hockey tradition, and seeing some future Capitals play at the Giant Center in central Pennsylvania should be on every fan's to-do list. Visiting the Hershey Park Arena, where the Bears played from 1938 through 2002 and still practice today, is also a worthwhile experience.

With most Bears home games taking place on weekends, the commute up to Hershey—about 130 miles north of Washington, D.C.—makes for an ideal day trip for local hockey fans.

Recent Capitals who played in Hershey before reaching the NHL include Karl Alzner, Jay Beagle, John Carlson, Braden Holtby, and Michal Neuvirth. All five were members of the 2009–10 Bears team that repeated as Calder Cup champions. Former Capitals head coach Bruce Boudreau also passed through Hershey, where he led the Bears to the 2006 Calder Cup title and another appearance in the finals in 2007. Tomas Fleischmann, Mike Green, Brooks Laich, and Jeff Schultz were among Boudreau's players both in Hershey and later in Washington.

It has been said before that Hershey is North America's best hockey market outside the NHL, thanks to a winning tradition, terrific facilities, and a rabid and knowledgeable fan base. Entering the 2017–18 season, the Bears had led the AHL in attendance in 11 consecutive seasons. Hershey has averaged about 9,000 fans per game for the last decade.

"It's like a mini-NHL," Boudreau told NHL.com in 2014. "The building they play in is state of the art. The dressing room is as good as most NHL rooms. You're coming into a town where it is really relevant to be a Hershey Bear. You have to understand that."

In addition to future NHL players and coaches passing through Hershey, a number of longtime NHL broadcasters also cut their teeth with the Bears. Mike "Doc" Emrick (NBC), Dan Kamal (Atlanta Thrashers), Dave Mishkin (Tampa Bay Lightning), and John Walton (Capitals) all served as Hershey Bears play-by-play voices before landing jobs in the NHL.

During the 2009–10 season, a package of 10 Hershey Bears games aired in Washington, D.C., on the Capitals' flagship radio station, WFED 1500AM. Multiple postseason games that spring were also carried on Comcast Sportsnet as the Bears repeated as AHL champions.

The relationship between the Capitals and Bears has strengthened over the last decade and after working primarily off of one-year deals, the clubs signed a four-year affiliation extension prior to the 2016–17 campaign.

"The success of our organization over the last decade speaks volumes about the strength of our relationship with Hershey," Capitals general manager Brian MacLellan said in 2016. "Our affiliation makes sense both geographically and on the ice, and we look forward to continuing to work with the Bears to develop our prospects into quality NHL players."

52 Game Over Green

Bruce Boudreau looked like a genius. He had Mike Green to thank.

Ahead of his first game as an NHL head coach in November 2007, Boudreau made one change to the Capitals' struggling power play.

"I had Green take [Alex Ovechkin's] spot up top and I moved Ovi to the slot," Boudreau recalled in 2017. "I said, 'Watch, they're all going to overplay Ovi and Green will be open.'"

Less than five minutes into the game, Green scored on Washington's first power play of the afternoon.

"I remember looking down the bench saying, 'See, I told you!' And that probably got them thinking, 'Hey, maybe this guy from the minors isn't a complete idiot.'"

The Capitals beat the Flyers 4–3 in overtime with Nicklas Backstrom scoring the game-winning goal on his 20th birthday. It was a sign of things to come. The Capitals went 37–17–7 after Boudreau took over on Thanksgiving and clinched a playoff berth on the last day of the season.

That first game was an early example of the trust Boudreau had in Green. The two had worked together with the American Hockey League's Hershey Bears, where they won the 2006 Calder Cup. When Boudreau arrived in Washington, Green's career took off.

"Bruce just let him go," said general manager George McPhee. "He just let him play. The game was really wide open after the lockout and players like Mike that could skate and generate offense could really showcase all of their abilities. Bruce brought it out in him."

In 113 games under coach Glen Hanlon, Green had six goals and 22 points. But in 261 games under Boudreau, he had 76 goals and 228 points.

As the Capitals rose from irrelevance to must-watch, Green was as much a part of the ride as Ovechkin, Backstrom, and Boudreau.

"He was the key to that quick-transition offense," said Capitals beat reporter Tarik El Bashir of CSN Mid-Atlantic. "All those huge numbers that the Caps put up under Bruce Boudreau, it started with Mike Green turning that puck up ice. He was a one-man breakout."

"He could make something out of nothing," said longtime teammate Brooks Laich. "He could pull pucks off the wall, invade a forechecker, and skate the puck up and push our team north."

The Capitals were the NHL's highest-scoring team during Boudreau's four-year tenure with Green emerging as the game's top-scoring defenseman over that span.

"Bruce knew what he could do," McPhee said. "He knew that the more you played Mike, the better he played. In a lot of ways, he was better with 28 or 29 minutes of ice time than he was with 20 or 21. He never pulled back on the reins with Mike. He just let him go."

Green finished second among defensemen with 18 goals and 56 points in 2007–08, but his 2008-09 season ranks among the best by a blue-liner in the last 30 years.

Despite injuries limiting Green to just 68 games, he finished with 31 goals and 73 points. He remains one of eight defensemen in league history with a 30-goal campaign and the only one since Capitals alum Kevin Hatcher scored 34 times in 1992–93.

Along the way, Green set an NHL record, becoming the first defenseman to score a goal in eight consecutive games. Green reached the milestone on February 14, 2009, in a 5–1 win in Tampa Bay.

"It was just magic," Laich said of Green's eight-game streak. "You knew he was going to score. He was going to pull the puck and drag it and he was going to release one and it was going to find its way through traffic and he was going to fist pump. When he got the eighth one, the whole team went over the boards and he was mobbed. His dad was there to see it. It was one of the special moments."

The record-setting game coincided with the Capitals' annual fathers and mentors trip, so Mike's father, Dave Green, saw the milestone in person from a suite with some of the other players' dads.

Boudreau received permission from the NHL for the entire team to leave the bench and join Green to celebrate the feat on the ice.

"It was pretty cool," Green said. "I thought it was just the next line that was coming out."

During the Capitals' Presidents' Trophy–winning 2009–10 season, Green had 19 goals and 76 points in 75 games. He became the first defenseman to average more than a point per game in consecutive seasons since Hall of Famers Al MacInnis and Ray Bourque in 1993 and 1994.

Green had established himself as an elite NHL defenseman, but the opinion wasn't universally shared. When Hockey Canada revealed its roster for the 2010 Winter Olympics from Vancouver, Green was not included among the seven defensemen named to the team. It was a difficult blow for Green, and for members of the Capitals organization who felt disrespected.

"It not only hurt him that he wasn't selected for his country," said El Bashir, "but it made him angry. It took a little while for him to get over it. I don't know if he ever did. His teammates were restrained in their comments, but behind closed doors, they were fuming."

"He had to settle me down," Boudreau said. "He seemed like the parent in this one. I was bummed out."

The Olympic team omission was the first in a string of events that took some of the shine off of Green's impressive run. Although he was a First-Team All-Star in 2009 and 2010, Green finished second in voting for the Norris Trophy both seasons.

Over the next two years, Green was slowed by injuries. He played just 49 games in 2010–11 and 32 games in 2011–12. The blue-liner who once scored 10 times in an eight-game scoring streak, had just seven goals across two seasons.

"They affected his performance, there's no doubt about that," McPhee said of the injuries. "I don't know how you control those things. You train hard, you prepare hard, and you hope you stay healthy."

"It's too bad, really," said Backstrom, Green's teammate for eight seasons. "When he was on, he was so mobile, all over the ice. It was amazing to see. I've never really played with anything like that. He was up in the rush, he was the first guy back. Great skater. That's how I choose to remember his time here."

Others will remember Green for his uncanny knack for scoring in overtime. His eight overtime winners in Washington earned him the nickname "Game Over Green." They are the most by a defenseman with one franchise.

The end of Green's run with the Capitals seemed inevitable when the Capitals invested more than $67 million in defensemen Matt Niskanen and Brooks Orpik on July 1, 2014. Exactly one year later, Green signed a three-year deal with Detroit.

In 575 career games with the Capitals, Green had 113 goals and 360 points.

"They're all great memories," Green said of his time in Washington. "I spent 10 years here and created a lot of friends and memories with those friends, especially a lot of the guys in the dressing room. I'll never forget that."

53 Bedeviled: Caps Let One Slip Away in '88

The demons had been exorcised, the 1988 Capitals were told. After years of blown leads and playoff disappointments, it was finally shaping up to be their year. As they prepared to skate in the Patrick Division Final for the third time in five years, the Capitals were a confident bunch.

Not only had they just completed their own comeback—rallying from a three-games-to-one deficit to eliminate the Philadelphia Flyers in their first-round series—but the Capitals did so in dramatic fashion, with Dale Hunter scoring an overtime game-winning goal in Game 7 on home ice.

For once, it seemed, everything was falling into place for the usually snakebit Capitals. While Hunter's overtime winner sent the Flyers into the off-season, the other Patrick Division Semifinal series saw the New Jersey Devils upset the regular season division champion New York Islanders.

Arguably the Capitals' biggest hurdle for a deep playoff run was out of the way.

The Capitals had faced the Islanders in each of their five previous trips to the Stanley Cup Playoffs, with New York eliminating Washington in four of those series.

But with the Islanders falling in the first round in 1988, the only thing standing in Washington's way from a maiden trip to the Wales Conference Final was a series with the surprising Devils, who the Capitals beat regularly since the franchise settled in New Jersey for the 1982–83 season.

"We didn't have to deal with the Islanders, we got by the Flyers, and we had owned Jersey for the five or six years we had played them," former Capitals forward Lou Franceschetti said in 2016. "They couldn't beat us at home. It was right there for us."

Dating back to the Devils' first year in the Meadowlands, the Capitals were 32–6–4 against their newest divisional rival, including 19–1–1 at the Capital Centre.

Beating up on the Devils was a widely shared experience league-wide, as New Jersey finished with one of the NHL's bottom-three records in five straight seasons from 1982–83 through 1986–87.

Finally, in their sixth season in New Jersey, the Devils clinched their first playoff berth thanks to a season-ending five-game winning streak. Even that was by the slimmest of margins, with John MacLean needing to score in overtime in New Jersey's final game of the season—a 4–3 OT win in Chicago—just to secure fourth place in the Patrick Division.

The Devils rode their late-season momentum into a first-round defeat of the Islanders in six games.

One round later, the Devils handed the Capitals one of the most disappointing playoff defeats in franchise history, eliminating the Capitals in seven games in the Patrick Division Final.

"They were a better team than we thought they were and I think maybe we didn't give them enough respect at first," said Mike Gartner. "Then we found ourselves just trying to catch up and trying to claw our way back in the series."

The Capitals won Game 1 at the Capital Centre 3–1, but the victory came with a tremendous price, as Rod Langway suffered a severe cut to the back of his left leg. Langway was cut by the skate blade of New Jersey forward Pat Verbeek.

The three-inch cut to an area of muscle and tendon just above the ankle sidelined Langway for the rest of the series and left the

Mike Gartner and the Capitals appeared to have a clear path to the 1988 Wales Conference Final, only to be upset by the surprising New Jersey Devils in seven games in their second-round series.

Capitals without their captain, their No. 1 defenseman, and the only player on the roster with a Stanley Cup ring.

"That was a team that I really thought could win the Stanley Cup," Langway said of the 1987–88 Capitals. "When I got my Achilles cut, I still thought we were going to win that series. We had a better team than they did."

The Devils evened the series with a 5–2 win in Game 2 with Aaron Broten recording a hat trick and Verbeek netting the eventual game-winning goal.

The Capitals argued that Verbeek should have been suspended for Game 2, given the severity of Langway's injury. Adding insult to injury, Capitals goaltender Pete Peeters insisted that Verbeek's game winner had been kicked in.

"Verbeek cuts Langway's tendon in Game 1," recalled Franceschetti, "then Game 2 they beat us and when you give a team like that any positive—because they didn't have history of beating us in our building—it gave them a little jump and a little bit of excitement. They got rid of that fear knowing that they could come into our building and beat us.

"When you give a team hope like that, they think they can walk through a wall and that's exactly what they did."

The series shifted to New Jersey for Game 3, where the Devils took command with an authoritative 10–4 win. Patrik Sundstrom set a Stanley Cup Playoff record with an eight-point game, including a hat trick (with his brother Peter suiting up for Washington that night), as the previously favored Capitals started to unravel.

The Capitals set a franchise record that still stands today with 123 penalty minutes, 32 of which belonged to Hunter.

Hunter was ejected in the third period after he protested a slashing penalty. On his way to the dressing room, he gave referee Denis Morel a choke sign, for which he received a gross misconduct in addition to a game misconduct. Capitals defenseman Greg Smith had already been ejected in the second.

Head coach Bryan Murray told reporters after the game that it was "absolutely embarrassing the way we played."

The Capitals bounced back with a 4–1 win in Game 4, but the injury bug struck again as Peeters and defenseman Garry Galley were both knocked out of the game with concussions. Peeters had to be taken off on a stretcher after he was knocked unconscious by a MacLean shot that hit his goalie mask.

Neither Peeters or Galley played in Game 5 in Landover, which the Devils won 3–1 to take a three-games-to-two series lead. Both returned, though, for Game 6, as the Capitals avoided elimination with a 7–2 win in East Rutherford.

Just as they had done in their first-round series against Philadelphia, the Capitals won Game 6 on the road by a 7–2 score to force a decisive seventh game on home ice.

With the win, the Capitals improved to 4–0 when facing elimination in the 1988 postseason after going 0–5 with their season at stake in the previous five years combined.

But there was still one more game to be played with a second Game 7 on home ice in two weeks. Dating back to the previous spring when the Islanders beat the Capitals in quadruple overtime in Game 7, this was Washington's third winner-take-all game at the Capital Centre in as many series.

"I think the seventh-game pressure has helped us already," Murray told the *Washington Post* before Game 7 against the Devils. "Last year's seventh game took a little out of us at the start of this season, but in the Flyers series, the guys looked back and there was good carryover value."

Against New Jersey though, the Capitals came up short. Devils captain Kirk Muller scored on the opening shift, 14 seconds in, to give New Jersey the early 1–0 lead. New Jersey led 2–0 in the second period before Washington defensemen Grant Ledyard and Galley pulled the Capitals even.

But MacLean would score the controversial winning goal with 6:11 left in regulation on a play the Capitals argued should have been called offside.

The Capitals tried in vain to tie the game in the final minutes—Dave Christian coming closest with a chance that was turned aside in close by Sean Burke.

The Devils were able to hang on for the 3–2 win in their first Game 7 experience. Sam Rosen had the call on ESPN:

> "New Jersey wins! The New Jersey Devils win! And Cinderella dances on to the Wales Conference Final. The unbelievable story of the New Jersey Devils continues. The team that made the playoffs on the last day of the regular season, in overtime, has won the Patrick Division playoff championship by defeating the Washington Capitals four games to three. What a story. Wow!

With Langway sidelined for the Capitals, Gartner wore the captain's "C" on his sweater and led his teammates through the postgame handshake line with the Devils.

"If the Game 7 against the Islanders [in 1987] was the toughest game, this was the toughest series to lose, for sure," said Gartner, who was held to three goals in 14 games that postseason.

"This was the toughest series, because we felt that we should have won. But they had played so well the last part of that season, and they just got into the playoffs and they just carried it right through."

Franceschetti missed Game 7 with a hip injury, and still thinks back to the missed opportunity.

"It was the most heartbreaking series that I've ever been involved in as a professional," Franceschetti said. "We knew that with Rod 100 percent, there's no way they would have touched us. We could have walked through them in four or five games."

"No sweat," Langway said. "I was probably in the best shape of my career at the time and I felt good playing. The games were easy."

Langway watched Game 7 from the bowels of the Capital Centre, riding a stationary bike in hopes of pumping some life into his legs after his Game 1 injury. It was, he said in 2017, the toughest injury of his career.

"My play went down after that," he said. "My conditioning and my speed were never the same because of my Achilles. It probably took two years away from my career."

And perhaps the Capitals' best chance to reach a conference final in the 1980s.

54 Halak, Canadiens Upset 2010 Capitals

Although Jaroslav Halak appeared in 12 games with Washington during the 2013–14 season, he is best remembered for what he did *to* the Capitals, rather than anything he did *for* them.

Nearly four years before the Capitals acquired Halak at the 2014 trade deadline, the former Montreal Canadiens goaltender was among the biggest factors in one of the greatest upsets in Stanley Cup Playoff history.

Halak stopped 131 of 134 shots in Games 5 through 7 as Montreal rallied from a 3–1 series deficit and beat the Presidents' Trophy–winning Capitals in seven games in a first-round matchup in 2010.

The Capitals became the ninth No. 1 seed to fall to a No. 8 seed, but the first to blow a three-games-to-one series lead along the way.

"Still to this day, one of the most frustrating defeats of my career because that group had special abilities," said Brooks Laich, one of seven 20-goal scorers on that team. "But it also is a fabulous lesson in this game that raw abilities don't just win. That iron will, desire, inches, determination, playing the right way, all those things matter—maybe more than raw ability—to try to win the ultimate goal."

It was an agonizing defeat for Washington following the best regular season in team history, complete with a 54–15–13 record and a franchise-best 121 points. The Capitals finished 33 points clear of the Canadiens, who hadn't clinched a playoff berth until their final game of the season.

"That playoff loss was the most disturbing," general manager George McPhee said in 2017. "We got up 3–1 in the series, everything was going well, we were healthy, and I remember leaving the Montreal rink that night up 3–1 and thinking, 'Okay, we've got three chances to win this series and we should be able to do this.'"

After an early-series wake-up call in the form of a 3–2 overtime defeat in Game 1, the Capitals came back from 4–1 down and earned a 6–5 overtime win in Game 2. Washington then took Games 3 and 4 at Bell Centre in Montreal by scores of 5–1 and 6–3.

Travel issues on the flight back to Washington, though, made for an unforeseen long night for the Capitals. With fog settling into D.C., the Capitals' charter flight was unable to land at Dulles Airport as scheduled. Reagan National Airport was also off limits, which meant that in the middle of the night, the plane was diverted to Baltimore.

"We were really fortunate to land in Baltimore," McPhee said, "but because we were unexpected, there was nobody from immigration to meet us, and so we sat on the tarmac in those people movers until 5:30 in the morning. And then we still had to go through customs and immigration and then we had to pick up our cars back at Dulles Airport and then get home."

The decision was eventually made to cancel that day's scheduled practice. There were no meetings or video sessions, either, as the team was told to rest and recuperate and be ready for Game 5.

"I remember walking in the door at 8:30 in the morning, having missed a whole night's sleep along with everyone else in the organization," McPhee said. "And we couldn't have been any worse in the next game; in the first 10 or 15 minutes, we just weren't very good. And that gave them life. They got up off the mat and the whole series changed."

With a chance to clinch the series on home ice, the Capitals came out flat in Game 5, falling behind 2–0 before the game was even eight minutes old. Mike Cammalleri and Travis Moen scored for Montreal on two of the Canadiens' first five shots.

"We let it slip away," said head coach Bruce Boudreau. "We have Game 5 in our building and we played like crap for the first 10 minutes and then the game's over."

Halak made 37 saves as the Canadiens held on to beat Washington 2–1 in Game 5. The series returned to Montreal for Game 6, where Halak had a game for the ages with 53 saves in a 4–1 win. With the Canadiens celebrating their centennial season, Halak set a team record for most saves in a regulation playoff game.

The winner-take-all series finale was more of the same in Washington, where the Canadiens eliminated the Capitals with another 2–1 win. The Capitals outshot the Canadiens 42–16, but again Washington couldn't beat Halak until the final moments of the third period (Laich scored with 2:16 remaining in regulation to pull the Capitals within one) and again their power play came up empty.

After leading the NHL with the No. 1 rated power play during the regular season (25.2 percent), the Capitals went 1-for-33 with the man advantage in their first-round series against Montreal.

The list of disappointments for the Capitals was lengthy.

Alexander Semin, who finished second on the team with 40 goals during the regular season, was held to just two assists against Montreal. Tomas Fleischmann, who had 23 goals during the regular season, had one assist in six games against Montreal before sitting as a healthy scratch for Game 7.

And Norris Trophy nominee Mike Green, who had 19 goals and 76 points during the regular season, was held to three assists against the Canadiens and had a miserable Game 7.

Green took an offensive-zone cross-checking penalty late in the first period before Montreal's Marc-Andre Bergeron opened the scoring on the ensuing power play. Then in the third, Green was beaten badly in the defensive zone seconds before Dominic Moore scored the eventual game-winning goal.

Alex Ovechkin led the Capitals with five goals and 10 points in seven games, but the Canadiens held him off the score sheet in Games 6 and 7. Led primarily by defensemen Josh Gorges and Jaroslav Spacek, the Canadiens believed they had Ovechkin figured out and that they could limit Washington's No. 1 weapon.

"Generally, you know what's coming," Gorges told reporters after Game 7. "When he comes in on the off-wing, he'll try to step to the middle and shoot through you. You can bait him into that."

Years later, McPhee and other members of the Capitals organization would agree that part of Ovechkin's game had become "predictable" and "stale." The first-round series against Montreal was an eye opener.

As the final seconds ticked down on Washington's 2009–10 campaign and the horn sounded at a stunned Verizon Center, Boudreau remained behind the bench, dumbfounded, staring blankly out at the ice.

"I thought we had a good chance to win the Stanley Cup," Boudreau said. "I would have bet my house that they wouldn't have beaten us three in a row and that we wouldn't have scored only three goals [in the last three games]."

Following the traditional postseries handshake line, Ovechkin and a handful of his teammates gave a half-hearted stick salute to the fans who had stuck around. Veteran Scott Walker, a healthy scratch in the first six games of the series but who played Game 7, saluted the crowd in what turned out to the final game of his NHL career.

Rookie defenseman Karl Alzner also saluted the crowd following his Stanley Cup Playoff debut. Alzner was recalled from AHL Hershey after veteran Tom Poti suffered an eye injury in Game 6.

"That team was expected to go very deep, they had so many good things going on and then all of a sudden I got thrown in there in an extremely important game, where things didn't go as anybody expected," Alzner recalled in 2017.

"You could tell how invested everyone was after the game, because it was such a shock and some seriously deflated spirits. When I look back at my career, it will be one of those 'what if' moments where, if that game went differently, then maybe that team goes a lot further, maybe they go to the end. Those are the things, if you don't end up winning, you look back on years later."

Today, members of the 2009–10 Capitals can point to that team and admit that despite a dominant regular season, the club was hardly flawless. Their run-and-gun style of play was only going to take them so far.

"We weren't always playing the right way," Nicklas Backstrom said in 2016. "In the playoffs, you have to find ways to win if you're not scoring a lot. We had to figure that out."

The Capitals were also a relatively inexperienced bunch, led by a core in their early 20s and a head coach working his first NHL job. According to Laich, given that the Capitals had built such an insurmountable lead atop the standings during the regular season, bad habits crept into their game late in the year that proved hard to kick come the playoffs.

"I didn't think our individual approach to practice was strong enough," Laich said. "We had so much success that I don't want to say there was complacency, but the work ethic kind of faded. The teams that we beat went home and practiced hard. So they're doing that, and if you want to stay on top and be on top, you have to come to the rink and practice regardless of whether you have success. If you fail, you'll be driven to come in and practice hard, but if you have the success you still need to work at it. I'm not sure that we always did."

Mike Marson's On- and Off-Ice Battles

It was a typical Career Day for the Grade 6 class at Buchanan Public School in Scarborough, Ontario, complete with the usual allotment of firefighters, policemen, nurses, and other accomplished professionals on hand to chat with students.

Mike Marson, who played for the Washington Capitals during their 1974–75 expansion season, still remembers sitting in the classroom that day in 1967 along with his childhood friend and future New York Rangers forward Wayne Dillon.

"They were trying to get us to think about more than being in Grade 6," Marson recalled in 2016.

"So Wayne was asked what he would someday like to do for a living, and he said he wanted to be a National Hockey League player. 'That's great, good for you,' he was told. Then I was asked the same question, and I gave the same answer. The [staff] just looked at each other and shook their heads as if to say, 'Kid, you have no idea the mountain that you think you're going to climb.'"

The doubters were always going to be there because of Marson's skin color. He was a black kid looking to make it big in a historically white sport.

Although Willie O'Ree had broken the NHL's color barrier with the Boston Bruins on January 18, 1958, his 45-game tenure ended after the 1960–61 season. By the time Marson was dreaming of his own NHL career in his Grade 6 classroom, no other black player had earned an NHL paycheck.

But as racial tensions increased in the United States and the race riots of the late 1960s dominated the news cycle, Marson was enamored by a different tone that was slowly building momentum in Canada. Sixteen days after Martin Luther King Jr. was assassinated in Memphis, Tennessee, on April 4, 1968, Pierre Elliott Trudeau was elected as Canada's 15th prime minister.

"We had the original 'Trudeau-mania' going on, and its message was that you could do anything you want regardless of your race, creed, or color as long as you applied yourself to it," Marson said.

The eldest of five children, Marson left home when he was 17 to play with the Ontario Hockey Association's Sudbury Wolves. In his mind, if he showed himself well in Ontario's top junior league, an NHL career would follow, regardless of his skin color. The politically active Marson believed in what Prime Minister Trudeau was selling.

"The whole thing in Trudeau's perspective was, 'Why shouldn't you be allowed?'" Marson explained. "You're black? Well, why shouldn't you be able to play in the National Hockey League and play at Maple Leaf Gardens? Why not?"

In his second season in Sudbury, Marson was the Wolves' leading scorer with 35 goals, 94 points, and 146 penalty minutes in 69 games. The 1973–74 season would be his last in the OHA.

On May 31, 1974, the Capitals began assembling their maiden roster at the NHL Amateur Draft and selected Marson with the first pick in the second round (19th overall).

Defenseman Greg Joly was taken first overall by the Capitals and Joly and Marson had plenty of expectations thrust upon them as the first two players selected in franchise history.

The expectations only grew when the Capitals signed Marson to a five-year, $500,000 contract, primarily to keep him from signing with the rival World Hockey Association.

Marson recorded a hat trick in his first preseason game, then made the team out of training camp and skated in the club's first regular season game on October 9, 1974, in New York. Marson became the second black player in NHL history and the first since O'Ree nearly 14 years earlier.

Playing for a struggling expansion team would have been difficult enough for Marson under normal conditions, but doing so as a well-compensated visible minority made for challenges he wasn't prepared for.

"It wasn't just that I was a 19-year-old kid playing professional hockey," Marson said. "I was the only kid in the world who was black and playing at that time. And with all of the different social ramifications and setups that were going on at that time in America, it was completely unheard of."

Without the benefit of any minor league seasoning, Marson played in 76 games during the Capitals' inaugural season—second on the team behind only Bill Lesuk, who played in 79.

Marson finished with 16 goals and 28 points as a rookie and entered the NHL as advertised—as one of the game's best skating prospects. The problem, Marson quickly found out, was that he couldn't escape the social realities of his situation quite as easily as he could elude a cross-check.

"It was a daily issue of things that were almost mind-blowing," he said. "There were times when I was refused lodging in hotels and the team would have to stick up for me. Or entering an arena like, say, Madison Square Garden, and being questioned by security staff because there were no black hockey players. So, to their credit, they were asking the right questions, only to find out that, yes, I was playing for Washington. For me, this was a daily thing. You'd go to preboard an airplane and you're questioned—'Well sir, I'm sorry, this is just for the hockey players.' I dealt with this kind of business all the time."

Perhaps most alarming were the death threats Marson received in the mail and over the phone both at the Capital Centre and at his suburban home in Silver Spring, Maryland. There was also a death threat called in one night at the Spectrum in Philadelphia.

"These are things that are not in the manual of a professional hockey player," he said.

According to Marson, the battles he dealt with off the ice carried over into the hockey arena as well.

"We're right in the pressure cooker of it, visiting cities like Chicago, Detroit, or Atlanta back then," Marson said.

"People still had an emotional attachment to the negative things that had transpired in America at that time in the big cities. So now you're a young black hockey player coming into this arrangement and you're going into arenas where the people are looking to see who is going to get you. It's a novel thing and hockey is a contact sport. They hear, 'Oh, the kid can throw them pretty good, let's see who's going to handle him.' So, it was just a nonstop thing."

According to some of his teammates, Marson was set up to fail. He was a teenage prospect on a lousy expansion team with little guidance and few mentors. The slurs and taunts were audible every game, not only from the stands, but on the ice too, where opponents regularly took extra liberties with slashes and high sticks.

"It was overt on the ice, and he played an aggressive style," said Ron Lalonde, teammates with Marson for parts of four seasons.

"He played like he had a chip on his shoulder. That's how he played junior—rough and tough. But guys in the NHL started to challenge him and you'd hear things that would get anybody upset and riled. Unfortunately, he had to spend too much time fighting and trying to defend himself rather than working on his game. He had the physical skills, but he needed some coaching and some patience and fitting in."

Yvon Labre led the Capitals with 182 penalty minutes during the 1974–75 season, but the expansion club, which lacked in many areas, didn't have a true enforcer or tough guy. On most nights, the 19-year-old Marson was left to fend for himself.

"You'd hear things from some of the tougher players in the league because they knew they could get him off of his game pretty quick," Lalonde said.

"There were racial slurs that were fired and he'd be quick [to react]. He had a short fuse. The next thing you knew, he'd be involved in something. It was hard for him to work on his game. And he could skate. He was one of the best skaters in the league, but he spent so much energy having to defend himself."

Decades later, Marson said he would have appreciated more support from his teammates, many of whom he admits were from rural settings and had had little contact with people of color until meeting him.

Off the ice, Marson battled weight issues and alcoholism during his playing career. In 1976, Marson nearly missed the Capitals' postseason trip to Japan because head coach Tom McVie said he wasn't in good enough shape.

"Me, Tommy, and the weight scale became good friends," Marson said of his regular trips to the trainer's room.

Marson's playing career fizzled, with his trying rookie season arguably serving as the peak. He spent four more seasons in the Capitals organization, all of which were split between the NHL and the minors.

"I enjoyed Mike," said former Capitals goaltender Bernie Wolfe. "He could skate probably better than anybody on our team. That guy could move and he was big. But Mike had difficulty, there's no doubt. He was making a lot of money, and there was big-time pressure.

"Mike could fight, though, so he wasn't going to put up with much shit [on the ice]. But I think the things that bothered Mike more were in his personal life. We were in Toronto one night, *Hockey Night in Canada,* and Coach comes in and says, 'Mike, I've got to talk to you.' And he tells him that an hour earlier, his brother had died suddenly. Mike had a lot of the personal things that he had to live with."

Marson's career lasted six seasons, five of which were spent shuffling between the NHL and AHL. After 193 games with the Capitals and three more with the Los Angeles Kings, Marson finished his NHL career with 24 goals, 48 points, and 233 penalty minutes. He retired at the age of 25, and returned to the greater Toronto area, where he worked as a martial arts instructor and a bus driver.

Despite the challenges, he looks back fondly on his playing days.

"You do your best," he said. "I was certainly up against many different challenges that there was no schooling for, there was no education that you can get or read up on. You had to be in tune with arrangements and situations. And at 18, just turning 19, I haven't met very many people that were playing in the National Hockey League at that level at that age and had a different ethnicity that was a visible minority. So I did my best."

As for that unspoken mountain from Career Day that Marson would have to climb to realize his dream:

"I did climb it," he said decades later. "And I put a flag on the top of it, too."

56 After Olie: The Kid Goalies

While longtime Capitals Peter Bondra and Sergei Gonchar were both traded during the 2003–04 season, Olie Kolzig was among the few veterans to survive Washington's prelockout fire sale. When the dust settled and the Capitals returned from the work stoppage in September 2005, Kolzig did so as the elder statesman on the rebuilding club.

Kolzig turned 36 late in the 2005–06 season and often paid the price for having a young team in front of him. The Capitals allowed a league-worst 35.7 shots per game that year and finished 29th in the 30-team NHL with a 3.66 goals-against average.

Kolzig split time with backup Brent Johnson, who was 29 by season's end. Down a level, the Capitals' top minor league affiliate—the American Hockey League's Hershey Bears—won the Calder Cup championship with journeyman goaltenders Frederic Cassivi, 31, and Kirk Daubenspek, 32.

In other words, as the Capitals began to rebuild with young players like Alex Ovechkin, Brooks Laich, Tomas Fleishmann, and Mike Green, the cupboard was void of any goaltending prospects.

That changed at the 2006 draft in Vancouver, where the Capitals owned a league-high four selections among the first 35 picks. The Capitals chose center Nicklas Backstrom with their first pick—No. 4 overall—securing a player who would emerge as one of the best in franchise history.

With their next two selections—Nos. 23 and 34 overall—the Capitals addressed their glaring need for young goaltenders by selecting Semyon Varlamov from Russia and Michal Neuvirth of the Czech Republic. The No. 23 pick originally belonged to the Nashville Predators, but the Capitals had acquired the pick as part of a trade deadline deal for veteran defenseman Brendan Witt months earlier.

The drafting of Varlamov marked the first time the Capitals took a goaltender in Round 1 since they picked Kolzig in the first round—No. 19 overall—in 1989. By selecting Neuvirth with the No. 34 pick, the Capitals landed two of the first five goaltenders taken in the 2006 draft class.

Two years later, Kolzig played his final game in a Capitals uniform. Three months after that, the Capitals selected another goalie, Braden Holtby, in the fourth round of the 2008 draft.

Add it up and the Capitals had three goaltending prospects in the system, with the expectation that one would ultimately emerge as a franchise goaltender like Kolzig.

Because Varlamov and Neuvirth were two draft classes ahead of Holtby, the thought was that they had the inside track on the goaltending competition. Based on age and development, they would get the first opportunities, but this would ultimately become a three-horse race.

"I wasn't a high pick, so I wasn't expecting anything to be handed to me at the start," Holtby said. "I knew I'd have to work to get there. With the other two in front of me, they were young too, they were trying to establish themselves and as a goalie, you just want to go to a place where there isn't a franchise guy who's been there forever where you're basically working to get traded. That's not the ideal situation, so I saw it as a perfect opportunity to hopefully get a shot."

Varlamov was the first of the three to get consistent work in the NHL, as he replaced veteran Jose Theodore as Washington's starting goalie during both the 2009 and 2010 Stanley Cup Playoffs. At the same time, Neuvirth led AHL Hershey to consecutive Calder Cup championships.

By the start of the 2010–11 season, the Capitals were all-in on the kids, handing the keys to a pair of a 22-year-olds in Varlamov and Neuvirth, with a 21-year-old Holtby lurking in Hershey.

Varlamov was viewed as the most athletic of the bunch, while Neuvirth was thought to be positionally sound and the most economical with his movement. Both struggled with injuries, though, and that opened the door for Holtby.

"He was the third-string guy," recalled forward Brooks Laich, "and I remember looking at Holts and how he worked and I remember thinking, 'He's going to turn this table. Somehow, give this kid a couple of years and he's going to turn this table upside down.'"

According to his teammates at the time, Holtby was the hardest working of the three, perhaps the product of his blue-collar upbringing on a farm in Saskatchewan.

"I saw how hard he worked from day one in development camp, in training camps, and in Hershey," said defenseman John Carlson. "You could tell that he was destined for success because of his work ethic and athletic ability and skill. I think that set him apart from every other guy. That's not to say that Varly or Neuvy aren't very successful—they're both great goalies—but Holtby certainly emerged as the crown jewel of the three."

Neuvirth was Washington's starter in 2010–11, compiling a 27–12–4 record with four shutouts for the regular season Eastern Conference champions. It remains the best season of his career. Injuries limited Varlamov to just 27 games (11–9–5) in what turned out to be his final season in a Washington uniform.

Holtby impressed in spot duty, going 10–2–2 with a 1.79 goals-against average and .934 save percentage. Midway through the season, Holtby made 35 saves in a 4–1 win in Toronto on *Hockey Night in Canada* and, although it was his seventh career appearance, he'd say years later that it was the first time he really felt like he belonged in the NHL. His teammates saw the same.

"I remember talking to [Mike Green] being like, 'Who is this kid? How is this guy in the minors?'" said defenseman Scott Hannan, who was acquired in a trade a month earlier.

"I mean, they had Varly and Neuvy so it was just a contract thing. But I remember playing in Toronto and he had an outstanding game, standing on his head and it was like, 'Who is this guy?' And they were all saying, 'Yeah, this guy is going to be good.' So now when you look back, yeah, we saw a glimpse of it."

"Out of respect to Varly," said Matt Hendricks, "he had a tough bout of injuries there and those are hard to control. Neuvy, same kind of thing, he battled some injuries and we just needed a guy like Holts to come in and say, 'All right, this is my job, I'm going to hold on to it, I'm going to take it and nobody is going to take it from me.' From day one, I felt like Holts was going to take the job and it was going to be his."

Soon after the 2010–11 season, Varlamov was traded to the Colorado Avalanche. In 2014, Neuvirth was dealt to the Buffalo Sabres. Both have had productive careers—Varlamov was runner-up for the Vezina Trophy after the 2013–14 season—but injuries have been a common theme for both.

Holtby, as some teammates predicted, eventually moved atop the Capitals' goaltending hierarchy, earning the Vezina Trophy in 2016 and matching the NHL record for most wins in a season that same year.

57 Attend Capitals Prospect Development Camp

Fans looking for their hockey fix to help break up the summer months can get an early look at future Capitals players during the club's annual Prospect Development Camp.

Typically held during the first or second week of July at the Kettler Capitals Iceplex, the camp offers both Capitals management and the club's fan base a glimpse into the future, with many of the organization's top prospects in attendance. All practice sessions and scrimmages are free and open to the public, with daily schedules posted on the team's official website.

The summer development camp provides Washington's most recent draft picks with their first chance to meet the team's coaches and trainers, in addition to some potential future teammates. The prospects also get a firsthand look at the amenities and facilities that await should they one day crack the Capitals' lineup.

Attendees include Capitals prospects who are under contract and recent Capitals draft picks who have not yet been signed. Since the Capitals started holding their summer development camp at KCI in 2007, participants have included future Capitals Nicklas Backstrom, Karl Alzner, John Carlson, Braden Holtby, Evgeny Kuznetsov, and Andre Burakovsky.

Several undrafted and free agent amateur players are also invited to the camp with an opportunity to impress Washington management.

Forward Liam O'Brien was an undrafted free agent when he was invited to the Capitals' prospect development camp in 2014. O'Brien made enough of an impression to earn an invite to Washington's rookie camp and main training camp that fall. After a strong performance in the preseason, O'Brien received a three-year, entry-level contract. He made his NHL debut on opening night in October 2014.

Among the highlights for fans during the weeklong summer development camp is the Caps Fan Fest. Activities during the Caps Fan Fest vary from year to year, but past itineraries have included an alumni exhibition game, the team's annual equipment sale (with the chance to purchase game-used gear), and autograph and photo sessions with Capitals prospects and members of the coaching staff.

For the prospects in camp, and for the fans who take in the festivities, the week culminates with a Saturday-morning scrimmage that has traditionally been very well attended. The main rink at KCI includes seating for 1,200 fans, and it's not uncommon for the final scrimmage of the week to be played before a standing-room only crowd.

Members of the winning team earn the Future Caps Cup—and perhaps a few bragging rights.

58 The Original Voice

Soon after the news broke in June 1972 that the NHL would expand to Washington, broadcaster Ron Weber set out to become the club's first play-by-play voice.

Having worked various talk shows and minor league broadcasts in the 1960s and early 1970s, Weber saw stability in a full-time gig in the NHL.

"That's a job that wouldn't be a stepping stone to something else," Weber told his wife, Mary Jane. "It's a job that if I got it, I could wind up doing that for the rest of my professional life."

Weber wasn't kidding. After beating out more than 250 applicants, Weber served as the Capitals' play-by-play voice for their first 23 seasons. Along the way, he never missed a day of work. Between the regular season and playoffs, Weber worked the first 1,936 games in team history.

"Not only was he a local guy and a D.C. native," said longtime Washington sports broadcaster Phil Wood, "but the bottom line was that his preparation for what he did was so complete. And knowing that he'd be working by himself, at least for the road games, they felt comfortable that he could ad-lib and inform the fans accordingly."

In retrospect, Weber played a critical role in developing a fan base in a market that didn't have a rich hockey history. Besides describing the action, Weber taught many of his listeners the intricacies of the game and introduced Washington sports fans to the players and personalities who made up the NHL.

Weber's influence was even greater given that he called all 80 games during the season, with only a dozen or so available on television. If Capitals fans wanted live updates, D.C.'s WTOP 1500AM was the source. Thanks to a powerful signal that went up and down the East Coast, Weber could sometimes be heard as far north as Canada and as far south as Florida.

"After all those years as a sportscaster doing shows and minor league this and that, I was finally the No. 1 guy on a major broadcast for a major sports team," he said in 2016.

Weber still has fond memories of his first few years on the job—despite calling only 19 wins in his first 160 games. He says that only he and winger Bill Lesuk—"the eternal optimist,"—were disappointed to see the inaugural 8–67–5 campaign come to an end in 1974–75.

"People kept asking me, 'How did you bear up under that?'" Weber said. "Well, hockey is such a fast sport that you don't have time to sit and dwell. I often wondered about the New York

Mets—their opening year they won 40 games out of 160. I often thought how did Lindsey Nelson and the rest of them bear up if they're playing in September and they're behind 8–0 in the 8th inning and it's going to be their eighth straight loss and they have time to reflect between pitches, 'Boy, how did I ever get into this?' But in hockey, I'm busy talking [all game], so I didn't have as much time to think about it. After the game it was different, it was like, 'Oh God, another loss.' But during the game, you're tied up in doing it."

Weber also had some training for the mounting losses, having worked as the No. 2 man on the Philadelphia 76ers' radio broadcast in 1972–73. That team went 9–73 and still holds the NBA record for the worst winning percentage in a season.

"I saw how the No. 1 guy, Bill Campbell, handled that year, so maybe that prepared me," he said.

Like the fan base, Weber eventually saw the Capitals turn the corner and after 720 regular season games, he called his first playoff game in April 1983. Four years later, Weber was working solo when Game 7 of the Capitals-Islanders first-round series went to quadruple overtime.

"I couldn't take a bathroom break," he said of the Easter Epic. "We came on the air at 7:15 and I signed off at 2:19 in the morning. I didn't leave my broadcast spot for seven hours and four minutes."

Only once during Weber's career did a Capitals broadcast not make air—the first night of the Gulf War on January 15, 1991, when coverage of the Capitals was preempted. Weber still worked the game from his broadcast position, filing periodic updates as the Capitals battled the Blues in St. Louis.

By the mid-1990s, though, as the Capitals underwent significant rebranding with new logos and uniforms plus a scheduled move to the downtown MCI Center, the decision was made to hire a new radio voice.

"I was told two years before," Weber said, "that I was only going to get two more years. It might be the longest lame-duck performance in the history of radio or TV."

The 1996–97 season was Weber's last. It was also the first time in 15 years the Capitals didn't reach the Stanley Cup Playoffs.

Just more than two weeks before Weber was to call his final game, his mother died on Good Friday. He worked the next night, as scheduled, as the Capitals hosted the Philadelphia Flyers. After the game, Flyers head coach Terry Murray took the stairs up to the Capital Centre broadcast booth to congratulate Weber on his career. Murray had been Washington's head coach for parts of five seasons from 1990 through 1994.

Weber was 63 when he called his final game on April 13, 1997—an 8–3 win in Buffalo, highlighted by a four-goal performance from rookie Jaroslav Svejkovsky.

Proud of the work he did, but yearning to continue, Weber gave his signature sign-off one final time: "It's been a two-point night, Caps fans."

Weber's biggest disappointment with the way his tenure ended is that he wasn't given the chance to call the final 10 games at the Capital Centre at the start of the 1997–98 season. The team did not move to the MCI Center until December 5, 1997.

But since then, in retirement, Weber has remained a constant at Capitals home games. He estimates that he attends about 35 games a year, splitting his time between the press box and the stands. Now in his 80s, Weber still rides the Metro to most home games, taking the Red Line from Montgomery County down to the Gallery Place–Chinatown stop next to the arena.

And along with six former Capitals players, Weber has been honored by the Hockey Hall of Fame. Weber was the recipient of Foster Hewitt Memorial Award in 2010 for outstanding contributions as a hockey broadcaster.

Weber received the news over the phone from longtime Carolina Hurricanes voice and president of the NHL Broadcasters Association Chuck Kaiton. When Kaiton called that spring, Weber had a feeling he knew the reason, so he immediately put the call on speaker so that his wife could hear it as well.

"That's the greatest moment of my professional life," Weber said of being honored at the Hockey Hall of Fame on November 8, 2010.

"As I gave my speech, my theme was that everyone has two lives. You have your professional life and your personal life. So I said this is the greatest moment of my professional life. This is it. It doesn't get any better than this."

59 A Comeback 13 Years in the Making

Forty-year-old goaltenders who haven't played pro hockey in more than 13 years don't get offered NHL contracts. It's more of an understanding than a rule. Some might call it common sense.

But in an effort to circumvent a rule that was actually in place, Capitals general manager David Poile tried to work some creativity in June 1992.

"It's a low point in my career," Poile said nearly a quarter century later.

With the expansion Ottawa Senators and Tampa Bay Lightning set to build their maiden rosters, the Capitals had to expose at least one goaltender for the 1992 expansion draft. The rules stipulated that the unprotected goalie must be under contract and must have at least one game of NHL experience.

The Capitals had three goalies who met the criteria in Don Beaupre, Jim Hrivnak, and prospect Olie Kolzig. Poile wasn't prepared to expose any of them, but he was willing to take advantage of a potential loophole in the rules: it was never specified when that one NHL game had to have been played.

"They make rules," Poile said in 2017, "and whether you're a coach or general manager, you try to use the rules to your advantage or extend them as much as possible."

So, in an attempt to protect Beaupre, Hrivnak, and Kolzig, Poile looked to acquire another goaltender with NHL experience. When trade possibilities fell through, Poile went outside the box. He called his financial advisor, Bernard Wolfe. That would be former Capitals netminder Bernie Wolfe, who was 40 at the time and already well into his second career as a certified financial advisor in Chevy Chase, Maryland.

Wolfe spent four seasons with the Capitals from 1975 through 1979, but hadn't played since. In 120 career appearances, Wolfe posted a 20–61–21 record with a 4.17 goals-against average and one shutout. Teams weren't lining up for his services, but he was exactly what Poile was looking for. Three days before the expansion draft, the Capitals signed Wolfe to a one-year deal for the NHL minimum of $100,000.

"It was very exciting for me," Wolfe said. "David says it's his most embarrassing moment. The whole plan was to make me available so he could protect a young kid named Olie Kolzig. So he said, 'Would you mind doing that? It might be some good publicity.' That was an understatement. Every TV, every radio, and [every] newspaper reporter was in my office."

The same day the Capitals signed Wolfe, they also completed a trade—some would say a legitimate hockey transaction—acquiring veteran Mark Hunter from the Hartford Whalers for Nick Kypreos.

"I felt bad because they traded for Mark Hunter that same day and his [acquisition] was given just a little space, and mine was in big headlines—Caps re-sign Wolfe at age 40! But it was all a publicity ploy. My business had already started to take off, and the free publicity was great."

Tampa Bay Lightning general manager and minority owner Phil Esposito wasn't impressed.

"What the hell is this?" he asked reporters at the time. "I'm not paying $50 million for Bernie Wolfe. He wasn't any good when I played against him."

Wolfe tried to quell the skeptics.

"I will be in 41 in December," he told the *Washington Post*. "But I feel a very young 40."

While Wolfe was having a good laugh, the NHL was hardly amused. The signing of Wolfe, the league said, was not in the spirit of the rules for the expansion draft.

"I got a call from [NHL President] John Ziegler that night," Poile recalled. "He told me unequivocally that I had 24 hours to rectify this."

Poile responded, signing free-agent goaltender Steve Weeks the next day for the sole purpose of exposing him in the expansion draft. Wolfe's short-lived NHL comeback was over.

"It's still something that I regret," Poile said. "It got a lot of publicity and a lot of attention. I can laugh at it, maybe, but I should have been smarter. Hopefully it got Bernie a few more clients."

The Capitals ultimately lost defenseman Shawn Chambers and forward Tim Bergland to the Lightning in the expansion draft, while Weeks was traded to the Senators later that off-season for future considerations.

Wolfe remains the chairman and CEO of Bernard R. Wolfe and Associates financial planners.

"Hockey opened up a lot of doors," he said. "There are a lot of people just as smart as me in the [financial] industry, but none of them had the background or the publicity that I got."

60 The Forgotten 60-Goal Scorer

Only two players in Capitals history have scored at least 60 goals in a single season. One is a bona fide Hall of Famer; the other describes himself as "the NHL's forgotten 60-goal scorer."

Washington's most recent 60-goal scorer is Alex Ovechkin, who set a single-season franchise record with 65 goals during his MVP campaign in 2007–08. Before that, it had been more than a quarter century since Dennis Maruk, an undersized forward known as "Pee Wee" to his teammates, became the Capitals' first 60-goal man in 1981–82.

"The year Ovi broke my record," Maruk said in 2016, "about 20 or 30 games into that season, they began showing the graphics each night on his chase of my record. I was cheering him on. If he broke it, that's great. It's an honor to be included on a list with him."

But, Maruk said, "When he broke it, I was surprised that they didn't invite me down to pass the torch. You know, recognize that my record stood for [26] years."

Now more than three decades removed from his becoming the first player in Capitals history with a 60-goal season, Maruk still wonders if his NHL career was ever fully appreciated. In the late 1970s and early 1980s, Maruk quietly emerged as one of the league's elite goal scorers.

"In Washington, the success of the team was not real strong," said Maruk, who spent five seasons with the Capitals from 1978 through 1983. "We didn't get total fan support; we were losing so much, so it was frustrating. But I pushed hard and fortunately had some pretty good years there."

Maruk broke into the league with the last-place California Golden Seals in 1975–76, finishing second on the team with 30 goals and 62 points in 80 games. In the summer of 1976, the Golden Seals relocated and became the Cleveland Barons.

The club would only last two years in Cleveland, though, with Maruk leading the Barons in scoring both seasons.

"When I was in Cleveland," Maruk said, "we were always told we were going to fold. At one point, we didn't get paid for a month and players really didn't know what was going on. I remember thinking, 'I thought the NHL was a lot better than this.' All I could do was keep my head up and play hard, and maybe another team would pick me up."

Soon after the Barrons merged with the Minnesota North Stars for the start of the 1978–79 season, Maruk was on the move again. Two games into his tenure with the North Stars, he was traded to Washington for a first-round pick.

Finally, in his fourth NHL city, Maruk had a chance to develop some continuity, albeit with another struggling franchise whose future was sometimes in doubt.

"There weren't many players back then who were happy to be joining the Washington Capitals," Maruk said. "I was one of them."

Maruk came to Washington in search of respect. He had heard the pundits suggesting that at 5'8", 165 pounds, he was too small. He knew of the critics who said that he was a one-dimensional player who didn't care to back-check. He also didn't appreciate how he and his former teammates had been treated while moving from Oakland to Cleveland to Minnesota.

"He had a real edge to him," said Maruk's onetime Washington linemate Tom Rowe. "He played with an enormous chip on his shoulder. He was pissed off at the world and he played like that. He definitely felt that he had to prove why he was such a successful player year after year. I think that wore on him after a while. I think he got frustrated with it, especially early in his career. But I'll tell you what, if I had to play with a centerman back then, he'd be in the top two or three guys I'd want to play with."

While in Washington, Maruk became a fan favorite, easily identifiable with his handlebar moustache and popular given his knack for scoring goals in bunches. He was also popular among his teammates, regularly hosting parties and get togethers at his home in Upper Marlboro, Maryland.

"Dennis Maruk was a fireball," said defenseman Robert Picard. "A lot of energy and he was feisty."

Despite his small stature, Maruk was a welcome addition for a Capitals team that ranked last in scoring the season before he arrived.

"Dennis was a natural goal scorer," said defenseman Rick Green, who also played junior hockey with Maruk with the London Knights. "It was a huge addition because he gave us the opportunity to keep games close. He was a true sniper, he loved to score, and he had great hands around the net. For a guy that wasn't that big, boy was he feisty. A hardworking guy that just wanted to score. And we needed that."

Maruk had his two best seasons in Washington in 1980–81 and 1981–82. Skating primarily with veterans Jean Pronovost and Bob Kelly during the 1980–81 campaign, Maruk became the first Capitals player to score 50 goals in a season. He reached the milestone with a hat trick in the regular season finale—a 7–2 win over Detroit at the Capital Centre.

"I can remember being so proud of him the night he scored his 50th goal," former head coach Gary Green told the Capitals Radio

Dennis Maruk recorded a hat trick on the final day of the 1980–81 regular season to become the first player in Capitals history to score 50 goals in a single campaign. He scored a career-high 60 goals in 1981–82.

Network in 2011. "I may have overplayed him a little bit that night, but the guys wanted me to overplay him. Dennis Maruk was a good heart-and-souler."

Green was fired 13 games into the 1981–82 season, but Maruk enjoyed a career year under his successor, Bryan Murray. Playing much of the season with captain Ryan Walter and rookie Chris Valentine, Maruk established franchise records across the board with 60 goals, 76 assists, and 136 points.

Walter (38 goals and 87 points) and Valentine (30 goals and 67 points) also established career highs as the trio accounted for 40 percent of Washington's scoring that season.

"The coach could make the difference, putting the right guys together," Maruk said. "Bryan kept us together all year. We'd go a stretch of eight or nine games without scoring, but he'd keep us together and we played together on the power play and so I have a lot to thank Bryan for my success there because he gave me the opportunity on the ice. I played a lot, he gave me the opportunity to do what I did best, and it just kept going."

Although Ovechkin set a new Washington record for most goals in a season, Maruk's 76 assists and 136 points remain single-season franchise highs.

"That record will probably stand," Maruk said of his 136-point campaign. "I don't think anybody will beat that. That will be pretty tough and 76 assists is the other one. Those are safe, I think."

Despite a drop in his ice time and productivity, Maruk led the Capitals in scoring once more in 1982–83 with 31 goals and 81 points in 80 games as Washington reached the Stanley Cup Playoffs for the first time.

But with the Capitals preparing to take another step in the mid-1980s and with younger players such as Bobby Carpenter and Dave Christian in the fold, Maruk was traded back to Minnesota, where he would spend the final six years of his NHL career.

"That was a shock," he said of the 1983 trade. "It was very disappointing, very frustrating. It was not a very happy time in my life. I put my heart and soul into that, I worked real hard, and to be traded like that, I was very disappointed. I felt I was part of it. And then all of a sudden, boom, you're gone."

Maruk's time with the Capitals was brief, but effective. In 343 career games with Washington, Maruk recorded 182 goals and 431 points. His 1.26 points per game remain a franchise high.

And although Maruk may not be remembered as an all-time great, consider the company he kept while consistently ranking among the league's scoring leaders during his first eight seasons.

Of the NHL's top 12 scorers from 1975 through 1982, Maruk is the only player on the list who is not in the Hockey Hall of Fame.

From 1980 through 1982, only Wayne Gretzky and Mike Bossy had more goals than Maruk. And in recording 136 points in 1981–82, Maruk finished No. 4 overall in league scoring behind Gretzky, Bossy, and Peter Stastny. It would take 20 years before another Capitals player finished in the top five in league scoring, with Jaromir Jagr doing so in 2001–02.

"Dennis Maruk, 5'8" or whatever the heck he was," said former teammate Wes Jarvis, "but let me tell you, he was good. Could he ever score goals! Today you hear about the Mike Bossys and the Guy Lafleurs and all of these guys and they were great players, but people forget about a guy like Dennis Maruk, who scored a lot of freaking goals. He just kind of got lost in the shuffle with all of those other guys.

"I could go around to people and you say the name Mike Bossy and people know who you're talking about. Then you say Dennis Maruk and it's like, 'Well, who's that?' These are people that followed hockey and they don't remember. So yes, I'd agree that he is the forgotten 60-goal man."

61 Niskanen and Orpik Come to Town

Say this about Capitals general manager Brian MacLellan: the man is a straight shooter. From instructing majority owner Ted Leonsis to change the tone of his blog to admitting a past trade was blunder to calling his shots and sharing his off-season game plan with reporters, MacLellan is as candid as they come.

That's why it should have come as little surprise when, on July 1, 2014, MacLellan attacked the first day of free agency with two high-profile signings.

Weeks before the Capitals hired MacLellan as the sixth general manager in franchise history, the club concluded a forgettable 2013–14 campaign with a makeshift blue line.

The Capitals were still battling for a playoff spot as they prepared for their 79th game of the regular season, a road contest in St. Louis.

Needing a win just to keep their slim playoff hopes alive, Washington's defensive unit that night consisted of mainstays Karl Alzner and John Carlson, plus a quartet of players who had just 285 career NHL games between them.

"When you look back at the blue line, it was an Achilles heel for the Caps," head coach Barry Trotz said years later.

Although the Capitals beat the Blues 4–1 that night, they were mathematically eliminated from playoff contention the next day. Many factors contributed to Washington's downfall in 2013–14, but instability and inexperience on the blue line certainly didn't help.

The Capitals dressed an NHL-high 14 different defensemen that season, including four who made their NHL debuts and two others who had fewer than 15 games of NHL experience.

"There were young players playing back there, some inexperience, some guys that were maybe a little bit undersized, and there wasn't a complete balance on what you needed," Trotz said.

Aware of Washington's defensive shortcomings, MacLellan discussed them at length with Leonsis and team president Dick Patrick while interviewing for the team's vacant GM position that spring. MacLellan wanted to sign not one, but two veteran defensemen.

Solidifying the back end topped his off-season to-do list, and on the first day of free agency he signed former Pittsburgh Penguins Matt Niskanen and Brooks Orpik to long-term deals worth a combined $67.75 million.

"We needed to shore up our defense," MacLellan said, "give us some depth, give us some leadership, and give us some experience."

Niskanen signed a seven-year, $40.25 million contract—the most lucrative free-agent deal in team history—while Orpik signed for five years and $27.5 million.

"There are defining moments for a GM," Capitals goaltender Braden Holtby said in 2017, "and you have to put things on the line and take risks. Signing those two, basically right after he got hired, sent a clear message through our team that he was serious and that he knew what we needed and he knew what the players wanted."

The signings also represented a new way of doing business in Washington, where, up until then, the biggest free-agent defenseman signing during the Alex Ovechkin era was a two-year, $7 million deal for 37-year-old Roman Hamrlik in 2011.

"Bringing those two in can change the whole dynamic of the team," Holtby said. "It's not easy to sign two guys like that, especially coming from Pittsburgh. For a first-time GM, that was a bold move and one that changed the shape of our team and direction that we were going."

The free-agent signings of Niskanen and Orpik were a sign of things to come from MacLellan, who showed a knack in his first three years on the job for making big-time moves. One year after shoring up his blue line, MacLellan strengthened Washington's top-six forward group with the acquisitions of T.J. Oshie and Justin Williams. At the 2017 trade deadline, he landed the most coveted defenseman on the market in Kevin Shattenkirk.

"He goes out there and does what it takes," Alzner said. "It doesn't seem to faze him whether he needs to go make a couple big signings or if he needs to move somebody, he's willing to do that. That's kind of what we've seen. He wants to win as bad as anybody. He's shown that he's ready to make those tough decisions if necessary."

Orpik arrived in Washington with 703 career games under his belt—the most by a defenseman in Penguins history. He had also played 44 games—regular season and playoffs combined—against Washington, the most of any player in the Penguins-Capitals rivalry from 2004 through 2014.

Shortly after Orpik settled in Washington, he began the sometimes tedious exercise of unpacking his personal belongings as he set up shop in his new home in northern Virginia.

Among the items that caught his attention was a painting from the 2011 Bridgestone NHL Winter Classic featuring the Capitals and Penguins.

"It was just kind of funny," Orpik said, "kind of fitting that those were the two teams on the painting and now they're the two teams that I've played for."

They also happened to be two of the NHL's fiercest rivals.

"It really wasn't hard for me to get past [the rivalry]," Orpik said. "It was maybe harder for fans. I think there's probably more emotion attached to it for fans than for us. It's just part of the business for us, guys moving teams. It was a quick hurdle for me to get over."

During his first season with the Capitals, Orpik came as advertised, providing a welcome boost of physicality on the back end. His 306 hits during the 2014–15 campaign were tops among all NHL defensemen.

"The impact is really kind of endless," forward Tom Wilson said of Niskanen and Orpik nearly three years after they signed. "They've done such a good job at kind of reforming this team. We really needed a couple solid rocks like them on the back end. Definitely stole two big pieces from [Pittsburgh]."

Niskanen had turned his career around in Pittsburgh after cracking the NHL with the Dallas Stars. The Minnesota native was the Stars' first-round pick in 2005, but was traded to the Penguins in February 2011—an additional piece to a deal that saw defenseman Alex Goligoski head to Dallas and forward James Neal move to Pittsburgh.

"It was a rough point for me," Niskanen recalled years later of the midseason trade. "I really had no confidence, things seemed to snowball on me, I fell out of favor with the coaches [in Dallas], I was scratched every other night, not playing a ton of minutes, so the trade happened and it was like a fresh start for me."

Success, though, didn't come immediately to Niskanen in Pittsburgh. Instead, it was a gradual process that included a "plan to restore his confidence," according to former Penguins assistant coach Todd Reirden.

"His career was heading in the wrong direction," said Reirden, a Penguins assistant coach from 2010 through '14 who joined the Capitals coaching staff in the summer of 2014. "But right away we had a really good connection and we worked to get his career back on track."

The work in Pittsburgh culminated in 2013–14 when injuries decimated the Penguins' blue line and allowed for Niskanen to embrace a bigger role. He finished the season with career highs across the board—10 goals and 46 points in 81 games. Months later, Washington made him the highest-paid free agent in the class of 2014.

While the money was attractive to both Niskanen and Orpik, they were also drawn to Washington by Reirden, who was hired by the Capitals on June 25—his 43rd birthday—six days before the start of free agency.

"As soon as I heard that Washington was interested in me, and knowing that Todd was already here, something kind of clicked there and sparked my interest," Niskanen said. "Obviously, my relationship with him is outstanding so I was kind of hoping things might work out that way and lo and behold they did."

Reirden's presence on the coaching staff also peaked Orpik's interest when the Capitals came calling about his services.

"I remember talking to Todd and the coaching staff here before I came and talking to [Niskanen] a couple days and the night before free agency just to kind of get on the same page," said Orpik, a Penguins first-round pick in the 2000 NHL Draft.

"I didn't know how it was going to play out, but I think myself and [Niskanen] and our wives were pretty happy with the decision and how everything worked out."

Although Orpik's ice time gradually declined in each of his first three years with the Capitals, Niskanen's role steadily increased. During the 2016–17 Presidents' Trophy–winning season, Niskanen emerged as Washington's top defenseman, leading the club in ice time and playing all situations.

62 The Wild Thing

Six months after Scott Stevens signed with the St. Louis Blues in July 1990, the Capitals helped fill the void when they landed defenseman Al Iafrate from the Toronto Maple Leafs.

Just as the Capitals needed Iafrate, the seventh-year pro needed out of Toronto. Selected fourth overall by the Maple Leafs in the 1984 NHL Draft, Iafrate had a pair of 20-goal seasons and two All-Star Game appearances before he turned 23.

But he also took multiple leaves of absence after going through a divorce with his first wife and later dealing with a paternity suit from another relationship.

"The way the media portrayed him, you'd have thought we were getting a troubled youth," former Capitals teammate Alan May recalled in 2017. "But we really got an awesome teddy bear of a guy who worked his ass off. He was obsessed with being the best. We had no idea that he was as good as he was. He was built like a Greek god. Just massive."

The Capitals acquired the 6'3", 240-pound Iafrate in January 1991 in a trade for center Peter Zezel and defenseman Bob Rouse. It didn't take long for Iafrate to develop a large, cult-like following from fans in Washington.

"He was the 'Wild Thing,'" said former Capitals broadcaster Kenny Albert. "He had the long hair, rode motorcycles, and had a booming slap shot. But he could play. He and Kevin Hatcher gave the Capitals a couple of big-time goal scorers on the blue line."

In 256 games with the Capitals over parts of four seasons, Iafrate recorded 58 goals and 176 points, while racking up 616 penalty minutes. His best season came in 1992–93, when he had

25 goals and 66 points in 81 games and was named a Second Team All-Star at year's end.

Iafrate also became the first Capitals defenseman to record a playoff hat trick, scoring three times in Game 5 of the 1993 Patrick Division semifinals against the New York Islanders.

"Big Al was a great athlete," said former teammate Kelly Miller. "There are probably not many guys [who] are better athletes than Al Iafrate. A tremendous athlete with his size and strength and the way he could shoot a puck and the way he could skate, he was a force. But for me, the thing that I remember about Al, because he certainly has the Wild Thing appearance to him, but really, a tremendous guy who really cared about his teammates. He could bring some flair to the game, but at the same time, I thought he was a teammate that cared about the locker room."

Iafrate's slap shot was among the hardest in the NHL, and it was on full display at the Superskills Competition at the 1993 All-Star Game at the Montreal Forum. With his long hair flowing, Iafrate set an NHL record with a slap shot clocked at 105.9 miles per hour. The record stood for 16 years before Zdeno Chara established a new mark at the 2009 All-Star Game.

"You'd get him and [Peter Bondra] shooting the puck and you didn't know where it was going, but you knew it was going to be hard," said Rod Langway. "It was a rocket. When we had scrimmages and stuff, you knew it was coming and you just hoped it wasn't going to hit you."

"I don't think I ever saw anyone block any of his shots," May said. "And he'd do this with old fiberglass wood sticks. He and Hatcher used to get a ton of goals. He called himself the human highlight reel. He was a wow factor, all the time. He had one knee brace that was a shin pad made into a knee brace. I had never seen that before. He had really bad knees, but he never took practices off, he never complained about being injured ever. He was just a machine."

Iafrate's habit of smoking cigarettes, often between periods with the aid of a blowtorch, didn't slow him down either.

"He used to break the cigarettes out, and he'd be smoking in the stick room," May said. "Coach [Terry Murray] would come in and he'd be smoking a cigarette, buck naked, with the filter off. And he'd light a cigarette, kind of like the Diceman [Andrew Dice Clay], the old comedian at that time—he kind of dressed like him too. Coach would come in and say, 'Al, no smoking in the dressing room.' And he'd say, 'Coach, once again, it's not the dressing room. It's the stick room.' And he'd blow smoke right at the coach. He would be naked on the UBE [exercise machine], and he'd be on there with a cup of coffee and a lot of times with a cigarette in his mouth."

Iafrate played hard on the ice and carried himself like a rock star off it. He rode Harley-Davidsons, decorated his body with tattoos, smoked cigarettes, and even had a weekly show on Baltimore's Rock 103 dubbed *The Afternoon Power Play with Al Iafrate*.

One year during the playoffs, May and Iafrate were rooming together on the road and Iafrate wanted to go shopping for some CDs. Iafrate was dressed in all black—boots, pants, a mock turtleneck, and a long leather jacket.

"He looked like a badass," May said. "Like a criminal right out of a movie. And he had the hair slicked back. So we go into this record store and he finds CD after CD. He must have bought more than 100 CDs—he's loading them into bags. And then he goes to pay and the guy [at the cash register] is shocked and mortified, like, 'Who is this monster buying all these CDs?' And he's waiting for his credit card, but Al whips out a wad that's about two inches thick of 100-dollar bills."

Iafrate loved carrying cash. Oftentimes, rather than depositing his paycheck at the bank, he'd ask the tellers to give him the money in cash—sometimes as much as $30,000.

"We'd go for lunch, he'd have all this cash," May said, "and then two hours later, he'd just go back to the bank and deposit the cash he had just made them get for him. That was Al. He was the best."

63 That's a Stretch

Somewhere between San Antonio and Houston, the Hershey Bears' team bus was making its way through Texas when head coach Bob Woods received a call from Washington.

Capitals goalie Jose Theodore had a hip flexor injury, Woods was told, and the team was going to recall prospect Simeon Varlamov.

The Capitals' first-round pick in the 2006 draft, Varlamov received the news in a separate call from Alex Ovechkin. It was Varlamov's first NHL promotion.

"It was a great moment on the bus," said Capitals play-by-play voice John Walton, who held the same position with Hershey from 2002 through 2011. "There was a lot of 'Hey, way to go Varly!'"

But then reality set in.

Walton was sitting across the aisle from Woods and overheard the details of Varlamov's travel itinerary. The 20-year-old Russian was to fly from Houston to Washington that afternoon, with the Capitals hosting the Ottawa Senators later that evening.

"I'm kind of listening to his conversation," Walton recalled, "and when he hung up, I said to him, 'Did you say the flight was at 1:30 out of Houston?'"

Woods confirmed.

"Listen," Walton told Woods, "we could have a jet engine on the back of this bus, we're not going to be in Houston at 1:30.

There's no way. We're nowhere near Houston, and we're not going to be for some time."

The bus eventually pulled over at a roadside stand in Gonzales, Texas—"nothing but tumbleweeds and a Sunoco station," Walton said—where Varlamov and his gear were loaded into a rental car the team's trainers had been driving.

"The car is going directly to IAH [Airport] in Houston, but there is no way he's going to be in Washington before puck drop. There is just no way. And we knew it."

Approaching Houston, the Bears had a problem. By extension, so did the Capitals.

"It started to set in at Kettler too," Walton recalled. "It started to set in that, you know what, 'We're not going to have a goalie in time. What are we going to do?' There was so much crazy about that in the hours leading up to it."

Back at the Kettler Capitals Iceplex in Arlington, Virginia, the Capitals completed their morning skate sans Theodore. Brent Johnson, who knew he would start that night against Ottawa, manned one of the nets at the morning skate, with the team's website producer, Brett Leonhardt, protecting the goal at the other end.

Leonhardt was 26 and two years removed from playing at Division III Neumann College. His playing days were behind him, but the 6'7" Leonhardt, whom coworkers affectionally called "Stretch," was equipped to fill the void at the occasional practice or morning skate if needed.

On December 12, 2008, the morning skate was just the start of a day that began like most others for Leonhardt, but wound up as anything but ordinary.

At about 1:00 PM, Leonhardt was working in his cubicle when general manager George McPhee tapped him on the shoulder.

"We may need you tonight," McPhee said.

Two hours later, McPhee called Leonhardt into his office to sign an amateur tryout contract. The website producer who shot and edited video was going to serve as the Capitals' backup goaltender in a regular season NHL game.

"When George called me into his office, it kind of scared me, to be honest," Leonhardt said eight years later. "Nerves set in right away."

With Varlamov not expected to arrive at Verizon Center until the second period, the plan was for Leonhardt to serve as the backup goalie for warm-up and the start of the game. When he arrived at Verizon Center after 5:00 PM, a No. 80 sweater reading LEONHARDT was hanging from his stall in the Capitals dressing room.

"I remember getting ready for the game and thinking how crazy it was to be in an NHL locker room before a game. It was the coolest feeling in the world, being in the room with the guys and just being a younger kid at the time. Going through the entire warm-up, I don't know how I got through it."

Leonhardt was expecting the Capitals players to have fun at his expense and to chirp him, but to his surprise, he wasn't treated any differently.

His pregame memories include Sergei Fedorov asking him about his college playing experience, Shaone Morrisonn sitting at the stall next to him, and Johnson including him as he went over the Senators' scouting report.

"The way pro sports and hockey can be," Leonhardt said, "I thought it was going to be a lot of jokes, I thought there were going to be a lot of headshots in warm-up and guys kind of laughing about it. But to be honest, it was 100 percent professional. Nobody let up in warm-up, so they treated me like I was supposed to be there, which may be the coolest part of the whole day."

Surviving warm-up was a relief for Leonhardt, but there remained an uneasy feeling on the bench knowing that he was one freak injury away from making his NHL debut.

"There was almost a goaltender interference penalty with Chris Neil running into [Johnson], so there was a moment" when his heart may have skipped a beat, he said.

As Leonhardt tried to maintain his cool, watching the game in full pads and a baseball cap, the arena scoreboard showed him on the bench with a graphic highlighting that it was his first game.

"It should have said that it was my first game and my last game," he said. "It was a lot going on. So, to be honest, when Varly got there, I was actually relieved. People may think I was actually disappointed, but I was like, 'Yeah, here's the guy who is actually supposed to be here, not me.' The circus act was over. I just went back to my regular job."

The Capitals beat the Senators 5–1 that night with Johnson making 32 saves in the win. One night later, Varlamov made his NHL debut as the Capitals beat the Montreal Canadiens 2–1 on *Hockey Night in Canada* at the Bell Centre—a far cry from the tumbleweeds of Gonzales, Texas.

64 Tim Taylor's Skate in the Crease

Olie Kolzig may have been the biggest reason the Capitals reached the Stanley Cup Final in 1998, but catching a huge break in their first-round series against the Boston Bruins didn't hurt.

After splitting the first two games at the MCI Center, the series shifted to Boston for Game 3, where the series ultimately turned.

The Capitals were playing without leading scorer Peter Bondra because of an ankle injury, but defenseman Sergei Gonchar scored twice as Washington built an early 2–0 lead. Undisciplined play from the Capitals, though, allowed Boston back into the game, with the Bruins scoring twice on the power play in the final 21 minutes of regulation.

Tied 2–2 through 60 minutes, the game went to overtime, where Boston rookie P.J. Axelsson beat Kolzig with just over four minutes remaining in the first OT.

The Bruins mobbed Axelsson and celebrated their Game 3 win, while the Capitals retreated to the dressing room, now facing a 2–1 series deficit.

"I remember they scored, and I remember I just stormed off," Kolzig said. "I'm pissed off and I'm in the dressing room starting to take my gear off. But then a minute later they called me back and said they were reviewing the goal."

Referee Paul Devorski called upstairs for a video review to determine if Bruins forward Tim Taylor was in the crease before the puck.

"This was back in the day when you couldn't even have a skate lace in the crease regardless of whether the guy influenced the goalie or anything like that," Kolzig said. "It didn't matter. Lo and behold, his foot was in the crease, and the goal got negated."

Replays confirmed that a few inches of Taylor's left skate blade crept into the blue paint on what otherwise would have been Axelsson's overtime winner. The goal was erased, the teams came back out, and the Capitals went from sudden death to sudden life.

"I can't remember having such a rapid swing of emotion," Kolzig said.

The Capitals weren't completely in the clear, as their parade to the penalty box continued late in the first OT. Captain Dale Hunter was called for a pair of minor penalties, but the Capitals successfully killed off their ninth and 10th shorthanded missions of the afternoon. The game remained tied through four periods.

"We got a couple of breaks, actually, in overtime," said head coach Ron Wilson. "And that's what we said between the first and second overtimes. That we've done enough shooting ourselves in the foot; that we had to get to work. And we did."

Just 6:31 into the second overtime, former Bruins prospect Joe Juneau beat Byron Dafoe to secure a stunning 3–2 double OT win for Washington. Another former Bruin, Adam Oates, drew the primary assist.

The Capitals somehow had a 2–1 series lead despite being outshot 54–27 and having to kill 10 penalties. There was also that matter of the potential winning goal being called back.

"It's highway robbery that we won that hockey game," Wilson said.

After the Capitals returned to the dressing room, this time for good, all the talk surrounded the unusual turn of events.

"Getting that goal called back was like a second life," Juneau told the *Washington Post*. "In my mind, they had scored. After that point, guys might have played a little better, because we felt very lucky."

Down the hall, then–Bruins head coach Pat Burns tried to pick up the pieces after having a potential victory snatched away.

"It's really disappointing, and it took the air out of us, too," he said.

"The rule is that and that's it. It's no goal and I could sit here and moan about it for 15 or 20 minutes, and it's not going to change nothing. He had maybe two inches of skate in the goal crease."

But for a Capitals franchise that has historically seen bad bounces and tough breaks spoil potentially deep playoff runs, there may be no greater exception to the rule than Game 3 in Boston in 1998.

"It was close enough that it had to be reviewed," general manager George McPhee said in 2016. "All [Devorski] did was throw it upstairs and let the guys upstairs make the decision. They said that his toe was in the crease. Those were the rules. They were just following the rules."

The NHL did eventually rid itself of the skate-in-the-crease rule after it made for a controversial finish to the 1999 Stanley Cup Final between the Dallas Stars and Buffalo Sabres. Despite Brett Hull's skate being in the crease before the puck, his series-clinching goal in triple OT of Game 6 was never reviewed or called back. It remains a sore subject in Buffalo nearly two decades later.

In Boston, the stakes weren't as high, but a case can be made that of all the goals that were in fact called back because of a skate in the crease, none had bigger ramifications than Axelsson's disallowed game winner.

"It was a major swing of emotions," McPhee said. "They thought they won the game; we end up winning the game. And then they weren't very good in the next game in Boston. We took that game too, and it probably had a lot to do with how they lost that third game."

After making 52 saves in in the double-overtime win in Game 3, Kolzig stopped all 38 shots he faced in Game 4. The Capitals beat the Bruins 3–0 with Oates netting the game-winning goal as the Capitals took a commanding 3–1 series lead.

"Who knows what would have happened in that series if that goal was allowed?" former Capitals and Bruins forward Anson Carter said in 2017.

Carter was among a young core in Boston in 1998 that included rookies Axelsson, Joe Thornton, and Sergei Samsonov.

"It was a real source of frustration for us," he said, "because we thought, as a young team, that we had a chance to do some damage that year. We thought we were the better team. That may have taken the air out of us because we thought we deserved a much better fate."

While momentum was on Washington's side after two wins in Boston, the Bruins avoided elimination with a 4–0 win in Game 5 at the MCI Center.

"The thing that I remember most is that the Caps had long histories of blowing 3–1 series leads in the playoffs," Kolzig said. "Ron Wilson just came right out and addressed it. We faced it head on. He didn't try to downplay it or skirt around it, we just came out and said that we're a different team than those teams in the past. Even when Boston made [the series] 3–2, I can still remember [*Washington Post* columnist] Tony Kornheiser writing, 'Here we go again.' But we went into Game 6 and still felt that we could finish it."

Again, the Capitals went beyond 80 minutes, but Brian Bellows ultimately secured Washington's first series win in four years, scoring the series-clinching goal 15:24 into double overtime.

"Having the goal in [Game 3] waved off suggested to me that maybe this is meant to be for us," Kolzig said. "Then [Bellows] goes down and scores the winner in Game 6 and we exorcise one of those demons. Just a great feeling, like it was starting to align for us."

65 Play Poker with the Capitals

Alex Ovechkin claims to be the best poker player on the Capitals, but his teammates have long called his bluff.

"He *thinks* he's the best," Justin Williams said in 2016. "He's always running the game on the [team] plane, and he's the loudest one at the table. But that doesn't mean he's the best. But hey, let him think that. We're always happy to play with him."

Fans looking to test Ovechkin's poker face or try their luck at blackjack against Nicklas Backstrom can do so at the annual Capitals Casino Night—an evening of gaming and socializing that provides fans the chance to interact with their favorite players in a relaxed environment, all for a good cause.

Entry to the Capitals Casino Night requires a purchased ticket, with all proceeds benefiting the Monumental Sports & Entertainment Foundation. MSE Foundation is the nonprofit arm of the Capitals that offers resources and programs to various charities and nonprofit organizations throughout the D.C. area on behalf of the team.

Cocktail attire is required and attendees must be 21 or over.

Giving back to the community has long been in the organization's DNA, with visits to local elementary schools and the hosting of holiday skates for military families among the highlights.

The Capitals also do their part in helping raise money for local charities and no single-day event raises more funds for the MSE Foundation than the Capitals Casino Night. More than 400 fans attended the event in 2016, raising $285,000 for the MSE Foundation.

In addition to the usual allotment of casino games like blackjack, Texas hold'em, roulette, and craps, Casino Night also includes a silent auction featuring Capitals game-used equipment as well as autographed memorabilia. A live auction offers fans the chance to win unique experiences with members of the organization.

Among the experiences that were auctioned off at the 2016 Capitals Casino Night: a night of bowling with five Capitals players, a round of golf with a Capitals foursome, and a Segway tour around the National Mall with a group of Capitals players.

The event also offers a limited number of VIP tickets, which provide access to an exclusive hourlong VIP reception where fans can meet players from the team and obtain autographs in a more intimate setting before the start of the event.

"It's awesome," defenseman Matt Niskanen told the Capitals' official website in 2016. "What a cause. It all goes to charity. People have fun...they have a couple drinks, people let loose a little bit and get to meet us. We get to talk to fans, great all-around event, really well run. I think everyone looks forward to it every year."

The first six Capitals Casino Nights combined to raise more than $1.7 million for charity.

For more information on the MSE Foundation, go to www. monumentalfoundation.org.

66 Ovechkin "Nose" Goal Scoring

A Gordie Howe hat trick is referenced in hockey circles when a player records a goal, an assist, and a fight in the same game. By that definition, Alex Ovechkin didn't earn a Gordie Howe hat trick on January 31, 2008, but his performance in a home win over the Montreal Canadiens that night had to make Mr. Hockey proud.

In what may go down as the best game of his NHL career, a 22-year-old Ovechkin had four goals and an assist, accounting for all five Washington goals in a 5–4 overtime win against Montreal. But that's only part of the story. Ovechkin was also a physical menace and a human piñata, inadvertently skating and colliding into harm's way all game long.

On Ovechkin's first shift of the night, he was struck in the face by an errant Alexei Kovalev stick. Ovechkin stayed down on the ice for several moments before making his way to the Capitals' bench, where stitches were applied on the inside of his cheek. Ovechkin later took a puck to the face, requiring additional stitches, this time on the inside of his lower lip. There was also a second-period collision with Canadiens defenseman Francis Bouillon, which left Ovechkin's nose bloodied and broken. Again, Ovechkin was treated on the bench, and repairs were applied, and by the next shift, he was back on the ice.

Just as the Canadiens couldn't slow Ovechkin down, neither could the accumulation of bumps and bruises.

Ovechkin didn't miss a shift, leading all forwards with 24:52 of ice time. He scored a goal in all four periods (overtime included) and had a game-high five hits, including bone crunchers on forward Steve Begin and defensemen Josh Gorges and Mike Komisarek.

Want to see "Alexander the Great" at his best, in his prime? Look no further than Game No. 53 during the 2007–08 season. Ovechkin won both the Hart Trophy and the Lester B. Pearson Award that year, with his four-goal game against Montreal serving as one of the signature moments of the MVP campaign.

"Today was a special day," Ovechkin said after the win. "I broke my nose, have stitches, [and] score four goals. Everything [went] to my face."

Ovechkin and the Capitals already had plenty of motivation entering the game, which was the back end of a home-and-home series. Two nights earlier, the Canadiens beat the Capitals 4–0 at Bell Centre. With Montreal leading 3–0 and less than a minute remaining in the third period, Canadiens head coach Guy Carbonneau summoned his No. 1 power play unit, which the Capitals didn't much appreciate. Kovalev scored with 47 seconds left to play, securing the 4–0 win.

In the rematch, it was Kovalev's stick that clipped Ovechkin on the opening shift.

"Ovi plays with an edge," goaltender Olie Kolzig told reporters after the game in Washington. "And you know the saying, 'Don't wake up a sleeping giant?' Not saying Ovi sleeps every night, but he threw it into an extra gear" after getting up close and personal with Kovalev's twig.

With just under seven minutes remaining in the first period, Ovechkin opened the scoring, blasting a one-timer from Milan

Jurcina past Cristobal Huet. In the process, Ovechkin became just the fifth player in the previous 25 years to begin his career with three straight 40-goal seasons.

Ovechkin added a goal and an assist in the second period before completing the hat trick in the third. His third goal of the night was vintage Ovechkin. In search of his fourth career hat trick, Ovechkin received the puck in the neutral zone and picked up speed down the left wing.

Once he gained the Montreal blue line, Ovechkin broke slightly to the right, with Canadiens defenseman Mark Streit keeping a watchful eye on the puck carrier. Ovechkin then used Streit as a screen, wiring a wrist shot *through Streit's skates* that found its way under the crossbar, just above Huet's glove hand.

It was Ovechkin's first hat trick on home ice, and the crowd of 14,930 at Verizon Center celebrated accordingly, littering the ice with their own hats as Ovechkin jumped into the glass as part of his usual celebratory routine.

Ovechkin's fourth point of the game moved him past Ottawa Senators forward Daniel Alfredsson for the overall NHL scoring lead, marking the first time he sat atop the overall scoring ledger.

Washington led 4–2, but the Canadiens would rally, thanks to a pair of third-period goals from Guillaume Latendresse. The Capitals were less than a minute away from winning in regulation, but Latendresse tied the game at four on a goalmouth scramble with 33 seconds remaining.

The Capitals, though, did not wilt. With less than 90 seconds to play in four-on-four overtime, a Mike Green point shot was blocked by Komisarek, but the puck ricocheted to Jeff Schultz to the left of the goal. Schultz made a cross-crease pass to Ovechkin, who beat Huet from the doorstep. Game over.

Joe Beninati had the call on Comcast SportsNet: "Ovechkin's fourth is the game-winning fifth!"

Ovechkin capped off January in style with 13 goals and 22 points in 13 games.

"The way Ovi scored the goals today, he's pretty amazing," linemate Viktor Kozlov said after the game. "Alex's game is excellent. Excellent. Hitting people, passing, scoring. I don't know what other forwards could do that."

"We scored five, and he was in on all five," Boudreau said after Ovechkin's winner with 1:26 remaining in overtime. "How can you say enough about him? He's an amazing person. Don't get him angry."

For the second time in just over a month, Ovechkin had a four-goal, five-point game. He also scored four times on December 29, 2007, in an 8–6 win in Ottawa on *Hockey Night in Canada*.

Three weeks after signing a 13-year, $124 million contract extension—the largest deal in NHL history—Ovechkin earned his money. So did the Capitals' training staff.

"The Caps got him at a bargain, really," Kolzig said after the Capitals' fifth straight home win. "He single-handedly won us that hockey game. Never leave our games early."

67 Best Men

When the Capitals used their first two picks in the 1989 draft to select goaltenders Olie Kolzig and Byron Dafoe, the thought was that one would emerge as Washington's long-term No. 1.

Kolzig and Dafoe knew each other from the Western Hockey League—their junior teams played each other that spring in a seven-game playoff series—but they were more colleagues than friends.

"We had major battles in the WHL," Dafoe said. "Definitely not buddies at that point."

Both had been heavily scouted by Washington's director of player personnel, Jack Button, and by the Capitals' head western scout, Barry Trotz. Despite emerging as a perennial contender by the late 1980s, the Capitals had a revolving door in goal.

"Trotz put me on the Caps' radar," said Kolzig, the 19th overall pick in 1989. "I had met him and Jack and then as we got closer to the draft I interviewed with [general manager] David Poile. I knew they were interested in both Byron Dafoe and me, so I really didn't know what to expect come draft day. I had no idea they were going to select a goalie in the first round but lo and behold, my name was called."

To Kolzig's surprise, the Capitals called Dafoe's name 16 picks later.

"Olie has told me the story," Dafoe said in 2017, "that he went back to the draft table and kind of piped up like, 'What's going on?!'"

Opponents in the WHL, Kolzig and Dafoe were expected to remain fierce competitors for years to come while battling for playing time with the Capitals. But a funny thing happened along the way—Kolzig and Dafoe developed a tremendous bond.

They clicked from the get-go, a couple of teenagers finding their way in Europe as the Capitals held their 1989 training camp in Sweden and Russia.

"It was really during that camp where Olie and I became friends," Dafoe said. "We were the young guys, the young goalies, so we hung out on the days off and it led to a great friendship."

Two years later, while Kolzig and Dafoe were battling for playing time with the American Hockey League's Baltimore Skipjacks, they shared an apartment unit in Columbia, Maryland, along with forward Reggie Savage.

"It was funny," Dafoe said. "I remember management, and specifically Barry Trotz, saying, "Are you sure you guys want to room together? You're kind of fighting for the same job here."

By the 1993–1994 season, the Capitals' AHL affiliate moved to Portland, Maine, where Kolzig and Dafoe again split the goaltending duties with the eventual Calder Cup champion Pirates. Dafoe handled the bulk of the workload during the regular season, but a late-season recall to Washington opened the door for Kolzig to emerge as the No. 1 heading into the AHL Playoffs. Kolzig wound up winning the Jack A. Butterfield Trophy as AHL Playoff MVP.

"I really felt I was starting to arrive," Kolzig said.

With another goalie climbing the organizational depth chart in prospect Jim Carey, the Capitals traded Dafoe to the Los Angeles Kings in July 1995.

Kolzig and Dafoe remained friends, though, even serving as the best men in each other's weddings. Their friendship has stayed strong for nearly three decades, but any story about their kinship wouldn't be complete without a mention of the events of November 21, 1998.

By then, Kolzig had finally emerged as the full-time starter in Washington, while Dafoe was plying his trade with the Boston Bruins.

The Capitals were visiting Boston that night, with the teams meeting for the first time since their first-round series the previous spring.

"Early in the game, Dale Hunter turned to me on the bench and asked if we should goon it up," head coach Ron Wilson said in 2017. "We were trying to even a score. Somebody on the Bruins had done something the year before during the playoffs and we said that we'd do something the next year to even the score. So this was our first chance."

With the Bruins leading 2–0 early in the first period, Hunter looked to light a spark.

"I remember Dale saying, 'Hey coach, it's time for a little rodeo out here.' And I said, 'You're right.'"

A line brawl ensued on the next shift with Hunter, Craig Berube, and Mark Tinordi among the heavyweights on the ice for the Capitals. Ken Belanger and Ken Baumgartner provided some muscle for Boston, and it didn't take long for all five skaters to pair off.

The fighting escalated quickly, with Dafoe and Kolzig eventually finding each other in the neutral zone. Goalie fights are rare under normal circumstances, but a goalie fight between best friends makes for a memorable tale. Here's how they each remember it, as something they both can laugh at nearly 20 years later:

> **Dafoe:** "Down at my end, Dale Hunter got into a third-man-in situation. So I felt obligated to jump in as everyone else paired up. I wasn't really thinking about who I was grabbing at the time, because that would never be a smart thing to do—to grab Dale Hunter."
>
> *With Dafoe engaged in the brawl, Kolzig left his crease at the other end.*
>
> **Kolzig:** "Well, I was actually going to help out Dale Hunter—again."
>
> **Dafoe:** "I'm surprised Olie was able to skate all the way down without having to stop by the bench for a water break. But he did, and he actually grabbed Belanger, who was one of our tougher guys. That actually would have been fun to watch, but I figured I better save my friend."
>
> **Kolzig:** "I was getting in the middle of it and the next thing I know, I've got this arm reaching over me, and it's Byron. So we pair off and we're looking at each other, and we're like, 'Okay, let's do it.'"

Dafoe: "Hockey crowds love it when the goalies get into the battle, so I think that kind of fueled us to laugh a little bit. We weren't going to throw any serious punches at each other, even though the 20,000 [fans] there wanted it to happen. So, when you see us dancing around, I think there were smiles on our faces."

Kolzig: "We were tangled up, pretty much just holding on to each other when we skated by their bench and [the Bruins players] just yelled out 'Will you two f——s stop smiling and start throwing them?!' So then, with a shot of adrenaline, he pulled my jersey over my head."

Dafoe: "I recall pulling his jersey over his head, which, for anyone who knows anything about hockey fights, that's the first point to a win. Obviously, no punches were thrown, because it would have been an unfair advantage with the jersey over his head."

Kolzig: "The jersey is over my head, we're dancing, and I can remember saying, 'Byron, don't you do it.'"

Dafoe: "There were 20,000 people going nuts, but I did hear him, clear as day, say, 'Bysie, don't bleeping do it. I will kill you.' I heard him loud and clear and I have to tip my hat. I think if it were fair circumstances, he would kill me. He's got a few pounds and a few inches on me. So I left it at that."

When the dust settled, everyone on the ice—all five skaters on each side plus the two goalies—were thrown out of the game.

Dafoe: "My wife was at the game, so she was freaking out knowing how close Olie and I are. So we got kicked out in the first period and I've actually got a picture of me, my wife, and Olie down in the dressing room concourse. We posed for a picture and we've got our arms around each other and it's funny because this is just a couple of hours after we were in a battle."

The Bruins went on to win what turned out to be an eventful game 5–4 in overtime. Former Capitals forward Jason Allison beat Rick Tabaracci with 31 seconds remaining in OT for the Boston win.

As for who won the goalie fight?

"The funny thing is that for years after it," Kolzig said, "we'd be at functions and that story would come up and people would ask, 'Who won the fight?' And I didn't know, but the little prick had a cut-out copy from the *Boston Globe* with the picture right as he was pulling the jersey over my head, and he'd pull it out and say.\, 'I don't know. Who do you think won it?!'"

Dafoe says the picture is now hanging from his home gym—a frequent reminder to one of the more unusual nights in his NHL career.

"It was surreal and funny at the same time," he said. "It makes for a great story."

68 Jagr Bombs

A quick glance at Jaromir Jagr's NHL career shows that the second leading scorer in league history took a three-year hiatus to play in Russia's Kontinental Hockey League from 2008 through 2011.

Some hockey pundits will argue that Jagr also took a three-year hiatus during his brief, but tumultuous, tenure in Washington from 2001 through 2004.

"I don't think he ever fully embraced being a Washington Capital," team president Dick Patrick said in 2017.

Jagr spent the first 11 years of his NHL career with the Pittsburgh Penguins, winning the Stanley Cup in 1991 and 1992.

He earned the Hart Trophy as NHL MVP in 1999 and was the league's leading scorer for four consecutive seasons, from 1997–98 through 2000–01.

Contending teams like Pittsburgh typically don't trade players like Jagr, but the financially troubled Penguins were motivated to move him, and his contract, after the 2000–01 season.

Jagr had two years remaining on his deal and was owed $20.7 million over the next two seasons.

The New York Rangers were among the few teams that could afford to add such a contract in the pre–salary cap era and were therefore thought to be the favorites to land Jagr, then 29.

In Washington, owner Ted Leonsis and the Capitals were prepared to go shopping themselves that off-season, but they were eyeing the first day of free agency on July 1. Despite back-to-back Southeast Division titles, the Capitals were coming off consecutive first-round exits in the Stanley Cup Playoffs (both of which happened to come against Jagr and the Penguins).

The Capitals were targeting big free-agent centers, but came up empty despite aggressive offers to Jeremy Roenick, Pierre Turgeon, and Doug Weight.

Still looking to make a splash, the Capitals discussed a deal with Pittsburgh before landing Jagr on July 11, 2001.

In one of the biggest trades in team history, the Capitals acquired Jagr and defenseman Frantisek Kucera for prospects Kris Beech, Ross Lupaschuk, and Michal Sivek, plus $4.9 million in cash.

General manager George McPhee made the trade, but had reservations, as he later revealed in an interview with the team's official website in 2014.

"I remember telling Ted at the time, 'Ted, I've seen this movie before.' We traded three young players for Alex Mogilny when we were in Vancouver and it didn't work out. And halfway through the season we were wishing we had those three young players back:

Mike Peca, Mike Wilson, and a [first-round] pick that turned out to be Jay McKee. I remember telling him that and he said, 'It's my team, it's my money, and I want to do it.'"

Within three hours of the trade announcement, the Capitals sold 300 season tickets.

"This puts us on the national scene, because we now have a really, really great hockey team," Leonsis said at the time.

"I hope we can get rid of the stigma that DC's not a hockey town, that we can compete with the elite teams, that we can be a 'have' as opposed to a 'have not.' I think we've answered that question."

Leonsis was so enthused with the Jagr acquisition that he soon made him the NHL's highest-paid player, with a seven-year, $77 million contract extension.

"We knew it was a risk," Patrick said of the trade, "but we probably compounded it with the extension. We got him at such a high cost, our thought was, 'Well, he's only got a couple years left on his contract, we better make sure we tie him down.' That's when salaries were crazy and we were right at the front of it, giving him the highest contract in the league."

Jagr made his Capitals debut before a sold-out MCI Center in Washington's home opener on October 6, 2001. Washington opened the year as a legitimate Stanley Cup contender—it hadn't lost any significant pieces during the off-season, and added one of the game's best. Jagr had a goal and an assist in the opener as the Capitals beat the two-time defending Eastern Conference champion New Jersey Devils 6–1.

"As good as the group was, I thought Jagr would come in and he'd be the missing piece for us," said former Capitals forward Jeff Halpern.

"And I remember thinking after that first game that we would probably make the Stanley Cup Final and we'd probably win. We left that game feeling like we had all the pieces in place. The team looked great and we had a ton of confidence. From that game on, though, I honestly can't tell you what happened."

Despite having the league's sixth-biggest payroll, the Capitals won four of their next 15 games and dropped to 12th place in the Eastern Conference. A late-season surge wasn't enough, as the Capitals missed the postseason by two points.

The club did see a spike at the box office as the Capitals set a team record for attendance during the 2001–02 season with an average of 17,341 fans per game. Jagr's first year in Washington also marked the first time that all 82 regular season games were available on local television. But Jagr's productivity couldn't match the hype.

A year after recording 52 goals and a league-high 121 points in Pittsburgh, Jagr had 31 goals and 79 points in his first season in

Golden Jet Could Have Flown with Caps

The headlines the Capitals drew when they acquired Jagr in 2001 are similar to what team president Peter O'Malley was picturing 22 years earlier.

In July 1979, with the Capitals having missed the playoffs in each of their first five seasons, they had an opportunity to sign one of hockey's most recognizable names.

Two-time NHL MVP and five-time 50-goal scorer Bobby Hull was eyeing a comeback a year after he had retired from the World Hockey Association's Winnipeg Jets. Even at the age of 40, Hull would be a draw for the fledgling Capitals.

"We will do everything in our power to land Bobby Hull," O'Malley told the *Winnipeg Free Press*. "It would be a great shot in the arm for the franchise."

Jets general manager John Ferguson even gave the Capitals permission to negotiate salary terms with Hull, whose rights still belonged to Winnipeg.

Despite the interest, O'Malley and the Capitals never completed a deal. The future Hall of Famer returned to the NHL in 1979–80 but played just 27 total games with the Jets and Hartford Whalers.

Washington. He was limited to 69 games because of wrist and knee injuries and at times seemed distant and unmotivated.

"At that time," said former head coach Ron Wilson, "Jags was really hard to work with."

"He wasn't a happy person here," Patrick said. "It was a difficult time in his life and I think that had a lot to do with it."

A 2003 report from *Sports Illustrated* revealed that by the time Jagr arrived in Washington, he had accrued $500,000 in online gambling debts. The Internal Revenue Service filed a tax lien against Jagr for $3.27 million for back taxes for the year 2001.

"He just wasn't in the proper frame of mind when he came on board with our team," Wilson said.

"It wasn't a great period in his life," McPhee told the team's official website in 2014. "He had lots of things going on. He wasn't in a good place. He wasn't excited to be here. It was really difficult for him to be traded out of Pittsburgh, and I think it took him a long time to recover from that."

Former captain Steve Konowalchuk remembers Jagr telling him that he just wanted to be a "regular player," without the demands and expectations that came with being the highest-paid player.

"The weight of the organization was on his shoulders," Konowalchuk said. "And at that time, with other stuff going on in his life, I don't think that he always handled the pressure that well. And it is pressure. In his shoes, that's pressure. They trade for him, they give him big money, there's an expectation to win, so that pressure was on him."

There was also pressure on the Capitals to cater to their new superstar. A successful power play unit that featured Adam Oates as the key distributor and Peter Bondra and Sergei Gonchar as the primary shooters started to change with Jagr on board.

"The guy that is that much of a star can be demanding teammate too," Patrick said. "We had a power play with Bondra and Gonchar bopping it from the point and coming in back door, but then it started to slow down with Jagr. I'm sure Adam felt pressure to get him the puck, too."

Adding to that pressure was the identity crises the Capitals were left to tackle with Jagr in the fold. As McPhee suggested to the official team website in 2014, the Capitals were a blue-collar team and Jagr was a white-collar player.

"I said at the time, 'This is the right player at the right time for us.' But I wasn't sure that it was the right player at the right time for us. We were building our organization with bricks and when we did that, we suddenly went to siding or a different material. We got on a different bus. It's always about team construction and we weren't really constructed the right way to absorb him."

Halpern agreed: "We had an identity as a group. Bringing in such a big player and such a big personality, you hoped that he would add to the identity and make it better and make the team better, but it kind of weighed on the team in a different way. We slowly started to build around Jagr and it was creating something different. Any time you try to create a new identity there are going to be some rocky times from it. And to be honest, I don't think Jagr bought into the system and the teachings that Wilson was trying to bring in. I can remember specific arguments or conflicts that they had on and off the ice. We were never a team; we never won games as a team, other than that first game of the season."

Attempts were made to please Jagr during the 2002 off-season, including the signing of his former Penguins teammate Robert Lang to a five-year, $25 million deal. It was the largest free-agent contract in team history. A year and a half later, though, both Jagr and Lang were traded as part of the Capitals' 2003–04 fire sale.

Jagr was sent to the Rangers for Anson Carter, with the Capitals agreeing to pay between $16 million and $18 million of the remaining $44 million on Jagr's deal.

In New York, Jagr rediscovered his scoring touch with 54 goals and 123 points in 2005–06. With his personal life settled, he'd also become a model teammate, playing well into his 40s with the Flyers, Stars, Bruins, Devils, and Panthers.

In 2015–16, Jagr was the recipient of the Bill Masterton Trophy, which is presented to the NHL player who best exemplifies the qualities of perseverance, sportsmanship, and dedication to the game.

"I remember seeing him playing in New Jersey a few years ago," Patrick said, "and thinking, 'Boy, this is a really happy hockey player, that's really performing at his peak and helping his teammates.' It was just a different personality than what we saw here."

Although Jagr and the Capitals did not produce a winner during his time in Washington, the lessons learned in acquiring him and signing him to a long-term deal would set the stage for the club's most successful seasons a few years later.

"What was more important was the lesson," McPhee said in 2014. "You've got to draft and develop your own stars. That's how you win. Draft and develop your own guys and your own elite players. And if you want to add somebody else's star late in the game, you can. But getting someone else's star to change your team, I'm not sure that culturally that's the right thing to do."

69 To Russia with Love

When it comes to ranking the top Russian goal scorers in NHL history, there is little debate that "the Great 8" is No. 1. Alex Ovechkin officially took his place as the greatest Russian sniper on November 19, 2016, when he beat Dallas Stars goaltender Kari Lehtonen at Verizon Center.

The goal was the 484th of Ovechkin's career, passing his former teammate, Sergei Fedorov, for the most all-time by a Russian player in the NHL.

"Obviously a huge honor," Ovechkin said. "To pass all the great names in Russian hockey and to be No. 1, it's huge."

Although Ovechkin made his mark in the NHL playing in the U.S. capital, he's taken tremendous pride throughout his career representing Russia and being part of his country's rich hockey history.

"He's very proud of the Russian culture," said head coach Barry Trotz. "Some guys are from countries and they are proud of coming from that country but with Alex he's proud about tradition and heritage. He's Americanized, if you will, but he's also very traditional when it comes to Russian traditions and he respects all of those things. That comes from his parents and his upbringing and the culture that he lives under."

Ovechkin's parents are former athletes themselves, with his father, Mikhail, a former professional soccer player, and his mother, Tatyana, a two-time Olympic gold medalist in women's basketball. Tatyana Ovechkina represented the Soviet Union at the 1976 and 1980 Summer Games.

Alex Ovechkin was drawn to hockey from an early age in Moscow and began playing in Russian youth leagues in the early 1990s, just as some of the country's best players were taking their talents to the NHL.

Fedorov was among the early wave of Russians to establish themselves as top players in the NHL. In 1994, Fedorov became the first European-trained player to win the Hart Trophy as NHL MVP and in 2004, he became the first Russian to record 1,000 career points.

By the time the Capitals acquired Fedorov in February 2008, he was a three-time Stanley Cup champion and a six-time NHL All-Star.

"He was my idol when I was growing up," Ovechkin said. "You have a dream just to meet those kinds of guys, "but I had the huge privilege to play with him and had the luck to be on the same team and same line. He was the best teammate I had."

Throughout Ovechkin's career, his supporting cast in Washington has had a strong Russian flavor with teammates such as Alexander Semin, Viktor Kozlov, Semyon Varlamov, Evgeny Kuznetsov, and Dmitry Orlov. But none has had the credentials of Fedorov, who was inducted into the Hockey Hall of Fame in 2015—the same month Ovechkin broke his Russian goal-scoring record.

"I respect what he did for Russian hockey and what he did for my career," said Ovechkin, who also played with Fedorov on Team Russia at the 2008 World Hockey Championships and at the 2010 Olympics.

Fedorov played parts of two seasons with the Capitals, embracing the opportunity to play with Ovechkin just as he was entering his prime.

"When I came to Washington," Fedorov said in 2015, "we became immediately good friends. I felt his respect and I gave him back the same. That particular year he scored 65 goals. It was great to see that a young guy like him got excited to see an old guy like me on the team and it was great to play together."

They're totally different players," said Trotz, who coached against Fedorov's teams for 10 seasons with the Nashville Predators.

"Sergei was a real cerebral player; he played with a lot of grace. He played hard, but he was a real smooth player and very efficient and very smart. When you see Ovi play, he plays with power. Not that he can't play with finesse; he's got some of the best goals that you'll ever see on the planet. But he's more of that loud player than Sergei."

Fedorov finished his career with 483 goals in 1,248 games, whereas Ovechkin recorded his 484th goal in career game number 777.

"Any time that you pass a great player, that's got to be pretty fulfilling," Trotz said, "and it's crazy that he's hundreds of games ahead of one of the greatest players that went to the Hall of Fame. That's pretty outstanding. He's doing it in an era when it's harder to score, when there's a lot of emphasis on playing a 200-foot game. When I see those numbers, that's what blows me away. Knowing how great Sergei was as player too, it's pretty outstanding."

70 Holtby's Coming-Out Party

The roller coaster painted on Braden Holtby's goalie mask during the 2012 Stanley Cup Playoffs was a tribute to the Hershey Park amusement park in central Pennsylvania.

Holtby wanted his 2011–12 mask to have a Hershey feel, figuring that he'd be spending most of the year with the Capitals' American Hockey League affiliate, the Hershey Bears.

But eight months into the season, the roller coaster may as well have been a symbol of the wild and crazy ride it had been for the 22-year-old, who went from making one emergency start in Washington's first 72 regular season games to emerging as its No. 1 goalie in the playoffs.

With Tomas Vokoun and Michael Neuvirth both injured that spring, Holtby stepped in and delivered one of the best goaltending performances in franchise history.

"You can call it a coming-out party or whatever you like," defenseman John Carlson said of Holtby, "but to me it was just him getting a chance to play regularly. We knew what he was capable of."

Loyal Capitals followers had seen glimpses of Holtby's potential—he went 14–4–3 in 21 appearances over the previous two seasons—but the 2008 fourth-round pick wasn't necessarily on the national radar. That changed with his first-round showing against the Boston Bruins.

Thanks largely to Holtby—and a sound defensive structure put in place by head coach Dale Hunter—the No. 7 Capitals upset the defending Stanley Cup champions in a classic seven-game series. For the first time in league history, all seven games were decided by one goal, including four in overtime. It also marked the first time the Capitals had ever eliminated the Stanley Cup champs.

"That was a big moment for Holts and for a lot of us," said forward Jay Beagle. "They were the defending champions but he was a rock back there. He was so calm and you could tell that nothing rattled him, be it a fluky goal or if they scored the first goal. Nothing shook him up. He was a rock. You knew after that series that he was going to be our No. 1 guy. He stole the show."

In seven games against Boston, Holtby had a 2.00 goals-against average and a .949 save percentage. He also made NHL history as the first rookie goalie to win a series against the reigning Conn Smythe Trophy–winning goalie. Boston's Tim Thomas had also won the Vezina Trophy twice in the previous four seasons and was still regarded as one of the top goalies in the league in 2012.

One of the Holtby's best performances that spring came in Game 4 of the first-round series. The Capitals trailed Boston two games to one and were without center Nicklas Backstrom in Game 4 because of a one-game suspension. Holtby made 44 saves, though, allowing Washington to win 2–1 and even the series at two games apiece.

Four years after breaking through during the 2012 Stanley Cup Playoffs, Braden Holtby tied an NHL single-season record with 48 wins in 2015–16. He later became the third Capitals goalie to win the Vezina Trophy.

Holtby was the first rookie to make 44 saves in a regulation win in the playoffs since Hall of Famer Ken Dryden pulled the feat with the Montreal Canadiens more than 40 years earlier.

"Looking back, it was pretty cool," Holtby said. "It established me in the league and gave me a chance to play here every day. As a goalie, it's extremely hard, especially at a young age, to have success and win the trust of your teammates and that could be the turning point of a career. When you're doing it in the moment, you're not thinking of that too much, but looking back, that was a great opportunity."

As the rookie call-up from the minors, Holtby was soft-spoken and largely kept to himself that spring. The Lloydminster, Saskatchewan, native oozed with confidence on the ice, though, and had a quiet, calm demeanor that teammates appreciated. While Holtby entered the postseason with only 16 games of playoff experience from the AHL and Western Hockey League combined, his successful NHL playoff debut didn't surprise those around him.

"I just remember it was a very quiet time for the team," said Brooks Laich. "Dale was quiet and it trickled down. After two or three weeks, we still barely knew the guy because nobody really talked. We just came to work, it was businesslike and we didn't worry about anybody. We never worried about Braden even though he was a young guy. He held his own. It was a turning point for him—it really got him on the radar."

Veteran forward Matt Hendricks was among the few Capitals who got to know Holtby fairly well during his occasional recalls from 2010 through 2012.

"I'd always be on the ice early [for practice] given my role on the team," said Hendricks, a fourth liner. "So I was always out shooting on the goalie way before practice and way after practice. Sometimes I'd get upset if the work ethic isn't there with my goalies, but that's one thing I could never say about Holts. He's an absolute animal; he's a workhorse, he has that western Canadian mentality.

"And not only is he a workhorse in practice and shooting drills, but he works through traffic, he had that calm presence back there and we ended up riding him into the playoffs that season and he was outstanding for us, especially in the Boston series."

One round after knocking off the Bruins, Holtby and the Capitals met 2012 Vezina Trophy winner Henrik Lundqvist and the New York Rangers in Round 2.

Holtby continued to show off his ability to quickly turn the page and rebound from defeats—a trait rarely seen in young goalies in such high-pressure situations. After dropping Game 3 in triple overtime to fall behind 2–1 in the series, for example, Holtby made 18 saves as the Capitals took Game 4 by a 3–2 score.

Then, after blowing a lead with seven seconds left in regulation and falling in overtime in Game 5, Holtby made 30 saves and was the first star in a 2–1 win in Game 6.

The next day, Holtby became a father for the first time when his fiancée, Brandi, was induced and the couple welcomed Benjamin Hunter Holtby to the world. (Hunter was his mother's maiden name, not a tribute to his head coach, which was a popular theory at the time.) Talk about a busy week!

The unexpected postseason run ended two nights later with a 2–1 defeat in Game 7 at Madison Square Garden. Holtby led Washington to within a game of the Eastern Conference Final and finished the playoffs with a 1.95 goals-against average and .935 save percentage.

"We all realized during those playoffs, 'Holy crap, this is going to be a good goalie for a long time,'" Hendricks said. "And he has been."

71 Washington's First Taste of Pro Hockey

When the NHL granted Washington an expansion franchise on June 9, 1972, there was only a sliver of hockey history in D.C. to fall back on.

The Washington Eagles represented D.C.'s first foray into pro hockey, taking the ice for three seasons from 1939 through 1942 in the Eastern Hockey League.

The Eagles played at Riverside Stadium, an outdoor rink right off the Potomac River, located on the grounds where the Kennedy Center for Performing Arts stands today.

The Eagles showed themselves well during their three-year run, winning the 1940–41 EHL Championship.

Among those who played for the Eagles en route to the NHL was an 18-year-old defenseman named Keith Allen, who began his pro career with the Eagles, skating in 60 games during the 1941–42 season.

After more than a decade toiling in the minor leagues, Allen made a 28-game cameo appearance with the Detroit Red Wings in the mid-1950s. While his NHL playing career was brief, Allen is best remembered for his work as a coach and executive with the Philadelphia Flyers.

Allen was hired as the Flyers' first head coach in 1967 and led Philadelphia to a division title in its inaugural season. He would spend two years behind the Flyers' bench before serving as the club's general manager from 1969 through 1983. It was Allen who constructed the "Broad Street Bullies" rosters that helped Philadelphia win consecutive Stanley Cup championships in 1974 and 1975.

Fifty years after making his pro debut with the Washington
Eagles, Allen was inducted into the Hockey Hall of Fame in the
Builders category in 1992.

The Eagles didn't have much time to churn out too many
future NHLers, though, folding after the 1941–42 season. That
happened to be the first season for the American Hockey League's
Washington Lions, and apparently supporting two professional
hockey teams was asking a bit much of the locals.

The Lions were the primary tenants at the new Uline Ice Arena,
which was built in 1941 just north of Union Station. Miguel L.
"Uncle Mike" Uline built the facility primarily to house the hockey
team, although it would also serve as the region's principal arena
and concert hall up until the Capital Centre opened in Landover
in 1973.

In addition to the Washington Lions, Uline Arena was also
home to the Washington Capitols—a charter member of the
Basketball Association of America (BAA) in 1946 and the National
Basketball Association (NBA) in 1949.

Basketball Hall of Famer Red Auerbach had his first pro coaching gig with the Capitols, leading them to a 115–53 record over three
seasons. Auerbach led the Capitols to the Finals in 1949, when they
eventually fell in six games to the Minneapolis Lakers. The George
Washington University alum then moved to Boston, where he'd
spend 56 years as a Celtics coach, manager, and executive.

As for Uline Arena's pro hockey team, the Lions played the
1941–42 and 1942–43 seasons in the AHL before suspending
operations during World War II. During their initial two-year run,
the Lions served as the Montreal Canadiens' primary minor league
affiliate.

The Lions would resume play in 1947–48 and 1948–49 before
moving to Ohio and becoming the Cincinnati Mohawks.

The Eastern Hockey League also had a strong presence at Uline
Arena, with a club also known as the Washington Lions playing

from 1944 through 1948, when their AHL counterpart suspended operations. After the AHL team left, the EHL returned, sponsoring a franchise for all but one year from 1951 through 1960.

Jack Riley played for the AHL's Lions during the 1947–48 season and was head coach of the EHL's Lions for two seasons starting in 1951. Riley later became the first general manager for the NHL's Pittsburgh Penguins in 1967.

The EHL Lions earned their first league championship in 1955, sweeping the neighboring Baltimore Clippers in four games with Art Dorrington leading the way for Washington.

Dorrington was the first black player to sign an NHL contract when he joined the New York Rangers organization in 1950. He was also the first black player to play professional hockey in the United States, although he never did reach the NHL despite a successful minor league career.

Among the other notable players who briefly suited up for Washington's EHL clubs were Hockey Hall of Famers Al Arbor, Emile "the Cat" Francis, and Eddie Giacomin.

Francis was the opposing head coach when the Capitals made their NHL debut with a 6–3 loss to the New York Rangers on October 9, 1974. Giacomin was the winning goalie.

The Lions became the Washington Presidents in 1957 and capped off the 1957–58 season with another EHL championship. Two years later, the Presidents missed the playoffs in what turned out to be their final season.

Shortly after the 1959–60 campaign, the Presidents moved to Haddonfield, New Jersey, and became the Jersey Larks. It would take 15 years for professional hockey to return to the District in the form of the NHL's Washington Capitals.

Uline Arena sold for $1 million in 1959 and was renamed the Washington Coliseum. On February 11, 1964, the Washington Coliseum hosted its most historic event when the Beatles held their first concert in the United States, just 48 hours after their maiden appearance on the Ed Sullivan Show.

72 Mr. Outdoors

When the 2011 Winter Classic in Pittsburgh was delayed seven hours because of rain, Capitals forward Eric Fehr looked on the bright side.

"I figured the playing conditions weren't going to be great and it might be more of a grinder's game," he said years later. "I thought it could work to my advantage and maybe I could have a big game."

It turned out to be one of the biggest of his NHL career.

The Capitals beat the Penguins 3–1 on January 1, 2011, with Fehr ringing in the New Year with a pair of goals. It was just the second multigoal game of his career, and it came less than two weeks after he sat as a healthy scratch.

Fehr was still the least-utilized Capitals player in the Winter Classic—skating a team-low 9 minutes and 55 seconds—but he made of the most of his ice time and etched his name in outdoor hockey lore.

Fehr scored the go-ahead goal after a Marc-Andre Fleury turnover behind the net in the second period and added an insurance marker on a breakaway in the third.

"It felt unbelievable," he said after playing in front of more than 68,000 fans at Heinz Field. "The first time we came out, the fans were loud and it was just everything you kind of dreamed of. It was a perfect night."

Six years later, Fehr said, it's still the game that Capitals fans ask him about the most. The win was especially memorable for the Capitals, given the stage, the opponent, and all the pomp and circumstance that surrounded the fourth installment of the NHL's outdoor showcase.

While Alex Ovechkin and Sidney Crosby were the faces of both franchises and the stars of HBO's *24/7* series in the weeks leading up to the game, it was a third-line winger from Winkler, Manitoba, who stole the show.

"I think if you asked every player, they had wanted to have the game that Eric had," Brooks Laich told the *Washington Post* in 2014. "They wanted to be synonymous with a Caps win in Pittsburgh in the first outdoor classic for our organization. So he did it first. He was the star."

Fehr was traded to the Winnipeg Jets in July 2011, but returned to Washington for the lockout-shortened 2012–13 season. A two-time 50-goal scorer in the Western Hockey League as a junior, Fehr adapted during his second tenure with the Capitals, embracing his role as a defensive-minded checking centerman.

He still had a knack for scoring big goals, though, and when the NHL announced that the Capitals would host the 2015 Winter Classic from Nationals Park, fans and teammates couldn't help but wonder what Fehr could do for an encore in another outdoor setting.

"He's one of those players that's sort of in the weeds but when he needs to step up and play in big games, he does," said longtime teammate Mike Green two days before the Capitals and Blackhawks played outdoors.

"He's a guy that can all of a sudden step up," Laich said. "It's almost like a home run hitter can step up and just crack one. He's got that game-breaking sort of ability to score."

Even team owner Ted Leonsis was hopeful that Fehr could rekindle that outdoor magic from four years earlier.

"I walked in and saw Eric and said, 'You're our X factor,'" Leonsis said.

Fehr didn't disappoint, opening the scoring on a breakaway just over seven minutes into the first period. Fehr outraced Blackhawks defenseman Brent Seabrook to a loose puck in the neutral zone before beating Corey Crawford with a wrist shot.

John Walton and Ken Sabourin had the call on the Capitals Radio Network:

> **Walton:** The puck is cleared away, off of Seabrook and now it's a race. Here come the Capitals, Eric Fehr moves in, a shot, he scores! Eric Fehr, outdoors, does it again! With 12:59 to go in the first, it's 1–0 Washington at the Winter Classic.
>
> **Sabourin:** Well, who other than Eric Fehr once again? He steals the puck, a bad giveaway by the Blackhawks, and Eric Fehr just puts on the jets and blows by them. He had a clear-cut breakaway from the blue line in, makes a nice move in beating Crawford five-hole. Eric Fehr loves the outdoors.
>
> **Walton:** He was born to play outside, apparently! Two goals in Pittsburgh and he leads off Washington's Winter Classic at Nationals Park by scoring here.

The Capitals beat the Blackhawks 3–2 with Troy Brouwer netting the game-winning goal in the final minute of regulation. But Fehr's contributions didn't go unnoticed, as his third career goal at a Winter Classic gave him the most in league history for games played in the elements.

"The goals feel extra special in the outdoor games," he said, "especially when there's a home crowd like this. They were really into the game and we really wanted to get them a win."

73 **Japan Trip**

NHL history was made in October 1997 when the Vancouver Canucks and Anaheim Mighty Ducks played a pair of regular season games in Tokyo, Japan. The games, which were played months ahead of the 1998 Nagano Olympics, marked the first time in league history that regular season competition was staged outside North America.

A year later, the Calgary Flames and San Jose Sharks played two games in Japan, and the Nashville Predators and Pittsburgh Penguins did the same to begin the 1999–2000 season.

The NHL's trips to Japan in the late 1990s were aggressively marketed and featured some of the league's best players. But they did not represent the NHL's first foray to the Far East.

Back during the 1975–76 season, the NHL reached an agreement with Japanese promoters to have two of its teams compete in a four-game exhibition series in Sapporo and Tokyo. The series was primarily funded by the Coca-Cola Bottling Co. of Japan, with the teams competing for the Coca-Cola Bottlers' Cup.

With the series scheduled for mid-April, the NHL needed two clubs that wouldn't be occupied at the time with the Stanley Cup Playoffs.

Enter the Capitals, who went 11–59–10 in their second season, and their expansion cousins, the Kansas City Scouts, who posted a marginally better 12–56–12 record.

"We were fortunate enough to be invited," said Ron Lalonde. "The NHL organized this series and the first two teams who were officially eliminated from the playoffs were going to be invited. Well, unfortunately for us, we were the first team officially invited and Kansas City soon thereafter was booked as well."

Some hockey pundits at the time thought that the NHL could have rounded up a better group of hockey ambassadors—a touring All-Star team, for example—as opposed to sending the league's cellar dwellers halfway across the world.

"Sending these two clubs on a Japan tour, to build up the image of the NHL, makes as much sense as having the Broad Street Bullies...represent the NHL at a meeting of the Mothers for Clean Hockey Society," wrote Pete Mossey in the *Medicine Hat News*.

The itinerary for the exhibition series called for two games in Sapporo and two games in Tokyo, with sightseeing sprinkled in throughout the week. The players were invited with their wives or girlfriends, and the all-expenses-paid trip included a five-day layover in Hawaii on the way back. All in all, not a bad way to begin the off-season.

"It was a great trip," said Mike Marson. "It was an eye-opener. You go on something like that, it's like leaving planet Earth and going to some other planet. For me, that was my experience. You're looking at all the different new things, it was very advanced. I remember we were on the Ginza Strip, sort of their main street at the time, and they had all these big televisions outside the way most cities now have TVs downtown."

Goaltender Bernie Wolfe concedes more than 40 years later that most players, on both teams, viewed the trip as a vacation with a few hockey games mixed in to work up a sweat.

"They had signs welcoming us," Wolfe recalled. "'WELCOME WASHINGTON CAPITALS—TEAM OF BRAVE MEN AND BEAUTIFUL WOMEN. It was fun for us. We went there to enjoy ourselves."

For Capitals head coach Tom McVie, though, it was business as usual.

"We are going to play as if they were league games," McVie told the *Washington Star* before the series. "I'm not going to throw away everything I've done and begin taking a half-hearted approach to this game. Maybe this sounds absurd. But I want—and I even expect—four victories over there."

To break up the trip even further, the Capitals had a stopover in Los Angeles en route to Japan.

"McVie wanted us to be in shape," Lalonde said. "There had been a little bit of time from the last game [of the season] to the time we went to Japan. So we went out to L.A. and Tommy got practice time at the [Great Western] Forum, so we were practicing. We arrived, we checked into the hotel, and the wives thought it was funny because they're going shopping and we go straight to practice as if the season is still going on. But [McVie] was relentless that way."

The Capitals were scheduled to fly from L.A. to Tokyo with a connecting flight in Hawaii. The connection was delayed, though, due to a tire blowout on the runway. Capitals players made the most of the opportunity.

"We went into the bar and we were all drinking Mai Tais," Wolfe said. "And McVie was pissed. He came in after several hours and we're just drinking. The season was over. What did we care? But he was really annoyed. So, after we finally land in Tokyo, I think it was about a ten-hour flight, he made us go to practice right away. And all the Japanese photographers are hanging over the boards taking pictures of us and guys are going over the boards and puking on their shoes. They were sick. McVie was pissed and he made us skate like you wouldn't believe—like it was training camp. It was tough! I know Yvon [Labre] puked—several guys puked. That was how we introduced ourselves to the Japanese media. It was something."

As for the hockey, the Capitals' extra practices may have been worthwhile, as Washington won the first two games in Sapporo by scores of 5–2 and 6–2. The back-to-back wins were a rare feat for the Capitals, who had not won consecutive games since their maiden preseason.

About 4,500 fans took in each of the first two games in Japan, but the crowds were subdued, according to the game reports that ran in the *Washington Post*.

According to McVie, it was as if "they'd put 5,000 mannequins in the seats."

The series shifted to Tokyo for the next two games, which were played on a makeshift ice rink that was built on top of an Olympic-sized swimming pool.

"I had about four diving boards above my head," said Wolfe, the starting goalie in the first game in Tokyo.

"I remember a big Olympic-sized diving board," Lalonde recalled. "Jack Lynch took a slap shot and someone deflected it from center and it hit the diving board and went out of play. It was different."

The Capitals clinched a series victory with a 6–2 win in Game 3 before a crowd of 9,200 at Yoyogi Stadium. Kansas City took the finale 4–2, ending an unofficial 30-game winless streak that combined the final 27 games of the regular season with the first three games of the exhibition series in Japan.

It also marked the last game the Kansas Scouts ever played, as the two-year-old franchise relocated and became the Colorado Rockies for the start of the 1976–77 season.

When the dust settled, the Capitals won the series three games to one and earned the Coca-Cola Bottlers' Cup. Each Capitals player also received pearls, a geisha doll, and a radio-cassette player for each of the three wins. The Scouts didn't leave empty-handed, though, with each player receiving a watch after they won Game 4.

"Tommy McVie wasn't happy about that last one," Wolfe said. "He wanted to win them all."

In addition to the Coca-Cola Bottlers' Cup, the Capitals may have landed the ultimate prize from their trip to Japan. Although the games had little at stake, McVie and general manager Max

McNabb were impressed with what they saw from Scouts' forward Guy Charron.

Management made it a point to acquire the Scouts leading scorer that summer, and finally on September 1, 1976, with the Scouts in the process of moving to Denver, Charron was traded to Washington.

"The story has been told that there was a decision made through that series from management," Charron said, "as far as potentially acquiring my services through a trade. It came as a surprise to some extent, given all the preparations in Kansas City to move to Colorado. But you try to look at it in a positive way. Tom said they had been looking into acquiring me throughout the summer. So you're wanted by a team and they see something in you that could benefit their organization, and that's how you have to look at it as an athlete. It was still an expansion team, but I looked at it as an opportunity to extend my career and to hopefully contribute in some capacity."

Charron enjoyed a career year in 1976–77, leading the Capitals with 36 goals and 82 points in 80 games. Perhaps buoyed by the Japan trip and the Charron acquisition, the third-year Capitals went 24–42–14, winning more games than their first two seasons combined.

"The whole experience was a treat," Wolfe said. "It was a rallying thing for us, something that we could build on for the next season. McVie took it so seriously—if you're going to play, you want to win."

74 Comeback Kids Go Streaking

Santa Claus must have been working overtime, Jason Chimera said after he was traded from the last-place Columbus Blue Jackets to the first-place Capitals on December 28, 2009.

The Capitals acquired Chimera for captain Chris Clark and defenseman Milan Jurcina—two key figures during the club's post-lockout rebuild.

Within days of the trade, though, Chimera must have felt like the Grinch. He met his new teammates in California, where the Capitals rang in the New Year with consecutive losses in San Jose and Los Angeles. Tack on a home defeat to the Carolina Hurricanes the night the trade was completed, and the Capitals had lost three straight in regulation for the first time all season.

"I come to this great team and as soon as I get here, it was like they forgot how to win," he recalled years later.

But by the start of February, the Capitals were playing like a team that had forgotten how to lose. Beginning on January 5, 2010—the night Alex Ovechkin was picked to replace Clark as team captain—the Capitals went 17–1–0 over an 18-game stretch, highlighted by a franchise-record 14-game winning streak.

During the typical "dog days" of the season in January and February, the Capitals went on a roll the likes of which the franchise had never seen before. By year's end, the 2009–10 Capitals would secure the Presidents' Trophy for the first time in team history with a 54–15–13 record and a team-best 121 points.

"It was one of the best times of my life," Brooks Laich said in 2016. "That group was so special. Just the ability that group had to crack games open—the talent, the way we played was just a lot of fun. The 14-game winning streak was such a special month. It was just a ride. It was a giant wave that we were riding."

The Capitals trailed in eight of the 14 games on the winning streak, which was bookended by a pair of three-goal rallies. The streak began on January 13 when Washington came back from 4–1 down and beat the Florida Panthers 5–4 in a shootout. It culminated in similar fashion with the Capitals overcoming a 4–1 deficit and beating the Pittsburgh Penguins 5–4 in overtime on February 7.

The streak included five wins on the road and nine at Verizon Center, where the 2009–10 Capitals would sell out every regular season home game for the first time in club history.

The Capitals outscored the opposition 67–33 over the course of the 14-game run, including 30–6 in third periods. They graced the cover of *The Hockey News* and were dubbed the "Greatest Show on Ice," thanks to a swagger and an up-tempo style that had them believing that no matter the deficit, they were never really out of any game.

Ovechkin had a hat trick and an assist in the 5–4 overtime win over Pittsburgh as the Capitals earned their 14th consecutive win and improved to 17–1–0 since he was named the 14th captain in team history. Ovechkin delivered 16 goals and 36 points over the 18 games.

The streak ultimately ended against the Canadiens on February 10 despite another valiant comeback attempt.

"We ended up losing in Montreal," said Laich, who recorded his first career NHL hat trick that night. "We were down 5–2 [in the third] only to come back and tie it 5–5 in the last minute and then lose 6–5 in overtime. But that was the resiliency of that team. To this day, it was probably the best team I've ever been on in terms of not caring what the score was. There was a belief the entire time that we were going to find a way to win."

Tomas Plekanec beat Jose Theodore with eight seconds remaining in four-on-four overtime to send Washington to its first defeat in four weeks. It also marked the end to Theodore's team-record 10-game winning streak.

"For a lot of us, it's a once-in-a-lifetime thing," said Bruce Boudreau. "You think it's going to happen again. But those things don't come back again. Give the players a lot of credit for the intestinal fortitude they had to put that thing together."

At the time, only the 1992–93 Pittsburgh Penguins (17 consecutive wins) and the 1981–82 New York Islanders (15) had longer streaks than Washington.

"In the age of the salary cap, there's no easy games to play," Boudreau said. "So I would have to say that 17 games for Pittsburgh might have been a tad easier, or the 15 games for the Islanders in the 1980s was [easier] than what we did in 2010."

In the immediate aftermath of the defeat, forward Tomas Fleischmann may have summed it up best.

"This is 14 times worse than just one loss," he said.

This wouldn't be the last time Plekanec and the Canadiens would hand the 2009–10 Capitals a crushing defeat. When the teams next met, in Game 1 of the Eastern Conference quarterfinals, Plekanec scored the OT winner to give Montreal a 3–2 series-opening win. The Canadiens would eventually upset the top-seeded Capitals in seven games.

75 Fan Favorites Move On

Rod Langway and Olie Kolzig are two of the biggest stars in Capitals history, but neither had the storybook finish he would have liked in Washington.

Langway was in his 11th season as Capitals captain during the 1992–93 campaign when his ice time and responsibility took a significant dip. Passed over on the depth chart, the 35-year-old played sparingly throughout the year, gave up the captaincy in February, and eventually walked out on the team in March. He never played in the NHL again.

"That was a sad day for all of us," said former teammate Alan May. "He came into the dressing room and told us, 'That's it, guys. I'm done.' He took his equipment off, left everything, and said, 'If they don't think I can play and be the top defenseman for key matchups and penalty kill and all of that, then I'm not playing anymore.' That completely changed things. That rocked our world."

Fifteen years later, with the 2007–08 Capitals making a late-season playoff push, the winningest goalie in team history also took a back seat. Soon after the Capitals acquired Cristobal Huet at the 2008 trade deadline, Kolzig was relegated to backup duty as Washington reached the postseason for the first time in five years. After 19 years as part of the Capitals organization, Kolzig signed with the Tampa Bay Lightning that off-season. He was the backup for the final 14 games of his Washington tenure.

"I was very heartbroken that that's how it had to end," Kolzig said in 2017.

No matter how long a star athlete has played for a particular team, there comes a time when the club inevitably moves on. Father Time remains unbeaten, and it sometimes falls on a coach or general manager to inform a veteran that he may no longer be part of the team's long-term plans.

In Langway's case, GM David Poile was the messenger. With younger defensemen such as Al Iafrate, Kevin Hatcher, Calle Johansson, and Sylvain Cote making up the top five and prospects Jason Woolley and Shawn Anderson pushing for ice time, Langway started sitting games out as a healthy scratch. On occasion, he served as an unofficial assistant coach behind the bench.

Langway's on-ice responsibilities may have diminished by his final season, but he remained a respected figure in the room. He trained hard, made rookies and fringe players feel welcome, and regularly looked after his teammates on the road. One of the oddities of Langway's serving as an assistant coach when he didn't play was his not knowing whether he could still hit up the watering holes with the other players.

"This is a sad day for me, and I know it's a sad day for Rod," Poile told the *Washington Post* in October 1992 after Langway was scratched for the first time. "It's not the end, but it's a clear indication that we're starting to prepare for life without Rod on the ice."

Langway briefly left the team that fall to visit friends in Atlanta and to ponder his future. When he returned, he underwent minor surgeries on his knee and shoulder. His body was breaking down, the speed wasn't there, and the end was fast approaching for the two-time Norris Trophy winner.

When he was in the lineup that winter, he only played five to eight minutes a game. Some nights were even spent behind in the bench in a suit and tie. The Capitals didn't know what to do with Langway, the most popular player in franchise history, who still viewed himself as an NHL defenseman.

"It's not easy to retire," Langway told the *Washington Post* in February 1993. "It's not easy for me to sit out a game when I'm not hurt. It's a new role and I've just got to adapt to it."

That proved easier said than done. Although nobody knew it at the time, a Capitals victory over the St. Louis Blues on February 21, 1993, proved to be Langway's final game. There was no scoreboard tribute or elaborate farewell announcement.

He remained with the club for three more weeks, but didn't play. On March 12, Langway decided to move on.

"It took three or four days to make the decision to tell [owner] Abe Pollin that I wanted to walk," Langway said. "You don't do that overnight. It was a big shock to everyone but me. But after the decision, I stuck to it. I didn't second-guess myself. Should I call and go back? I never thought about it."

"When he left, it was almost like your father left," said May, Langway's dressing room stallmate. "You just go home one day and your dad isn't there anymore. So, it was a shock. It was hard to take. The one guy that you can count on isn't there anymore."

The Capitals officially released Langway in the off-season, but no other NHL team signed him. He retired just six games shy of 1,000 for his NHL career.

"I played more than 100 playoff games, [52] more in the WHA, so I'm way over 1000 professional games," he said in 2017. "It doesn't bother me. The only regret is that as a captain I didn't win the Stanley Cup. That's the biggest void in my career. Fortunately, I won one [as a rookie] in Montreal."

While Langway's departure was hardly ceremonious, neither was Kolzig's in 2008.

The Capitals' first-round pick in 1989, Kolzig backstopped Washington to the Stanley Cup Final in 1998, won the Vezina Trophy in 2000, and survived the fire sale of 2004.

"I made it clear to [GM] George [McPhee] that I didn't want to get traded," Kolzig said. "I wanted to be one of those athletes who played his whole career in one city."

Kolzig also wanted to be part of the Capitals' turnaround coming out of the 2005 lockout. But when the rebuilding club was

Rod Langway is the only Capitals player to win the Norris Trophy as the league's top defenseman. Langway earned the award in 1982–83 and 1983–84—his first two seasons in Washington.

finally fighting for a playoff berth in 2008, McPhee acquired Huet from Montreal. Kolzig was 37 and had a league-worst .890 save percentage among qualified goalies when the deal was made for the 32-year-old Huet.

"That was a difficult time," McPhee said in 2017. "Olie was a little bit off his game and he had a hip-labrum issue going on. Huet was available and so we made the move. It's my job as a manager to figure out who's playing well and who isn't and then to address it. So I did. You try to take the emotion out of it, but that was a hard thing to do. But it was done and Cristobal gave us the goaltending we needed."

Huet had an 18-save shutout in his Capitals debut—a 4–0 win over the New Jersey Devils on February 29—and ultimately took over the No. 1 job. At first, head coach Bruce Boudreau tried to establish a rotation with his goalies, but Kolzig started just five of the final 17 regular season games.

"It was tough," said Kolzig, who earned his 300th career win in his third-to-last start. "Not so much in the fact they got Huet—I understood that, I wasn't getting younger and in the last game I started before the deadline we lost to Carolina [6–3]. But I think the thing that upset me the most is that it stubbed the relationship George and I had. I get it—I'm a player, he's management. I just thought that we had the relationship where he would have come to me and told me what he was doing. Just the way things were handled, I wasn't happy with."

The Capitals fell to the Chicago Blackhawks 5–0 on March 19 in what turned out to be Kolzig's 711th and final game in a Washington uniform. Huet started the final seven games of the regular season and went a perfect 7–0–0 over that stretch. Washington secured a playoff berth in the season finale.

According to Kolzig, Boudreau had told him to be ready should Huet falter in their first-round series against Philadelphia.

Kolzig was hopeful he'd get the nod when the Capitals fell behind three games to one, but Huet started the must-win Game 5.

"I just wasn't happy with the way things were handled between Bruce and myself," Kolzig said. "I was told one thing and it never transpired even though the circumstances were playing out that way. I remember Game 6, we're down 2–0 quickly into the game and he didn't even look my way. So, at that point, regardless of how far we went, I knew I wasn't going to see the ice again as a Capital."

The Capitals were eliminated with an overtime loss at home in Game 7. Kolzig never got in the series.

"In hindsight, I should have probably retired after that season, but I didn't want my career to end on that kind of a note. I knew I wasn't going to be back in Washington, so when the opportunity came up [to sign a free-agent deal] in Tampa, I decided to take it."

Kolzig retired after posting a 2–4–1 record in eight appearances with the Lightning in 2008–09.

Despite the disappointing endings for both Langway and Kolzig, their careers rank among the best in franchise history. Langway's No. 5 sweater hangs from the rafters at Verizon Center, and Kolzig's No. 37 could soon join it.

Langway regularly represents the Capitals in the community and at alumni functions, while Kolzig, who rejoined the organization in 2012, has worked as a goaltending coach and as a player development consultant.

76 Brian MacLellan's Long-Awaited Promotion

It wasn't going to be an easy sell to the fan base. Weeks removed from announcing that George McPhee would not return for an 18th season as general manager, the Capitals promoted McPhee's longtime assistant, Brian MacLellan.

Even to the most loyal Capitals fans, MacLellan was hardly a household name. Sure, he had had spent more than a decade with the organization, including seven years as McPhee's top aide, but MacLellan lived and worked out of Minnesota and was one of many in the team's front office hierarchy who handled business behind the scenes.

But if the idea was to bring in a "fresh set of eyes and a new voice," as majority owner Ted Leonsis had previously outlined, handing the keys to the previous GM's right-hand man under-standably raised a few eyebrows.

"I felt that new leadership at this time was needed," Leonsis said at a news conference a month earlier while addressing the dismissals of McPhee and head coach Adam Oates. The Capitals were coming off a forgetful 2013–14 season in which they missed the playoffs for the first time in seven years.

"Let's start with a clean slate," Leonsis said.

But how clean of a slate would MacLellan really provide? Not only had he served as McPhee's assistant for the previous seven seasons, but MacLellan had spent a total of 13 years with the club, first as a scout and later as an executive.

MacLellan and McPhee were also longtime friends. They first played together as teenagers in Ontario with the junior Guelph Platers and were later part of the same class at Bowling Green

University in the early 1980s. Both reached the NHL as undrafted college free agents and were reunited as teammates with the New York Rangers during the 1985–86 season.

MacLellan had the lengthier playing career, suiting up in 606 career games spread over 10 seasons with five teams. He won the Stanley Cup in 1989 with the Calgary Flames.

After graduating from business school in the mid-1990s, MacLellan successfully transitioned into the financial world as a stock analyst. He settled in Minnesota with his wife and two daughters and figured he would make his second living in finance.

But when McPhee called in 2000 to offer MacLellan a part-time scouting position with the Capitals, he took it. A year later, he became a full-time pro scout and put the business career on hold. He eventually became Washington's director of player personnel and oversaw the club's American Hockey League affiliate, the Hershey Bears.

If not for McPhee, it's possible that MacLellan would never have returned to hockey, let alone emerged as one of the game's top executives.

Given that relationship, though, while MacLellan may have had his own values and beliefs, surely some of McPhee's methods had to have rubbed off on him during their time together. McPhee encouraged MacLellan to pursue the position, and MacLellan didn't think their relationship would threaten his chances at landing the job.

"I think I'm a different person," MacLellan said. "A different personality, different experiences, different education, different playing experience. I think all of that stuff forms your attitudes and your philosophies."

At first, though, even Leonsis and team president Dick Patrick wondered whether MacLellan could in fact offer anything different from his predecessor. But as a monthlong interview process was about to commence, the Capitals still had off-season business to tend to, and there was, at the very least, a trust and comfort with MacLellan. Patrick reached out to him with a short-term offer, and a long-term proposal.

"When the decision was made to make a change, I called him up right away and said, 'We'd like you to be the interim GM,'" Patrick said in 2017.

"But I also asked Brian if this is a job he'd like [full-time]. He had a pretty good life at that point, he's living in Minnesota, he can set his own schedule and this would involve moving here, so I asked if he'd like to consider it, and he said yes."

According to Patrick, the monthlong interview process included three categories of candidates: those with prior GM experience, up-and-coming assistant GMs, and a few internal candidates.

Nashville Predators assistant GM Paul Fenton and former Pittsburgh Penguins GM Ray Shero were among those considered for the position in May 2014.

Although MacLellan's original invitation to interview for the job may have been little more than a courtesy to a hard worker who had put in his time with the organization, he approached the exercise seriously. He took advantage of the one edge he had over the other 14 candidates—his inside knowledge of how the Capitals had been run and what needed to change.

"He rose to the top and we felt that he was the best equipped at the time," said Patrick, who has hired just three GMs in his more than 30 years with the club.

"He showed Ted and [me] a more in-depth view or side of him. He was so quiet and when he was working with George. I knew him and had spoken to him, but he hadn't exactly sought me out to have conversations. He sort of kept things to himself. But as part of the interview process, he was expressing his views regarding our strengths and weaknesses and which way we should go. It was very eloquent. He was very determined. There wasn't any waffling—he expressed himself very well. So he eventually became the person who we wanted."

In his first few years as Capitals GM, MacLellan has proved to be candid, openly sharing his off-season shopping lists with the media and explaining in great detail how he envisions certain scenarios playing out.

That openness and honesty was evident to Leonsis and Patrick early in the interview process.

"When Brian had his interview with us, he was very, very straightforward," Leonsis said. "It really wasn't an interview where he was trying to impress us or impress me, it was pretty straightforward. He led off with some of the things that I have to do to be a better owner.

"I like the brutal honesty that he brought. 'Here's what we have to do better as a franchise, and here's what you have to do better as an owner.'"

Among other things, MacLellan told Leonsis to limit his blogging on his personal website—*Ted's Take*—and to focus on the team as a whole rather than on individual accolades whenever he felt inclined to post an entry and communicate with the fans. A team-first culture had to be established from the top down, MacLellan said. That had not always been the case, from what MacLellan had observed. Everyone had to be better, the owner included.

"I didn't think I had anything to lose," MacLellan said at the time. "The important point I was trying to make is I think the team feels there's a disconnect or there's not a unified philosophy from ownership to management to coach."

"I thought that was very brave and very astute," Leonsis said, "because you don't want to hear things like that. I thought that was very, very straightforward and honest and authentic to him."

MacLellan also laid out elaborate plans on how to restructure a roster on the fly. He discussed the need to bolster a decimated blue line via free agency and his desire to develop Evgeny Kuznetsov into a second-line center.

Leonsis and Patrick were open-minded and announced MacLellan's promotion on Memorial Day 2014. They anticipated a skeptical fan base.

"We felt that there might be some blowback from fans and media because it's like, 'Well, what did you change?'" Patrick said. "Frankly, we didn't think we were that badly off that we needed to change everything. We had a down year, a dysfunctional year for a couple of reasons and it was determined that we'd make a change. So we just felt that we'd do whatever we felt was the best decision for the Washington Capitals. A lot of fans didn't think it was enough, and we knew that might happen and that we'd have to live with it, but we were very impressed."

77 Capitals Deal Bondra for Laich

As a teenager in the late 1990s, Brooks Laich often played the EA Sports–produced NHL games on his Sega Genesis. He constructed and customized his rosters and always made sure to include a familiar Capitals All-Star.

"Every single time, I wanted Bondra on my team," he said.

Years later, Capitals general manager George McPhee was configuring his own roster—with slightly more at stake—when the decision was made on February 18, 2004, to trade Bondra to the Ottawa Senators.

The return included the Sega-playing student turned 20-year-old NHL prospect named Brooks Laich and a second-round pick in the 2005 draft.

The Capitals were limping toward a last-place finish for the first time in more than two decades during a forgetful 2003–04 campaign. McPhee had already traded captain Steve Konowalchuk and All-Star Jaromir Jagr, and dealing the 36-year-old Bondra—at the time, the franchise leader in goals and points—was a necessary next step as Washington began to rebuild.

Veterans Sergei Gonchar, Robert Lang, and Mike Grier were also dealt before the 2004 trade deadline, but none had the impact on the Capitals of Bondra.

"He was our Ovi at that time," said goalie Olie Kolzig, teammates with Bondra for parts of 12 seasons in Washington. "Just a guy who could score big goals and carry the team…. Popular among the fans. But it was a really weird year in the organization's history and when he got traded, you knew that times were changing."

More than a decade has passed since the Capitals dealt one of the greatest players in franchise history for a prospect barely two weeks removed from his NHL debut. Bondra and Laich have unique perspectives on the day that forever changed their professional careers.

"It was an emotional time and I remember it came as a really big sock when I talked to George in his office that day," said Bondra, whose 472 goals and 825 points were franchise highs at the time.

"The trade deadline was still a few weeks away, so I was expecting maybe a heads-up from George that this was a possibility—something like, 'There are three or four teams that are interested if you want to make a decision on where you want to go.' But there was nothing like that. I didn't have a clause or detail in my contract like that, but it was a shock."

About 350 miles north of D.C., Laich was making sense of the news in central New York, where had been told to stay off the ice that morning as the Binghamton Senators prepared for an American Hockey League game against Syracuse.

"That was really my first taste that this is a business," said Laich, who 15 days earlier made his NHL debut with Ottawa. "At that stage in your career, you're almost naïve a bit and you pretty much tattoo yourself to the organization. So I was caught off guard, but I flipped the script pretty quick."

The Senators were coming off a trip to the 2003 Eastern Conference Final and had a deep pool of NHL talent. Laich recalls the night before his NHL debut having dinner with veterans Bryan Smolinski, Chris Phillips, and Wade Redden and thinking, "Man, these are established NHLers. These are pros.

"It would have been very tough to crack [as a prospect] and as a young player looking to make the NHL, to have an organization trade for you and say, 'You're going to be part of a rebuild for us and we want you here,' that was music to my ears. I was very excited about that."

In theory, Bondra should likewise have embraced the chance to join the Stanley Cup–contending Senators, but leaving his family in Maryland along with 14 years of memories with the Capitals proved difficult.

In 23 games with Ottawa, Bondra recorded five goals and 14 points. He was then held pointless in seven playoff games as the Senators were eliminated by the rival Toronto Maple Leafs. With a lockout wiping out the entire 2004–05 season and the final year of Bondra's contract, his time with Ottawa is little more than a footnote in his 16-year career.

"I grew up as Capital; I grew up as a person here and this team sort of raised me," said Bondra, Washington's eighth-round pick in the 1990 draft (156th overall) and a nine-time 30-goal scorer.

"They gave me, from the beginning, a lot of help. [Former general manager] David Poile and his staff looked after me from day one. And that's why I was emotional when you're told after 14 years that you have to go play somewhere else. That was tough. I was fortunate to play for such a long time with one team, so that was the hardest part for me."

Bondra eventually played two more NHL seasons with the Atlanta Thrashers and Chicago Blackhawks before retiring in 2007. Bondra returned to Maryland once his playing career was done, and continues to represent the team at alumni functions while serving as a team ambassador in the community.

Laich, meanwhile, would blossom into a key cog during the Capitals' multiyear rebuild and a reliable two-way player on rosters that were often chock full of skilled players who could score.

"As this organization took off with [Alex] Ovechkin, [Nicklas] Backstrom, [Alexander] Semin, and Mike Green," said former Capitals captain Jeff Halpern, "I think Brooksie was the guy in there, that while he may not have had the points that those guys had, he was a guy that this organization needed to help create an identity and to allow those players to do what they did all those years."

Laich lists Halpern, Kolzig, and defenseman Brendan Witt as veterans who welcomed him to the Capitals organization, but it was his first meeting with McPhee in the MCI Center that remains a lasting memory years later.

"George shook my hand and he said, 'Welcome to D.C. We hope you're here for the next 15 years.' And as a 20-year-old, bright-eyed kid looking to make the NHL, it's a moment that stands out in my life that I'll never forget."

Laich didn't quite make it to 15 years in a Capitals sweater, but he came close.

On February 29, 2016, more than a dozen years after he was acquired by the Capitals, Laich was traded to the Toronto Maple

Leafs, along with prospect Connor Carrick, for forward Daniel Winnik.

"I made it 12 [years], and that's longer than most," he said. "I'm very thankful."

Between them, Bondra and Laich combined to play 1,703 regular season games with the Capitals, recording 605 goals and 1,149 points across 25 seasons.

"I just have such an empty feeling that we never got the ultimate goal," Laich said three days after being traded for the second time in his career. "I really, before my time ended in D.C., wanted to [win the Stanley Cup] with Alex. I really wanted to do it with Nicky, and I really wanted to do it with Mike Green, who, unfortunately, wasn't back this year. But those guys meant a lot to me. They really did. Very special people. Very special players, and just tough to not be able to do it with them."

78 The Capitals' Miracle on 33rd Street

Stay-at-home defenseman Shaone Morrisonn scored goals about as often as he celebrated his birthday. On December 23, 2008, he got to do both on the grand stage of Madison Square Garden.

It was all part of a memorable 26th birthday for Morrisonn and one of the most stunning comebacks in Capitals history.

The Capitals were in their usual perch atop the Southeast Division as they prepared to visit the New York Rangers for their final game before the NHL's mandated holiday break. Washington had won seven of its previous nine games, but a win against the Atlantic Division–leading Rangers wouldn't be easy.

In fact, winning at Madison Square Garden was never easy for Alex Ovechkin early in his NHL career. The Capitals were looking to snap a franchise-worst seven-game losing streak at MSG, which included six defeats since Ovechkin's rookie season in 2005–06. Although Ovechkin scored his 100th career goal in New York on October 12, 2007, it was his only goal in those six games.

Making matters worse for this latest encounter, Ovechkin didn't have his usual cast of characters around him.

The Capitals were without injured forwards Chris Clark, Sergei Fedorov, and Alexander Semin, plus four of their regular defensemen—John Erskine, Mike Green, Tom Poti, and Jeff Schultz—forcing the Capitals to dress four blue-liners who had started the year with the AHL's Hershey Bears.

Tyler Sloan was skating in his 22nd career NHL game that night, which was still more than the combined total of fellow call-ups Karl Alzner (playing in his 14th NHL game) and Sean Collins (appearing in his seventh game). Veteran defenseman Bryan Helmer was also up with the big club.

Up front, minor league journeyman Alexandre Giroux was suiting up for his 17th career NHL game, while prospect Andrew Gordon was making his NHL debut.

Predictably, the Rangers pounced on the Capitals early. Markus Naslund opened the scoring 3:38 into the first period before Michal Rozsival doubled New York's lead at 11:04. Eleven seconds later, Ryan Callahan gave the Rangers a 3–0 cushion.

Starting goalie Jose Theodore was pulled after allowing three goals on five shots. An irate head coach Bruce Boudreau berated his team during a timeout, and called on backup Brent Johnson to stop the bleeding.

Johnson stopped all three shots he faced in the final 8:45 of the first period, but that was all he could provide the Capitals on a night in which he was also ailing, dealing with both illness and injury.

So Theodore returned for the second period and just 4:48 into the frame, the Rangers welcomed him back, with Callahan netting his second goal of the night. Callahan broke free past Ovechkin before beating Theodore on a deke.

Not even halfway through the game, the Capitals trailed 4–0 with their top line of Ovechkin, Nicklas Backstrom, and Viktor Kozlov a combined minus-10.

After a 7–1 blowout loss in Philadelphia just three days earlier, the shorthanded Capitals appeared headed down the same road in New York.

"I just said this is not going to happen again," coach Bruce Boudreau told reporters after the game. "We're not going to die. We're going to keep battling and we're going to succeed. Just keep believing. Keep believing. You say those things, you never know they're going to happen, but people that follow us know that we have a penchant for either coming back or, at the very least, making an exciting hockey game."

The rally started with 7:25 remaining in the second period when an Ovechkin centering feed from the left-wing wall deflected off of Rozsival's stick and snuck in past an unsuspecting Henrik Lundqvist. The Capitals were on the board, but still trailed 4–1 heading to the third period.

That's when Washington's power play took over. Just 1:12 into the frame, Rozsival was the culprit again, receiving a two-minute penalty for hooking Sloan.

On the ensuing man advantage, Tomas Fleischmann redirected a shot from Backstrom to narrow the Rangers' lead to 4–2 with 18:19 remaining in the third period.

The turning point of the game may have come just over a minute later. With New York's top line buzzing in the offensive zone, trying to restore the three-goal lead, Theodore made a series of stops on Naslund before robbing Nikolai Zherdev with a spectacular glove save from in close.

"When he came in and he stopped Zherdev, you need defining moments, you need saves at the right time," Boudreau said. "And that was a save at the right time. The guys knew on the bench that we had the opportunity to come back after he made that save."

Minutes later, the Capitals pulled within one, as Kozlov beat Lundqvist with another power play goal. Kozlov received a pass from Backstrom just inside the Rangers' zone before splitting defensemen Dan Girardi and Wade Redden and beating Lundqvist high blocker side.

With 12:56 remaining in the third period, the Capitals trailed 4–3.

It was the third assist of the night for Backstrom, who had turned 21 exactly one month earlier and was wearing the alternate captain's "A" on his sweater for the first time.

Ovechkin then brought the Capitals even, taking advantage of a Nigel Dawes turnover at the Rangers' blue line, breaking in all alone and beating Lundqvist on a deke to tie the score 4–4 with 7:22 remaining.

"[The Rangers] stopped playing hockey," Ovechkin said after the game. "They probably believe 4–0, they win the game. They try to play [conservative]. But we play different way. We played a hard, physical game, take lots of shots, and you see the results. Tonight was very important for our mentality."

The game stayed deadlocked through regulation, setting the stage for the overtime heroics from Morrisonn.

Less than a minute into the four-on-four OT session, veteran Michael Nylander scooped a loose puck below the Capitals' goal line and charged up ice. He gained the Rangers' blue line on the left side and tried throwing the puck on net. It deflected off Girardi's skate but found its way to a wide-open Morrisonn in the high slot.

Morrisonn uncorked a slap shot that beat Lundqvist glove side, giving the Capitals a stunning 5–4 win just 59 seconds into OT. Collins had a secondary assist on the play for his first NHL point.

Steve Kolbe had the call on the Capitals Radio Network: "Nylander drops back and Morrisonn scores! Shaone Morrisonn with his first goal of the season. It's the game winner in overtime at Madison Square and the Capitals erase a 4–0 deficit and they walk away a winner! The final score: the Capitals 5 and the Rangers 4 as the Capitals have pulled off a miracle on 34th Street!"

The Capitals bench emptied as the team piled on the unlikely game-winning goal scorer. It was Morrisonn's first goal in nearly 10 months, dating to the previous season, providing the icing on the cake in the final hours of his birthday.

"The guys have great character in here," Morrisonn said after the game, sporting the red construction hat that was awarded to the team's hardest-working player after wins during the 2008–09 season. "We felt it, we kept coming and pushing, and I saw the puck and I just blasted it through him.

"It came right back to me. It was on edge and I just fired hard and got a break. It was huge."

So was the comeback win, which matched the largest in franchise history.

79 Island Time for the Big Cheese

It wouldn't be a stretch to say that Joel Ward was a model teammate during his four years with the Capitals. Ward was a key cog in Washington from 2011 through 2015, a versatile piece who could play up and down the lineup and on both special teams units.

On the ice, he had a knack for scoring big goals in big games—none more memorable than his Game 7 overtime winner in the Eastern Conference quarterfinals against Boston in 2012.

Away from the rink, teammates were drawn to Ward's laid-back ways and easygoing nature. Passionate about the Baltimore Ravens and Bob Marley and reggae music, Ward was a different cat.

"His demeanor made him a popular guy in the locker room," said defenseman John Carlson. "He could get along with every-body. You could be any type of personality and he'd always be able to play to those strengths. He could be everyone's best friend."

Nicknamed the Big Cheese, which teammates would not confirm or deny had anything to do with flatulence, Ward embraced the handle.

"You know, I'm just a big guy," he would say with a sly smile.

For what it's worth, the Capitals marketing department also embraced the nickname, splashing it across promotional videos and publications.

"Fun guy to be around," said Jay Beagle, who carpooled with Ward to and from Dulles Airport throughout their four seasons together. "I sometimes catch myself missing those car rides or those late-night chats. He could talk about anything, really."

But as well liked and respected as the veteran was among his teammates, Ward wasn't flawless.

"I thought it was funny," defenseman Karl Alzner said, "when-ever Wardo came to a new team, he would warn the coach, 'Hey, just so you know, I'm good for at least one or two sleep-ins every year. I'm sorry, it happens, there's nothing I could do about it. I just love my sleep.'"

"Oh yeah, that was Wardo," Carlson confirmed. "He was always good for one sleep-in a year. Sometimes coming back from the West Coast with the time change, he'd have a tough time getting up. But at least he was open and honest about it."

The Capitals can laugh about it now, but nobody was laugh-ing in November 2011 when Ward overslept and missed a team meeting. Head coach Bruce Boudreau, who was on a mission to establish a culture of accountability to start the 2011–12 season, scratched Ward for the Capitals' next game. Boudreau acknowledged that in previous years, the discretion would likely have been handled with a fine.

Ward sat and apologized, but his affinity for shut-eye would follow throughout his Capitals tenure.

"I don't think I've ever seen a grown man that could sleep as sound as he could," Alzner said. "On the plane, he'd fall asleep right away. He was just a relaxed guy.

"He warned me when I went to the Bahamas on the Olympic break, he told me, 'You'll understand why I am the way I am once you go to the Bahamas. Us island people, we're on island time.' First thing when I got there, I saw people kind of walking around like Wardo and I started to get it. They were in no rush at all, very laid-back. That kind of summed up his personality pretty well."

One day in Dallas, Ward was running late for an entirely different reason. Following a team breakfast at the Omni Hotel, Ward made his way to the washroom. It turned out to be a lengthy stay.

"Hey, did you guys hear?" Troy Brouwer said as he boarded the team bus outside the hotel. "Wardo is stuck in the shitter!"

Stuck in the men's room when the door of his stall wouldn't open, Ward texted Alzner to notify him of the situation and to inquire if he may be able to help.

"Karl came in, but he was no use," Ward said. "We tried everything. We pretty much had the Dallas SWAT team in there at one point."

Carlson soon joined Alzner in the washroom as they tried to come up with a solution. All the while, they tweeted pictures with the hashtag #OperationSaveWardo. Back in Washington, on a Saturday morning, Twitter followers kept tabs on the developing story.

"At one point, it was just a Photoshop gallery, so I'm pretty sure they were laughing at me," Ward said. "Karl kept me company, but we were mostly just listening to toilets flushing."

Finally, after 40 minutes, a maintenance worker came through with a ladder that allowed Ward to climb out of the stall and make the team bus just in time.

"To be honest, I didn't think it would spiral into such a big story," he said. "We were just having fun with it, and then the next thing I know, I have my own mother texting me, asking me what's going on in the bathroom."

80 Unleash the Fury

Years before head coach Scott Brooks was patrolling the sidelines for the NBA's Washington Wizards, the Capitals hired a different Scott Brooks to work at Verizon Center.

The Capitals' Scott Brooks came from the Atlanta Thrashers, where he was part of the team's game operations department and oversaw the in-game entertainment. Among his productions in Atlanta was a rally video that played on the jumbotron during media timeouts in the third period.

The video was designed to energize the crowd and featured recognizable clips from movies such as *Varsity Blues*, *Remember the Titans*, and *Blazing Saddles*. There was also a clip of Tom Green's character in *Road Trip* yelling, "unleash the fury!"

Yes, an early version of the Unleash the Fury video, which has become a staple at Capitals home games during the Rock the Red era, actually came from an old Southeast Division rival.

When Brooks joined the Capitals' game ops department during the 2007–08 season, a modified version of the video was produced in D.C. The Capitals' version included additional clips from *Animal House* and *Hoosiers* and ended with Green's "unleash the fury!" line.

While the original video was popular in Atlanta, the updated version took on a life of its own in Washington.

As the 2007–08 Capitals climbed the standings and clinched an improbable playoff berth on the last day of the season, the Unleash the Fury video grew into a late-game fixture. Fans would scream the line in unison at the end of the video, which immediately led into the playing of Guns N' Roses' "Welcome to the Jungle" as arena PA voice Wes Johnson encouraged the crowd to stay loud.

A decade later, Unleashing the Fury remains as much a part of the game-day fan experience at Verizon Center as wearing red and cheering on Alex Ovechkin.

The video has gone through a few changes over the years, with Capitals highlights and shots of raucous fans now mixed in among the movie clips, but the premise has remained the same—get the crowd on their feet making noise at a potentially key moment in the game.

Perhaps the biggest change to the video came in 2010, when the Capitals' production crew actually met with Green and had him reenact the Unleash the Fury scene while wearing a Washington sweater. The new video debuted on opening night of the 2010–11 season.

"We were playing the New Jersey Devils and the game was actually a blowout," said Mike Wurman, director of game entertainment with Monumental Sports and Entertainment. "Usually, we prefer to play the video in a close game at a critical juncture, but we had been waiting all summer for this, so with the Caps up [7–2], we played it in the third period. Tom Green in a Caps jersey. Some people didn't believe it was him."

Years later, the Capitals went one step further when Green's stand-up tour brought him to Washington during a Capitals homestand. Naturally, the club invited Green to come to Verizon Center for a live rendition of Unleash the Fury on January 14, 2016.

"What a rush being out there and being able to do that live," he said. "I've known about it for years but just haven't been able to get out to a game until now, but it was amazing being up on that jumbotron with the whole stadium going crazy. Pretty incredible. A real unifying moment, unleashing the fury together, as one.

"It's one of those movie lines that people repeat, certainly in D.C. There's something about it. There have always been little things or lines from shows or movies that catch on and that people remember. But this is the only one that's really been taken and used in this fashion and really, it's cool to see how much it's taken off and it's really fun to be a part of it."

81 McVie's Weight Scale and the Capital Mile

Tom McVie was 40 when he was hired as Capitals head coach in December 1975, and although he exercised daily, he still found it troubling that he was in better shape than some of his players.

A noted disciplinarian, McVie introduced the Capitals to two-a-day practices, preached hard work and conditioning, and also implemented a system of random weigh-ins with his players. Each Capitals player was required to meet a specified playing weight, with additional conditioning and financial penalties going to those who didn't.

Veteran Ace Bailey went as far as dehydrating himself and spending hours in the sauna in order to shed a few extra pounds if he anticipated a spot weigh-in.

Bailey and Mike Marson had the most frequent dates with McVie and the weight scale, including an episode that Marson still remembers more than 40 years later.

Late in the 1975–76 season, Marson was sent down to the Baltimore Clippers of the American Hockey League, where bus trips and beer were the norm. Naturally, the second-year pro indulged and put on a few pounds.

To his surprise, Marson was invited to rejoin the Capitals after the regular season, as the Capitals and Kansas City Scouts (two nonplayoff teams) prepared for a series of exhibition games in Japan.

Upon his Washington return, Marson met with McVie and the scale. Marson checked in at 212 pounds. Far too heavy to make the overseas trip, he was told.

"But he counseled me," Marson said, "and he spoke softly and said, 'We're going to L.A. on Thursday,'—this was on a Monday morning—and he said, 'If you're not down to what you're supposed to be,'—I think he wanted me down to 197 or 198—he said, 'you and your bride will be getting back on a plane and flying back to Washington.'

"So I spent those few days doing everything I could. I was chewing gum and spitting. I was taking saunas, riding the bike, and sweating just to lose that water weight. At that stage, it's just water. When we landed in L.A. I remember on the inside I was dizzy like you wouldn't believe. But we get to the scale and he weighed me, and I was down under the weight I was supposed to be. I was down 14 pounds in three days. And he just said, 'Good job, Michael.'"

Marson played for five different head coaches over parts of five seasons with the Capitals. None, he says, compare to McVie.

"Tommy McVie was arguably the best hockey man I ever worked with or trained under or was coached by," Marson said.

"We used to do these skating drills at the end of practice, I remember Tommy saying, 'Okay, you six stay out with me'—usually guys he wanted to lose some weight. And he had a big, booming voice and he'd say, 'Okay, down and back!' And we'd begin the exercise, no pucks, just skate. But he would be doing it right along with us, so when it was his turn he wouldn't say, 'Okay, I've done three or four and that's enough for me.' He would just be right in there with us doing the same laps and same drills. So I was most impressed by the fact that he was a guy that doesn't just talk the talk, but also walks the walk."

Former Kansas City center Guy Charron was acquired just before training camp in September 1976 and was quickly introduced to McVie's Weight Watchers program.

"When I came to camp, he expected me at a certain weight," Charron said. "And because I had just been involved in a big trade, maybe my thinking was that I was going to come in and be someone special. But right away, he puts me on the 'Fat Squad.' And I say to myself, 'Is this for real?' He had me doing some real hard extra work in training camp to lose those extra pounds."

Charron went on to have the best season of his 11-year NHL career, leading the 1976–77 Capitals with 36 goals and a personal-best 82 points. One year later, Charron was named team captain and led the Capitals again with 38 goals and 73 points.

"When Tom left, I remember him inviting me over for dinner," Charron said, "and as a present, he gave me a pair of paints. Size 36. He said that when I'd retire, I'd probably be fitting into those pants. So I kept them all those years and it was great, because I always wanted to make sure that I'd never fit into them. He motivated you a lot of different ways, but I really liked him as a person and a coach."

The same applied to then-prospect Tom Rowe, the Capitals' third-round pick in 1976, who 40 years later became an NHL head coach himself with the Florida Panthers.

"He was a conditioning nut," Rowe said of McVie, "but he taught me a lot about being in shape and making sure that you come to training camp in shape every year. I know my first time that I got called up, I was a typical young guy right out of juniors. I didn't have a clue about pro hockey, the pace that you have to play at, the conditioning that you have to be in, and the mental toughness that you had to have to make it in the NHL. That's what he taught me an awful lot about."

When McVie was hired midway through Washington's second season, he found that every Capitals player had gained at least 10 pounds since the start of the year, with one player having put on 17 pounds.

At the end of the season, following the team's four-game series in Japan, McVie gave his players binders with personalized off-season conditioning programs. While this has become commonplace in the 21st century, it was a fresh practice in the 1970s.

Back then, players often used training camp to work themselves back into game shape. McVie demanded that his players arrive at camp already in top shape. He gave them no choice, implementing the Capital Mile—a one-mile run on the first day of camp that had to be completed within five minutes and 40 seconds.

"If you didn't [train] during the summertime, you didn't look too good that first day," said Ron Lalonde. "The first year, training camp was in Dayton, Ohio, and the track was the parking lot and it was like 80 degrees on a September day with the sun beating down on the asphalt. He had the pylons set up, and that's where we had to run the mile. The next year, we did it in Hershey, where at least we were running around a track. But you'd go to training camp and the next day you're trying to find muscles you didn't know existed because they were barking at you."

Journeyman forward Craig Patrick posted the fastest time in both 1977 (5:05) and 1978 (5:00), winning a $200 cash prize and a reclining chair from a furniture company.

Only 29 of 50 players completed the mile within the time frame in 1977, with additional workouts assigned to those who didn't. A year later, 37 of 53 players completed the mile within the designated time.

"He pushed everybody, and a lot of guys didn't like it at the time," Rowe said. "But he made us all better players and a lot more disciplined than we were before we had turned pro. He was tremendous for all of us, and in a lot of respects, he was ahead of his time. Certainly on the conditioning side."

82 A Mystery Fit for a Net Detective

The timing could not have been better for the Capitals' marketing department. Just as a Canadian comedian named Jim Carrey broke through in the mid-1990s with starring roles in *Ace Ventura, The Mask*, and *Dumb and Dumber*, the Capitals unmasked a Jim Carey of their own.

Carey—with one "R"—emerged as the Capitals' starting goalie as a 20-year-old rookie in 1995. Teammate Randy Burridge nicknamed him "Ace," and Carey soon became known as Washington's *Net Detective*. Although clips from Jim Carrey movies played on the Capital Centre jumbotron during timeouts, the Carey in goal was no joke.

After opening the lockout-shortened 1994–95 season with three wins in 18 games, the Capitals recalled Carey from AHL Portland on March 1. Thirty-one days after making his NHL debut, he was named NHL Player of the Month. Carey remains the only player in NHL history to receive the honor after just one month in the league.

By the end of his first pro season, which he split between Portland and Washington, Carey was named Rookie of the Year and Goaltender of the Year in the AHL and finished as a finalist in both categories in the NHL.

"Has any goalie burst on to the scene, other than maybe Tom Barrasso, and had more of an impact than Jim Carey?" general manager David Poile said in 2017. "He came to us and took off. The guy was a star."

Carey followed his rookie campaign with one of the best goaltending seasons in franchise history. In 1995–96, he set team records with 35 wins and nine shutouts. He also became the first Capitals goalie to win the Vezina Trophy.

"What was so impressive about him is that he literally just stepped in and took off," said former teammate Kelly Miller. "He did so well right from the get-go."

Carey was 21 and the first goalie in NHL history to be a Vezina Trophy finalist in each of his first two seasons. At long last, the Capitals appeared to have found their franchise goalie. Carey won a gold medal with Team USA at the 1996 World Cup that summer and signed a four-year, $11 million contract at Capitals training camp the following fall.

It would be the last contract of his hockey career.

Just as quickly as Carey rose to the top of the NHL, his career came to a skidding halt. By the time he was 25, Carey wasn't even playing in the minors, let alone in the NHL.

"I knew early that Ace wasn't going to be a long-term stay in Washington," said Olie Kolzig, who watched Carey pass him briefly on the organizational depth chart.

"We had conversations and you knew that hockey wasn't the driving force in his life. He was good at it, he was making money at it, but he looked at it as a way to make just enough money to retire."

After going 53–30–12 with 13 shutouts in his first two years in Washington, Carey went 26–35–4 with three shutouts over the final three seasons of his NHL career.

On March 1, 1997, the second anniversary of his first NHL call-up, the Capitals traded Carey to the Boston Bruins along with Jason Alisson and Anson Carter for a trio of veterans in Bill Ranford, Adam Oates, and Rick Tocchet.

The Capitals missed the playoffs for the first time in 15 years that season, but thanks largely to Kolzig's play in goal, Washington reached the Stanley Cup Final for the first time in team history one year later.

Carey was never able to recover from a subpar 1996–97 campaign, which saw him go 17–18–3 with the Capitals and 5–13–0 with Boston.

The next year, Carey appeared in 10 games with the Bruins and in 10 games with their AHL affiliate, where he went 2–7–1 with a 3.97 goals-against average and .878 save percentage.

"Jim bore no resemblance to the goalie who had won the Vezina," former Bruins general manager Harry Sinden told the *Washington Times* in 2000. "He was flopping and diving and guessing. Everything was wrong. That was as big a drop-off as I've ever seen in a player."

Poile wasn't necessarily looking to unload Carey when he completed the six-player trade with Boston in 1997. But he was in the market for veterans and when he inquired about Ranford, Sinden said that Boston would need a goalie in return. Given the choice of Carey or Kolzig, Sinden chose Carey.

"Of course, I went for the younger guy who had won the Vezina," he told the *Washington Times*. "Obviously, that wasn't one of my smarter decisions."

Despite playing for his hometown team in Boston, Carey couldn't reestablish the passion or the drive that had once helped him reach the NHL.

"Some guys are just wound differently," said Kolzig. "I wouldn't say hockey was life or death for me, but obviously it was a passion. But everybody is different."

Miller spent 12 years with the Capitals and can't recall too many examples like Carey.

"When I look at the guys that I played with," Miller said, "you look at a guy like Dale Hunter and one of the reasons probably why he had such a long career is that he's so passionate about the game. You can just tell that he loves to play the game, he loves to be at the rink, and he can't get enough hockey. When I look at Jim, I see a lot of very good skill and obviously a very good goaltender, but I don't know that he had that same passion that it requires to have a long career."

On March 1, 1999, four years after earning his first NHL call-up and two years after being traded to Boston, the Bruins released Carey.

He signed with the St. Louis Blues and went 1–2–1 in his final four games in the NHL.

Carey retired that summer.

"There was definitely something missing in terms of the ultimate passion," Poile said. "Even though he was the best, or could have been the best, it wasn't the focal point of his life. When we traded him, it could have been a huge mistake because you could rekindle that fire. But it just wasn't important to him and his career ended prematurely."

Carey majored in business and health care management and has worked in the health care industry since 2003. He is the president and CEO of OptiMED Billing Solutions and prefers not to discuss his playing career.

"What a goalie," Poile said. "What a talent. The way he started out, he could have been one of the best."

83 See the Capitals Play Outdoors

As the snowflakes fell in Orchard Park, New York, on New Year's Day 2008, Capitals owner Ted Leonsis watched the NHL's inaugural Winter Classic on television and immediately thought ahead.

With a growing fan base in Washington, D.C., a city known for hosting large-scale events, and an established NHL superstar in Alex Ovechkin, why not bring the league's marquee regular season game to the U.S. capital?

"I first emailed the commissioner right as the puck dropped on January 1, 2008," Leonsis recalled. "I was watching the first Winter Classic with my family and I had goosebumps. I thought, 'This is the greatest thing I've ever seen and we want one here in Washington.'"

Over the next several weeks, months, and even years, Leonsis constantly reminded NHL Commissioner Gary Bettman of his desire to bring outdoor hockey to Washington.

"He said, 'If you can come to the nation's capital and reward a fan base that is devoted, passionate, and growing, what better opportunity could you have than to celebrate New Year's Day in Washington, D.C.?'" Bettman said of Leonsis' message. "He pushed a little harder than that, but that's it at 10,000 feet."

The NHL ultimately announced in September 2013 that the Capitals would host the 2015 Winter Classic, later revealing the Chicago Blackhawks as the opponent and Nationals Park as the venue.

"I worked real hard on whatever the league asked me to do," Leonsis said in 2014. "I think it's really important to have all eyes on Washington, D.C. I think we can show the league and show the world that this is a great hockey town."

The Capitals and their fan base didn't disappoint. Four years after defeating the rival Penguins at the Winter Classic in Pittsburgh, the Capitals beat the Blackhawks 3–2 before 42,832 at Nationals Park. It was the largest crowd to attend a hockey game in the District.

On Memorial Day 2017, the NHL announced that the region would host another outdoor game during the 2017–18 season with the Capitals facing the Toronto Maple Leafs from Navy's Marine Corps Memorial Stadium in Annapolis, Maryland.

It will be the Capitals' third outdoor game in eight seasons and the NHL's 24th stadium game since 2008. There's a thought that the novelty of the outdoor games has worn off, but don't trying telling the fans who attend them or the coaches and players who partake. Each outdoor game has a unique feel and can be a celebration of the game for the host market.

"I thought that the Winter Classic that we had at Nationals Park was one of my favorite hockey experiences ever," said Capitals president and minority owner Dick Patrick, who has worked with the team since 1982.

"It was home, it was really mostly our fans because Chicago fans were a bit farther away so they weren't necessarily coming in for it. It was a beautiful day—it was sunny, it was cold, we won the game. I don't know how it could have turned out any better."

Former Blackhawks forward Troy Brouwer scored the game-winning goal for the Capitals with 13 seconds remaining in regulation. Eric Fehr and Alex Ovechkin also scored in the Washington win, while Braden Holtby made 33 saves.

"In the end, it was extremely worth it for the fans and the city," Holtby said. "The way the game ended was storybook. It was a storybook ending. It was a lot of fun to be a part of that. It was a lot of buildup for one regular season game, but it was something that we'll always remember."

As much as the television broadcast may capture the scenic shots that aren't available in a traditional indoor game, there is something to be said for experiencing the outdoor festivities in person. From the throwback uniforms to the décor that fills the stadium to the pomp and circumstance that surrounds the pregame

The Capitals celebrate Troy Brouwer's game-winning goal with 13 seconds remaining at the 2015 Bridgestone NHL Winter Classic. The Capitals beat the Chicago Blackhawks 3–2 before a crowd of 42,832 at Nationals Park.

player introductions, there is just a different feel to an NHL-produced outdoor game.

"There's a lot of emphasis on the little details that make it special and exciting," said defenseman John Carlson. "It's not just plopping a rink in the middle of a field and calling it an outdoor game. There's so much that goes into it."

In 2015, the NHL and the Capitals worked to give the Winter Classic a uniquely Washington feel. As players from both teams made their way to the ice rink, they entered through a model U.S. Capitol Building and skated along a mock Lincoln Memorial Reflecting Pool. Fireworks and F-16 jets flying overhead were also part of the pregame festivities.

"Skating out of the Capital Building at the beginning," said forward Tom Wilson, "I heard [teammate Michael Latta] say behind me, 'This is one of the coolest days of my life.' Just coming out to more than 40,000 fans was so awesome."

"When we came out on the reflecting pond, that was a neat moment," said Brooks Laich. "And then you see the fireworks go off and then the jets fly overhead, it's like, 'Okay, this is showtime.' Really cool experience."

The 2018 Stadium Series game from the U.S. Naval Academy will be the first NHL regular season game played on the campus of a U.S. military service academy. Given the quaint nature of Annapolis, the Capitals' next outdoor game should also provide a unique local flavor with plenty of opportunities to celebrate hockey and the work done by one of the branches of the U.S. military.

84 Capitals Go 3-D

Ron Wilson was a fairly conservative head coach during his five seasons in Washington, but midway through the 2001–02 campaign Wilson overtly went outside the box.

As the Capitals hit the dog days of the season in mid-January, Wilson's bunch had dropped out of a playoff position with just two wins in their previous 10 games. The Capitals also had a growing injury list, with seven regulars out of the lineup, including leading scorers Peter Bondra and Jaromir Jagr.

Washington was so banged-up offensively Wilson felt the only way the Capitals could win was with shrewd defensive play.

So Wilson drew on a strategy he had seen while playing in Switzerland 20 years earlier and dressed 10 forwards and eight defensemen, as opposed to the traditional 12 and six.

Given the players at his disposal, Wilson took it one step further, putting three defensemen on the ice at all times, along with two forwards. It was a highly unusual approach and went against decades of conventional wisdom that called for three forwards and two defensemen at even strength.

The strategy debuted at MCI Center on January 11, 2002, in a home game against the Maple Leafs. Wilson positioned his players in a 2–1–2 formation with two forwards up front, a defenseman in the middle, and two defensemen in back. The two most mobile defensemen, Ken Klee and Sergei Gonchar, rotated in and out of the middle spot, which Wilson referred to as the "rover" position.

Despite Toronto scoring on the opening shift just 21 seconds in, Klee and Gonchar were among the Washington goal scorers as the Capitals rallied for a 3–3 tie.

Wilson kept the alignment in place the next night as the Capitals beat the Florida Panthers 1–0. One game later, the Capitals beat the Boston Bruins 1–0 in overtime. Dainius Zubrus scored 13 seconds into OT with Adam Oates picking up his 1000th career assist.

Olie Kolzig made 55 saves in the back-to-back shutouts, and the Capitals won 1–0 in consecutive games for the first time in team history.

"The shutouts were a reflection of the way they played as much as it was me," said Kolzig, who went on to post a career-high shutout streak of 164 minutes and 24 seconds.

Looking to smother opponents and win every game 1–0 was hardly sustainable, but Wilson was willing to try.

Two nights later, in Montreal, the Capitals played a fourth consecutive game with the 10 forward, eight defenseman alignment, but their luck ran out with a 2–0 loss to the Canadiens.

The 2–1–2 rover system lasted just four games, but the loss in Montreal sent the Capitals on another tailspin as they lost seven of their next eight games.

The Capitals ultimately missed the playoffs that season after having won the Southeast Division in the previous two. Wilson was fired in the off-season, ending his five-year run in Washington with a 192–159–51–8 record. Wilson's 410-game tenure behind the Capitals' bench is the second longest in team history, behind only Bryan Murray (672). He remains the only head coach to lead the Capitals to the Stanley Cup Final.

85 Holtby Pays the Price of Success

It was a hefty parking bill that Braden Holtby didn't mind paying. Recalled from the American Hockey League's Hershey Bears in March 2012, the 22-year-old figured his latest NHL call-up wouldn't last more than a day or two.

Holtby was behind goalies Tomas Vokoun and Michael Neuvirth on the club's depth chart during the 2011–12 season and had only made one NHL start that year—a 5–0 loss to San Jose in mid-February.

But with Vokoun out with a groin injury a month later, Holtby was summoned again. He was told on a Saturday night in Hershey that he'd fly out the next morning to meet the Capitals in Detroit.

"I was basically told, 'See you at the start of the week,'" he said of the message he received from the brass in Hershey. "Basically, just go up there for a couple of days."

With the understanding that he'd soon return to Hershey, the Capitals goaltending prospect packed light—two suits, a shirt, and a pair of jeans. He also left his car in the airport's *short-term* parking lot.

"It was an early flight [to Detroit], so I thought I'd chance it with day-to-day parking at the airport in Harrisburg," he said.

But a funny thing happened once Holtby joined the Capitals. He didn't leave for the rest of the season.

An expected one- or two-day stay turned into a memorable two-month run that essentially served as Holtby's coming-out party in the NHL. Just over a week into his late-season recall, with Washington in a heated playoff race, the Capitals' third-string goalie was suddenly their starter.

Holtby sensed that he might stick around a bit longer, so he went shopping for some new clothes. But at risk of affecting the good karma, he kept his car stationed in the Harrisburg lot.

"It's collecting a pretty big paycheck there right now," he told the Capitals Radio Network after earning a shutout in his third start since the recall. "I don't want to tell somebody to go get it. I don't want to change things up."

Earning an NHL income no doubt eased the cost of the growing parking bill—$25 a day—as did Holtby's play down the stretch. Promoted with 10 games remaining and the Capitals clinging to eighth place in the Eastern Conference, Holtby went 4–1–1 in six appearances as Washington clinched a playoff berth in the penultimate game of the season.

Neuvirth actually started that second-to-last game of the regular season, but left the game with a knee injury in the second period. Injuries were a common theme during Neuvirth's tenure with the Capitals, and his setback in April 2012, combined with Vokoun's groin injury, opened the door for Holtby.

The goaltender who less than a month earlier had been pulled from a minor league game in St. John's, Newfoundland, was Washington's No. 1 option going into the Stanley Cup Playoffs.

Holtby didn't disappoint. He won the regular season finale at Madison Square Garden in New York before leading the No. 7 Capitals to a first-round upset of the defending Stanley Cup champion Boston Bruins. Holtby's performance in the playoffs ranks among the best by a rookie goalie in NHL history.

As Holtby's car sat in the short-term parking lot at the Harrisburg International Airport, the Capitals' long-term starting goalie took flight.

86 20/20/20 Vision

Records are made to be broken, but former Capitals defenseman Sylvain Cote can think of at least one exception.

During the 1992–93 NHL season, Cote was one of three Washington defensemen to top 20 goals. He joined Kevin Hatcher and Al Iafrate. No other team in league history has had three blue-liners score 20 or more goals in a single campaign.

"It was a special year," said Cote, who played parts of nine seasons with the Capitals. "I don't see that record being broken any time soon."

The 1992–93 season was the highest-scoring year in league history, with an average of 7.25 goals per game. A record 21 players scored at least 100 points that season and a league-high 14 players scored at least 50 goals.

To further Cote's point, since the '92–93 Capitals produced three 20-goal scorers from the back end, no team has even produced as many as two defensemen with at least 20 goals in the same season.

In 2016–17, San Jose's Brent Burns was the only defenseman in the entire league to crack 20 goals.

"The game has changed so much," Cote said. "Everyone now is so reliable defensively that you're not going to have scoring numbers like we had."

Hatcher led the '92–93 Capitals with 34 goals, while Iafrate had 25 and Cote chipped in with 21. All established career highs in the process.

Tack on another 14 goals from Calle Johansson, Paul Cavallini, and Shawn Anderson, and Washington blue-liners combined for a league-record 94 goals—a mark that still stands today.

"That's offense where you don't necessarily expect to get it," said goaltender Don Beaupre, "and that in itself is a plus."

Hatcher was Washington's first-round pick (No. 17 overall) in the 1984 draft and made three consecutive All-Star game appearances from 1990 through 1992. He eventually replaced Rod Langway as captain midway through the 1992–93 campaign.

Hatcher's career-best season left him in elite company, as he joined Bobby Orr, Paul Coffey, and Doug Wilson as the only defensemen with at least 34 goals in a season. No blue-liner has reached the mark since, although Capitals alum Mike Green came closest when he finished with 31 goals in 2008–09. Hatcher's 34 tallies also established a record that still stands for most goals by an American defenseman.

"For a big man, Hatcher was very smooth," Cote said. "He was 6'3" and 230 pounds, but he had some of the best hands of any big man I had ever seen play at that height and size."

Hatcher spent 10 of his 16 seasons in the NHL in Washington and he remains the Capitals' all-time leading goal scorer among defensemen, with 149 tallies in 685 games.

Like Hatcher, Iafrate was a Michigan native and a physical presence with a 6'4", 240-pound frame.

"Guys would try to line him up with a hip check," recalled former teammate Alan May, "and Al would hurdle over them and step into a slap shot and goalies were dumbfounded. You couldn't take him down. He was built like an NFL player."

"Big Al was a freak of nature," said Cote, who was primarily paired with Iafrate during the 1992–93 season. "Just a big man and so strong. He worked really hard at it, but he was one of the natural talents. He could skate like the wind and had unbelievable offensive skills."

The Capitals acquired Iafrate in a trade from Toronto in 1991, and the "Wild Thing" quickly became a favorite among the fan base and inside the dressing room.

"He had a presence," Beaupre said. "Such a big, strong, guy and he could shoot the puck. He'd command a lot of respect from the other team. And for me as a goalie, the front of the net, he owned it and not too many guys in the league wanted to challenge him. That's a big deal."

Iafrate had career highs across the board with 25 goals and 66 points in 81 games. He also had six goals in as many games in a first-round loss to the New York Islanders. With three goals in Game 3, Iafrate became the first Capitals defenseman with a post-season hat trick.

Cote's 21-goal output during the regular season came as a mild surprise. Considered one of the best-skating defensemen in the 1990s, Cote enjoyed a 16-year NHL career, but he only scored more than 11 goals twice.

"His skating was perfect," May said. "Al was power, but Cote was so smooth—he probably played in the wrong era because of how good of a skater he was. He always made the simple play and I remember most of his goals being wrist shots. A sneaky wrist shot and he could find openings in the net. He was good then, but teams would be lining up for him today."

While Hatcher, Iafrate, and Cote combined for a record-setting year in 1993, it wouldn't last much longer. Iafrate was the first to go, traded to Boston for Joe Juneau in March 1994, while Hatcher was later sent to Dallas for Mark Tinordi just before the start of the lockout-shortened season in January 1995.

Cote was eventually traded to Toronto in March 1998, three months before the Capitals reached the Stanley Cup Final for the first time. He'd later return for a second stint in Washington from 2000 through 2002 before retiring and settling in the area.

87 Listen to *Hockey Diaries*

For all the media coverage made available to Capitals fans through mainstream outlets and a plethora of well-established blogs, two journalists have set themselves apart both in the content they create and in how they present it.

Beginning with the 2008–09 season, producers Gemma Hooley and Chris Nelson have chronicled the journeys of several Capitals personalities through a series of long-form audio documentaries called *Hockey Diaries*.

The *Hockey Diaries* series uses rich sound, behind-the-scenes access, and terrific storytelling to offer a view into the day-to-day lives of Capitals players and coaches.

Each documentary is based on first-person narratives from two or three people in the Capitals organization who are asked to keep audio diaries from training camp through the playoffs. They are trusted to periodically record themselves and share their thoughts at various points in the season, be they low points or high.

Hooley and Nelson work with the team's media relations department to pick appropriate and willing participants. Ideally, each year they select personalities who may be at different stages of their careers or are likely to have different experiences and thoughts on what it takes to make it in the NHL.

For the first few years of the series, for example, the subjects often included a prospect or a fringe player trying to reach the NHL and an established veteran who could offer perspective on the ebbs and flows of an NHL regular season.

Veteran Mike Knuble and depth defenseman Tyler Sloan were the subjects in 2009–10.

Braden Holtby and goaltending coach Mitch Korn happened to be the two subjects during Holtby's Vezina Trophy winning season in 2015–16. The three-part series, *Hockey Diaries: Alone in Front,* provided unique perspective from the pupil and his teacher.

The documentaries are easy listens, thanks to the amount of work Hooley and Nelson put into the project. Hundreds of hours of audio are recorded throughout a season, with the project produced in the off-season and typically released the following fall.

Not only do players keep their own audio diaries, but Hooley and Nelson also conduct additional sit-down interviews throughout the season, and talk with players and coaches in the dressing room after games and practices. They also work to capture a wide range of stereo sounds that can help set a scene, move a story along, or serve as a transition from one subject to the next.

The series also often includes interviews with family members of the featured personalities, who offer background, insight, and anecdotes only those closest to the subjects would know.

If you're looking for clichés and packaged answers, this isn't the place. But if you're interested in thoughtful breakdowns and analysis, *Hockey Diaries* may be for you. It's a softer tone than you'll find from a typical sports talk radio show—think NPR style—but it works tremendously well for both longtime fans and even novices to the game.

Listeners get to hear the results of a long-term relationship built over time between the producers, the players, and coaches. And the craft of long-form storytelling, combined with unusually rich and textured audio recordings, delivers an in-depth and unique listening experience.

The *Hockey Diaries* series has been featured on NPR, Sirius XM's NHL Radio, and on the Capitals' official team website and the Monumental Sports Network. Archived episodes can be found online at www.monumentalsportsnetwork.com/hockey-diaries.

88 Capitals Host 1982 All-Star Game

Dennis Maruk was the last player introduced at the 1982 NHL All-Star Game, but the crowd's clamoring for the Capitals forward started long before he even stepped onto the ice for pregame warmup.

"Maroooooooook!" the sellout crowd of 18,130 chanted at the Capital Centre on February 9, 1982.

The 1982 All-Star Game remains the only time the Capitals have hosted the NHL's midseason classic, and with Maruk serving as Washington's lone representative, the spotlight shone brightly on the man with a Fu Manchu mustache.

"It was a day and a time that I'll never forget for our fans and for our team," Maruk said nearly 35 years later.

At the time, Maruk was playing in his fourth of five seasons with the Capitals and coming off the first 50-goal campaign in franchise history. He would finish third in the league in 1981–82 with 60 goals, while setting Capitals records that still stand today with 76 assists and 136 points.

As the Capitals lost 14 of their first 15 games that season, Maruk was among the few bright spots. When New York Islanders head coach Al Arbour selected Maruk to his Wales Conference All-Star team on January 27, 1982, Maruk ranked No. 3 in the NHL in overall scoring.

Less than two weeks later, Maruk was rubbing elbows with the likes of Wayne Gretzky, Paul Coffey, Denis Savard, Dino Ciccarelli, and Larry Robinson.

"I was introduced last in front of the home crowd, and it was pretty chilling and pretty exciting," Maruk said in 2016. "I had my parents down pretty much the whole week so I could share it with them. I can say that was kind of my Stanley Cup—that All-Star Game."

Back then, the All-Star Game was hardly the spectacle that it has become in the 21ˢᵗ century, but that didn't keep the NHL from coordinating a few special events. Among the highlights was a White House luncheon with President Ronald Reagan and Vice President George H.W. Bush.

"I understand Washington has been trying to trade for Gretzky," Reagan said in his address to the players. "When I asked what we could possibly give Edmonton for such a great player, they said, 'Two first-round draft choices and the state of Texas.'"

NHL President John Ziegler presented Reagan with an All-Star jersey with the No. 1 on the back, while Reagan suggested that the game was a benefit to relations between the United States and Canada.

"It's a day that I'll never forget," Gretzky told the *New York Times*. "I sat at a table with the President, Gordie Howe, Phil Esposito, Bob Hope, John Ziegler, [Speaker of the House] Tip O'Neill, and Canada's Ambassador to the U.S., and I did what Gordie advised me. He said that God had given him two ears and only one mouth for a reason, so I just sat there and I listened."

Maruk can still remember the tight security—"you couldn't go too many places"—but adds that all of the players were appreciative of the opportunity to shake hands one by one with President Reagan, First Lady Nancy Reagan, and many of their top aides.

Of the 40 All-Star Game participants, only Buffalo Sabres defenseman Mike Ramsey had previously met President Reagan. Ramsey was a member of Team USA's Miracle on Ice team in 1980 and was invited to the White House shortly after the Lake Placid Winter Games.

A black-tie All-Star Game benefit dinner was held the night before the game at the Washington Hilton, where Emile "the Cat" Francis received the Lester Patrick Award. Tickets for the event sold for $150, with proceeds benefitting the Juvenile Diabetes Foundation. The featured entertainers included Bob Hope, Rich Little, and Gloria Loring. The All-Star Game itself was played on a Tuesday evening in Landover, with tickets ranging from $10.00 up to $17.50.

The Wales Conference beat the Campbell Conference 4–2 with Islanders forward Mike Bossy scoring twice, including the game-winning goal, en route to being named Most Valuable Player.

Maruk picked up an assist on a goal from Boston Bruins defenseman Raymond Bourque and finished the game with memories to last a lifetime.

"The All-Star Game was an honor," said Maruk, who previously represented the Cleveland Barrons in the 1978 midseason showcase.

"I had one earlier in '78, but that time in Washington was probably my highest highlight playing in the National Hockey League besides scoring my first goal and making it to the NHL.

"We had other guys who could have played in that game— Ryan Walter and Mike Gartner—but I have to say that being the lone Capital and being able to represent the team was a real honor that I'll never forget."

89 Capitals All-Star Game Highlights

Hosting the 34th annual NHL All-Star Game in 1982 ranks among the most memorable All-Star moments for the Capitals organization, but there have been other highlights throughout the years as well. Below is a look at some of the other notable moments in Capitals All-Star Game history:

January 21, 1975: Denis Dupere Is First Player to Represent Capitals at All-Star Game

Aided by the fact that all 18 teams were guaranteed at least one representative at the All-Star Game, Denis Dupere of the expansion Washington Capitals earned his only All-Star Game invitation during the 1974–75 season.

The Capitals, who would finish a league-worst 8–67–5 during their first year, selected Dupere from the Toronto Maple Leafs in the 1974 expansion draft. Dupere quickly became part of Capitals history by scoring twice in the club's first-ever win—a 4–3 victory over the Chicago Black Hawks on October 17, 1974.

Dupere would later become the first Capital to earn a point in an All-Star Game when he assisted on the eventual game-winning goal as the Wales Conference beat the Campbell Conference 7–1 at the Montreal Forum.

Less than three weeks later, the Capitals traded Dupere to the St. Louis Blues for Garnet "Ace" Bailey and Stan Gilbertson.

February 12, 1985: A Club-Record Four Capitals Represent the Wales Conference

For the first time in franchise history, the Capitals had multiple players selected to the All-Star Game as the NHL's best gathered in Calgary in February 1985.

The Capitals led the Wales Conference with four players on the All-Star roster—forwards Bobby Carpenter and Mike Gartner and defensemen Rod Langway and Scott Stevens. Carpenter, Langway, and Stevens were all named to the Wales Conference starting lineup by the Professional Hockey Writers Association.

The Wales Conference beat the Campbell Conference 6–4, with Gartner becoming the first Capital to score a goal in an NHL All-Star Game.

The four players representing the Capitals in a single All-Star Game remain the most in club history.

February 5, 1993: Al Iafrate Sets Record with 105.2 MPH Slap Shot

Capitals defenseman Al Iafrate impressed the Montreal Forum crowd at the 1993 Super Skills Competition, firing a 105.2 mph cannon to win the Hardest Shot event.

Iafrate's record stood for 16 years before Boston Bruins defenseman Zdeno Chara hit 105.4 mph at the 2009 Super Skills Competition.

One day after Iafrate's performance, his Capitals teammate Peter Bondra made his NHL All-Star Game debut. Bondra would go on to appear in a then team-record five All-Star games, winning the Fastest Skater event in 1997 and 1999.

In 1993, Bondra had a goal and an assist as the Wales Conference beat the Campbell Conference 16–6. Former Capitals forward Mike Gartner was named the game's MVP after tying an All-Star Game record with four goals.

February 1, 2003: Caps Rookie Brian Sutherby Named YoungStars Game MVP

The Capitals' first-round pick from the 2000 NHL entry draft, Brian Sutherby, was named MVP of the 2003 NHL YoungStars Game in Sunrise, Florida.

Sutherby scored twice, including the game-winning goal, and had an assist as the YoungStars East beat the YoungStars West 8–3.

The YoungStars Game featured rookies and top prospects and was played from 2002 through 2009 as part of All-Star Game festivities.

January 24, 2009: Alex Ovechkin Wows Bell Centre Crowd

Alex Ovechkin has never shied away from the spotlight, and one of the game's most exciting players stole the show at the Mecca of hockey in Montreal.

Ovechkin brought some swagger to the Super Skills Breakaway Challenge, loading up on props before heading to the net with not one, but two hockey sticks. Among Ovechkin's additional accessories was an oversized pair of sunglasses, a safari hat, and a Canadian flag.

One day later, Ovechkin had a goal, two assists, and the shootout-deciding tally as the Eastern Conference beat the Western Conference 12–11 before an All-Star Game–record crowd of 21,273 at the Bell Centre.

January 25, 2015: Alex Ovechkin Taken Third to Last in Fantasy Draft; Still Wins Car

Back when the NHL turned to a Fantasy Draft to determine All-Star rosters, the final pick in the draft received both ribbing from fellow NHLers and a new set of wheels in the form of a Honda Accord.

With this in mind, Ovechkin made headlines at the 2015 All-Star Draft, begging captains Nick Foligno and Jonathan Toews to pick him last. "I want to be last. I need a car," Ovechkin said on the live broadcast.

Ultimately, Ovechkin was picked third to last by Team Foligno and finished with three assists in a 17–12 loss to Team Toews.

But the story didn't end there. In the hours and days following the Friday-night draft, it was revealed that Ovechkin wanted to win the car so that it could be donated to the Washington Ice Dogs, a hockey team for children with special needs. When word reached the NHL and the folks at Honda, arrangements were made and the vehicle was in fact donated to the American Special Hockey Association.

90 Hunter's Cheap Shot

In his 19-year NHL career, Dale Hunter skated in 35 playoff series for the Nordiques, Capitals, and Avalanche.

The 1993 Patrick Division Semifinal series between the Capitals and New York Islanders was among his best. Hunter scored seven goals in six games. It was the highest-scoring series of his career.

But 25 years later, it's merely a footnote in a series that is best remembered for an ugly cheap shot.

"It was a real down time in our history," former general manager David Poile said in 2017.

With the Capitals facing elimination in Game 6 at Nassau Coliseum in Uniondale, New York's Pierre Turgeon picked off a Hunter clearing attempt, beat Don Beaupre, and gave the Islanders a 5–1 third-period lead.

As Turgeon celebrated, Hunter slammed him into the boards with a vicious elbow to the head. A line-brawl ensued while the Islanders' medical staff tended to Turgeon.

"All hell broke loose," recalled Capitals president Dick Patrick, who watched the game with Poile in a suite.

The Capitals knew their season was winding down. Their first three defeats in the series all came in overtime, including two in double OT. Game 6 was a blowout.

"The frustration was building," said former Capitals forward Alan May. "You're already upset about the series, then they score and then you see at the top of the circles, way after the play was over, Dale absolutely crumbles him. And you're thinking, 'Oh, no! Oh geez, we didn't need that.'"

Hunter was ejected. Turgeon suffered a concussion and a separated shoulder.

"Dale played for keeps and that's what he did when he hit Turgeon," Beaupre said. "His motto was, 'You've got to get on the score sheet somehow.' Maybe it's not a goal or an assist, but you've to let them know that you played. Well, he didn't let anyone forget that game."

As the final minutes of Game 6 ticked off the clock and Washington's management team prepared to head downstairs, first-year NHL Commissioner Gary Bettman barged into their suite.

"He told us that he wanted to see Dale in his office in New York the next day," Patrick said. "And he starts talking to us and using all these medical terms—and this is after he had been sitting with the Islanders owners during the game. I thought it was the wrong time to come into our suite."

The Islanders held on for a 5–3 win and the Capitals were bounced in the first round for the second consecutive spring.

All-Star Dale

Although Bettman issued Hunter's 21-game suspension in 1993, he threw him an olive branch four years later. Back then, the Commissioner added two players of his choice to the All-Star Game after the original rosters were announced. In 1997, Bettman chose veterans Hunter and Dale Hawerchuk.

The usually stoic Hunter choked up when he later spoke to reporters.

"I don't know what to say," Hunter said after learning of the news in a meeting with Poile. "Give me a few minutes."

Hunter was in his 17th NHL season, but had never been selected to the All-Star Game. Bettman had the power to change that.

"When the suspension ended, the matter was over," Bettman said at the time. "His career was viewed in its totality, and that makes him an All-Star this year."

May remembers a chaotic postgame scene outside the Capitals' dressing room. Head coach Terry Murray refused to speak to reporters. Hunter tried his best to explain his actions.

"I didn't hit him dirty," he said at the time. "I went after him to finish the check."

Hunter claimed to have not heard the whistle.

"It was not a good thing what he did," May said in 2017, "but he should have never been made available to the media. They were throwing him to the wolves with the press. It was a bad move by him, but it should have been a 'no comment' type of thing."

The Capitals flew home that night while Hunter and Poile stayed over in New York and met Bettman the next day. Bettman had been on the job for less than three months. This was the first act of discipline the new sheriff would be handing down.

"Obviously, he wanted or felt that he needed to set a tone," Poile said.

Hunter received a 21-game suspension without pay. At the time, it was the longest suspension for an on-ice incident in NHL history. Hunter was barred from being around the team during the suspension. This meant that he could not practice or skate with his teammates for the first two months of the 1993–94 season.

"It was a very severe penalty that took the wind out of our sails for both Hunter and our team," Poile said. "It took us a little bit of time to recover. Terrible way to end the year."

"The punishment was way too extreme," Patrick said. "Turgeon did miss the next series, but they won and he was back playing after that in the third round. It was the harshest penalty I had ever heard of. They took him out of the picture completely, and I thought it was way too much."

Patrick is not only still bitter over the severity of the suspension, but also in how it was handled.

"I heard later that Gary had spoken to at least one other general manager to get a gauge on how many games Dale should be suspended," he said. "I didn't like that either."

Without Turgeon, the Islanders still pulled off one of the NHL's biggest upsets when they beat the two-time defending Stanley Cup champion Penguins in seven games in Round 2. Turgeon returned for the Wales Conference Final, but the Islanders' magic ran out with a five-game defeat to Montreal.

Without their leader, the Capitals lost their first six games the following season. They climbed back to a respectable 10–11–0 by the end of Hunter's suspension, but two games into his return, he suffered a knee injury.

After playing all 84 games in 1992–93 and recording 20 goals and 79 points, Hunter played just 52 games in 1993–94 and was limited to nine goals and 38 points. Although Hunter continued to play with an edge and intensity to his game, he was never the same player after the suspension.

"Dale was one of my favorite Caps of all time," Patrick said. "What he did was wrong, he deserved a punishment, but the punishment, I thought, was out of line."

91 Fedorov Joins Capitals in 2008

Hockey Hall of Famer Sergei Fedorov may be best remembered for his 13 seasons with the Detroit Red Wings, but don't try telling members of the 2008–09 Capitals.

Although Fedorov spent parts of just two seasons with the Capitals to cap off his 18-year NHL career, the impact he left in Washington was lasting.

"He had a presence, a legendary status around him all the time," said Karl Alzner, a rookie defenseman during the 2008–09 season. "He's one of the guys that everybody looked up to and wanted to be like."

Even when it came to fashion sense, Alzner can remember the elder statesman Fedorov becoming the trendsetter on a Capitals team chock full of young pros.

"Everybody looked up to him," Alzner said. "I remember, he was one of the first guys that had the little Ugg boot cutoff slipper things. And when you first see those, you think, 'Okay, those don't belong at the rink.' But he wore them to the rink all the time. He wore them and legitimately five or six guys had them within the next few weeks. It was just, whatever Sergei did was cool. He was 'the guy,' so if it was okay for him, it was okay for everybody. That was just what everyone thought of him. He was a legend."

When Fedorov arrived in Washington in 2008, he gave the once-rebuilding Capitals instant credibility. Alex Ovechkin was already on his way to winning his first career Hart Trophy as NHL MVP that season, and as the trade deadline approached, the Capitals were in a playoff race.

"Our plan all along had been that when this team is ready to win, we'll spend money and we'll add players," general manager George McPhee said in 2017. "And the players had demonstrated in that season that they were ready to win. So we went for it at the deadline."

McPhee made three significant moves at the 2008 deadline, acquiring goaltender Cristobal Huet as well as forwards Fedorov and Matt Cooke.

The feeling around the Capitals was that, although they were making a second-half push under first-year head coach Bruce Boudreau, something was missing from a roster that was oozing with raw talent and youthful exuberance.

Enter Fedorov, the three-time Stanley Cup champion and wily veteran acquired from the Columbus Blue Jackets for prospect Theo Ruth. While Ruth never reached the NHL, Fedorov came to D.C. with more than 1,300 regular season and playoff games combined.

"I thought it was quite a statement to make to our players, our team, our marketplace, and to the league that we thought that we were good enough to make the playoffs and do something special in the playoffs," McPhee said.

Fedorov was 38 and immediately became a mentor to a core group of Capitals that included Ovechkin, Nicklas Backstrom, Mike Green, Brooks Laich, and Alexander Semin—all 24 and under.

"We needed that," recalled Backstrom, a 20-year-old rookie when Fedorov joined the club. "We needed that experience. That was maybe the one thing that we were missing those years. You need those players that have been through it too.

"When a guy like him walks into the dressing room, that's a guy you really listen to. He's been in a good organization for many years with the Red Wings and you have a lot of respect for him. We were young and a lot of the guys were listening to him. He came with a lot of pointers for everyone. He was really important for us that year."

The Capitals went 15–4–0 after the trade deadline, highlighted by a seven-game winning streak to end the regular season. The Capitals needed every one of those seven wins down the stretch, clinching a playoff berth with a 3–1 triumph over the Florida Panthers in the regular season finale. Fedorov had the game-winning goal and an assist as the Capitals ended a five-year playoff drought.

"He was almost like a dad," said Ovechkin, 16 years Fedorov's junior. "Bruce [Boudreau] didn't have experience in the playoffs as well and so [Fedorov] kind of was a player and a coach at the same time. He obviously gave us the right thoughts with what we had to do on the ice."

The Capitals returned to the postseason one year later, capturing a second consecutive Southeast Division title during the 2008–09 season. This time, the playoff run did not end in the first round, thanks largely to a 39-year-old Fedorov. In what turned out to be the final goal of his NHL career, Fedorov beat Rangers goalie Henrik Lundqvist with just under five minutes remaining in Game 7 of the Eastern Conference quarterfinals at Verizon Center. His 52nd career playoff goal stood as the eventual series clincher. The Capitals held on for a 2–1 win in Game 7, and completed a comeback from a 3–1 series deficit to advance to the second round for the first time in 11 years.

"His poise was something that I hadn't seen before," said Laich. "His poise in the hockey game with momentum swings and how he handled the game, he was always calm. I always said about Sergei, he could show up for the team plane a half hour late and still walk on with a smile and brushing his hair back and look as happy as ever. He was just so calm, he never seemed to get rattled or shaken—just very poised."

Fedorov retired from the NHL in the summer of 2009, returning to Russia where he played the final three years of his professional career in the Kontinental Hockey League. Still, the impact he made in Washington goes beyond the 13 goals and 46 points he collected in 70 regular season games spread over parts of two seasons.

"Sergei came in and gave us terrific play his first season and then the next full season," McPhee said. "We added a few other pieces but Sergei was the big one. He was a guy that a lot of the guys on that team had looked up to growing up. Some of them had his poster up on their walls in their bedrooms. But he lived up to everything that they had thought of him as a player and as a person."

92 The Loch Ness Monster Arrives

Not long after Sergei Fedorov played his last game with the Capitals in May 2009, general manager George McPhee signed veteran free agent Brendan Morrison to fill the void as the club's second-line center.

And so began a multiyear revolving door at a critical position within Washington's lineup. With Nicklas Backstrom locked in as the No. 1 center, the Capitals tried in vain to find a complementary piece that could form a reliable 1-2 punch down the middle.

Morrison was serviceable, but toward the end of his first and only season in Washington, the Capitals acquired center Eric Belanger at the 2010 trade deadline.

After a disappointing first-round exit at the hands of Montreal that spring, neither Morrison or Belanger returned. In the following years, the Capitals tried in-house options Tomas Fleischmann, Marcus Johansson, Brooks Laich, and Mathieu Perreault, but none proved to be a long-term fit at the position.

The 2011 trade deadline brought another second-line center in the form of Jason Arnott, but he too was a short-term rental. Mike Ribeiro was acquired in 2012 and lasted just one lockout-shortened season, while Mikhail Grabovski also spent one year in Washington after signing as a free agent in 2013.

All the while, Backstrom and Alex Ovechkin played out some of the prime years of their NHL careers without a consistent No. 2 pivot on the roster.

As the Pittsburgh Penguins (Sidney Crosby and Evgeni Malkin), Boston Bruins (Patrice Bergeron and David Krejci), and Los Angeles Kings (Anze Kopitar and Jeff Carter) all won the

Stanley Cup with formidable centerman tandems, the search continued in Washington.

If the mission to find that second-line center seemed like an exercise in patience, so was the Capitals' wait for one of their top prospects to make his NHL debut.

Back in June 2010, the Capitals used their first-round selection (26th overall) on a Russian forward named Evgeny Kuznetsov. He was one of the highest-rated prospects in the draft, ranked No. 3 among European skaters by Central Scouting. Teams shied away from Kuznetsov, though, unsure when, or if, he would come to North America.

At the time, Kuznetsov was playing for his hometown team, Traktor Chelyabinsk of Russia's Kontinental Hockey League, but his move to the United States was further delayed in 2012 when he signed a two-year deal to remain in Europe.

Along the way, Kuznetsov was named MVP at the 2012 World Junior Championships, developed into a two-time KHL All-Star, and represented Russia at the 2014 Sochi Games. He was widely considered the best professional prospect not in the NHL and remained part of the Capitals' long-term plans.

"You have to weigh that risk with the reward," McPhee said. "When it got to that pick, we said, 'We've got to take that guy. He's that good.' We might not see him for a couple of years—didn't expect it to be four."

Kuznetsov finally came to Washington in March 2014 and signed an entry-level NHL deal after five seasons in the KHL.

"It's kind of like seeing the Loch Ness Monster," McPhee said of the then-21-year-old. "We've heard of you, but we haven't seen you. I found it hard to believe he was standing there after all this."

Kuznetsov had a brief 17-game taste of the NHL late in the 2013–14 campaign before becoming a full-fledged NHLer the following season. It was during his official rookie season that first-year

Capitals head coach Barry Trotz moved Kuznetsov to the middle. By year's end, the Capitals, at long last, had their No. 2 center.

"He's very cerebral," Trotz said. "He's one of those guys who knows what's happening on the ice not only from his position but from everyone else's perspective too. He's one of those top players that has the ability to process things quickly—you only have to tell him something once and he gets it—and with that ability he's had a good start to hopefully a great career here."

Goaltender Braden Holtby has also admired Kuznetsov's smarts.

"He's got an absolutely amazing hockey IQ," Holtby said. "He's an intelligent guy, very good set of skills, skatingwise, puck-handling wise, and he's got great vision, but also very good in all three zones. He can be a top-10 player in this league."

As a teenager in Russia, years before he reached the NHL, Kuznetsov often skated in the off-season with former Capitals winger Alexander Semin. Kuznetsov did not have a television growing up, but he watched NHL highlights on YouTube and studied the ways of his countrymen, most notably Alexei Kovalev and Pavel Datsyuk.

Since turning pro, Kuznetsov has also developed a conditioning program with Datsyuk, the former Detroit Red Wings center and three-time winner of the Selke Trophy as the NHL's best defensive forward.

"Kuzy's his own player," said T.J. Oshie. "There's not a guy, I don't think, that he really plays like. He kind of has his own style. You don't want to put expectations on guys or put guys up on pedestals or things like that, but he's got a very promising future, I think, and [is] a guy that I think one day you can build your franchise around."

Kuznetsov quickly became a favorite in the Capitals' dressing room, where his light-hearted ways made him a popular teammate.

It's not uncommon for Kuznetsov to recruit his teammates in the players' lounge to watch his favorite show, *Family Feud*.

"We watch the show before the game, always after morning skate," he told NHL Network in 2015. "I don't watch a lot of American TV, but this show I really like."

He also developed an unlikely friendship with his locker room stallmate Brooks Orpik, the veteran American stay-at-home defenseman. Their families grew close too as Orpik helped Kuznetsov acclimate to life in North America during his first full season in Washington.

"I think it's really important to make younger guys, whether they're European or North American, feel comfortable off the ice," Orpik said, "because if they don't feel comfortable off the ice, they'll never feel comfortable on the ice."

Kuznetsov gave Orpik, 10 years his senior, the nickname "Batya," a good-natured Russian term for a father figure, similar to "Pops."

In 2015, teammates Tom Wilson and Michael Latta gave Kuznetsov the nickname "Harry Potter" (which Kuznetsov had stitched into one of his suits), comparing the Russian's use of his hockey stick to a magician and his magic wand.

Perhaps his biggest trick was erasing the Capitals' long-standing search for a second-line center and providing Washington with stability down the middle.

93 Baltimore's Bid for the NHL

Before the NHL doubled in size with the addition of six teams in 1967, the league considered 13 expansion applicants, representing eight cities.

Washington was not among the markets in the running for an NHL franchise, but just up I-95, Baltimore was an early favorite.

"San Francisco and Baltimore are both dealing from strength since each city has only one applicant," Toronto Maple Leafs president Stafford Smythe told *The Globe and Mail* in February 1966.

"The Baltimore people particularly are the sort we like for partners."

Baltimore's expansion bid was led by sports industry moguls Zanvyl Krieger and Jake Embry—a tandem who owned 90 percent of the American Hockey League's Baltimore Clippers. Krieger was also a shareholder in Major League Baseball's Baltimore Orioles and had previously invested in the NFL's Baltimore Colts.

At the time Baltimore was also home to the NBA's Bullets, who were owned by Abe Pollin.

"Baltimore is big-league in other sports," Krieger said, "and we think it should be in hockey, too."

Days before the NHL's Board of Governors made their decision in February 1966, Embry had no doubts.

"I can't see how they can resist our bid," he said.

Despite the optimism, Baltimore's application fell short, mostly because of shortcomings at its proposed home, the Baltimore Civic Center.

Although the Civic Center had just opened in 1962, the home of the AHL's Clippers did not meet the NHL's standards.

When league president Clarence Campbell visited the arena for a site inspection, he was turned off by a permanent stage at one of the ends that limited seating to just three sides of the building for a hockey game.

"Who designed this place—Frank Lloyd Wrong?" he asked.

Ultimately, on February 9, 1966, the NHL granted expansion franchises to Los Angeles, Minneapolis–St. Paul, Philadelphia, Pittsburgh, San Francisco–Oakland, and St. Louis. The expansion to St. Louis seemed odd at the time, given that the league never received a formal bid from the city.

The move was done as a favor to Chicago Black Hawks co-owner Jim Norris, who owned the St. Louis Arena and was looking to either sell the building or find a permanent tenant.

Baltimore was on standby if an ownership group couldn't be found in St. Louis or if any of the five other expansion clubs skidded before the start of the 1967–68 season. All went according to plan, though, and Baltimore missed out on arguably its best chance to land an NHL franchise.

Charm City flirted with NHL expansion again in 1970 and 1972, but the league expanded instead to Buffalo, Vancouver, Long Island, and Atlanta.

When the Washington Capitals joined the NHL for the 1974–75 season and began play in the new Capital Centre in Landover, Maryland, any talk of the NHL coming to Baltimore was put to rest.

Despite the lack of an NHL team in Baltimore, the Civic Center housed the AHL's Baltimore Clippers from 1962 through 1976, the Baltimore Skipjacks from 1982 through 1993, and the Baltimore Bandits from 1995 through 1997.

The Skipjacks served as the Capitals' top minor league affiliate from 1988 through 1993, and in the early 1990s, both teams practiced at the Piney Orchard Ice Arena in Odenton, Maryland.

"Sometimes we'd call a player up or send a player down," said Capitals president Dick Patrick, "and all he'd have to do was cross the hallway. The Caps had one dressing room and the Skipjacks had theirs across the hall."

Olie Kolzig, Byron Dafoe, and Keith Jones were among the future Capitals to cut their professional teeth in Baltimore. Barry Trotz also had his first professional coaching job in Baltimore and longtime sports broadcaster Kenny Albert was the Skipjacks' play-by-play voice right out of college.

Minor league hockey left the area for good the late 1990s, although the Capitals played a pair of preseason games in Baltimore in 2011 and 2013.

The games were marketed as the Baltimore Hockey Classic, but poor ice conditions were a common theme in both exhibitions and the second game only drew an announced crowd of 7,634.

94 The Dueling Hat Tricks

As much as Alex Ovechkin and Sidney Crosby try to downplay their individual rivalry, there is no denying that their battles make terrific theatre.

Few of their meetings are as memorable as Game 2 of the 2009 Eastern Conference semifinals. Ovechkin was 23 and Crosby 22. Each was in his fourth NHL season, and the 2009 series marked the first time they were meeting in the Stanley Cup Playoffs.

For all of the headlines Ovechkin and Crosby made since breaking into the NHL on October 5, 2005, the hype reached frantic levels in May 2009.

Somehow, the series—and the play of the superstars—exceeded expectations.

The Capitals won Game 1 at Verizon Center, with Ovechkin and Crosby both scoring in the series opener.

Two nights later, the Capitals won again 4–3 in a game that is best remembered for Ovechkin and Crosby scoring three goals each. It marked the fourth time in NHL history, and the first time in 13 years, that a player from each team recorded a hat trick in the same playoff game.

"It's good for the fans to see great players play against each other and two great teams play against each other," Ovechkin said after the game. "It's unbelievable when we play against great players and you win the game like this. If I was a Capitals fan, I'd be really happy right now."

Game 2 had a real back-and-forth feel to it, with Crosby opening the scoring in the first period and Ovechkin answering early in the second.

Crosby scored again midway through the second to give Pittsburgh a 2–1 lead, but once more the Capitals came back. With 4:11 remaining in the second period, Washington's David Steckel beat Marc-Andre Fleury to tie the score at two. Steckel was the only player other than Ovechkin and Crosby to score in Game 2.

As tension built in a tie game in the third period, Ovechkin broke through with two goals in the final eight minutes. First, Ovechkin scored a power play goal on a one-timer from the left faceoff circle with 7:07 remaining. Ovechkin's second goal of the game gave the Capitals their first lead of the night. On his next shift, just 2:29 later Ovechkin wired a wrist shot through a screen and past Fleury to secure his first career postseason hat trick.

The capacity crowd of 18,277 at Verizon Center erupted, with several fans showering the ice with their own hats. When the ice crew appeared to have cleared all of the hats off the playing surface, a second wave of hats poured down, further delaying the resumption of the game. Crosby wasn't amused, and asked the officials if they could move things along.

"People kept throwing hats," Crosby said. "And I was just asking if they could make an announcement to ask them to stop."

When play finally resumed, Crosby went to work and completed his own hat trick in the final minute of the third period. That pulled Pittsburgh within one, but the Capitals were able to hang on for the one-goal win to take a 2–0 series lead.

It was also Washington's team-record fifth consecutive win the playoffs, dating back to its first-round series against the Rangers.

"Sick game," said Ovechkin, who celebrated each of his third-period goals by jumping into the glass. "Sick three goals by me and Crosby. It's unbelievable to see how fans react, how fans go crazy. The atmosphere right now, it's unbelievable in town."

The NHL's brightest young stars were delivering on the game's biggest stage.

"That's why Crosby and Ovechkin are who they are," said Capitals head coach Bruce Boudreau. "Not too many people can do what they did tonight.

Hat Tricks by Opposing Players (Same Game) in Stanley Cup Playoffs

May 4, 2009	**Alex Ovechkin, WSH (3)** and Sidney Crosby, PIT (3) WSH 4, PIT 3
April 25, 1996	Joe Sakic, COL (3) and Trevor Linden, VAN (3) COL 5, VAN 4 (OT)
April 26, 1993	**Al Iafrate, WSH (3)** and Ray Ferarro, NYI (4) WSH 6, NYI 4
April 14, 1983	Mark Messier, EDM (4) and Paul Reinhart, CGY (3) EDM 6, CGY 3

"It's great for our sport. When you build up hype about super-stars playing against each other, and then the superstars play like superstars, it's a neat thing."

Ovechkin had a game-high 12 shots on goal and four hits, and was tops among forwards with 23:32 worth of ice time. Crosby's three goals came on five shots on goal and he led all Pittsburgh forwards with 22:26 of ice time.

"It's a battle of the two best players in the league, and tonight both of them carried their teams," said Washington defenseman Mike Green. "We were fortunate we had Alex at the top of his game, and then had some guys like [Steckel] and these guys that are fourth-line guys pitch in, and that's all it takes to win."

Added Crosby: "It was nice to score but it's better to win. I'm sure it's entertaining for people to watch, if I were to look at it from a fan's point of view. As a player, you don't like when a guy on the other team gets a hat trick. That's usually not a good sign."

Although the Capitals had a 2–0 series lead, the Penguins would rally to win the series in seven games. Ovechkin had eight goals and 14 points in the series; Crosby eight goals and 13 points. Game 7 was the only blowout—the Penguins won 6–2 before a stunned crowd in D.C.—with the dueling hat tricks from Game 2 remaining a lasting memory.

"There are nights you never forget when you cover sports," *Hockey Night in Canada*'s Elliotte Friedman wrote on CBC.ca after Game 2. "This was one of them…. On Monday night in Washington, Sidney Crosby and Alexander Ovechkin pushed one another to the highest of levels, raising their games to places only the best can reach. Maybe it wasn't a Game 7. Maybe it wasn't the Stanley Cup final. But it was something special, something spectacular, something we can only hope to see again."

95 Five Alive for Gusty and Bonzai

Although it may seem like Alex Ovechkin owns just about every Capitals scoring record, there are a few exceptions. Washington's single-game goal-scoring mark is among them.

That franchise record is shared by Bengt Gustafsson and Peter Bondra—the only two Capitals players to score as many as five times in a game.

Through his first 12 NHL seasons, Ovechkin has maxed out at four goals on three occasions.

Gustafsson became the first Washington player to score five goals in a game on January 8, 1984. Head coach Bryan Murray decided to put his top three scorers on the same line ahead of that night's game in Philadelphia, and the decision paid off immediately.

The Capitals beat the Flyers 7–1 before a sellout crowd of 17,191 at the Spectrum. Washington's newly configured top line of Gustafsson, Dave Christian, and Mike Gartner combined for six goals and 11 points.

"It was just one of those nights when everything goes in," Gustafsson told reporters after the game. "Just close your eyes and keep your stick on the ice. That's how I felt. I didn't have to do much. It was like five empty nets."

Gustafsson was particularly efficient, scoring five times while taking five shots on goal. He beat fellow Swede Pelle Lindbergh for all five tallies.

Nearly two years earlier, Swedish forward Willy Lindstrom scored five goals for the Winnipeg Jets in a win in Philadelphia. Christian remembered that game from his time with the Jets and encouraged Gustafsson to try to do the same.

"After the second period, Dave told me, 'You have to get five too,'" Gustafsson said. "It's easy to say. I didn't expect to do it."

Gustafsson's five-goal game in Philadelphia is still fondly remembered by his former teammates.

"I marvel at his five-goal game," Craig Laughlin said in 2017. "That was unreal. We were all joking at the end of the game asking if he could keep that going. And he said, 'No, not really. I'm good for the next month now.' I remember that quote like it was yesterday. And he was right. I really don't think he scored for the next three weeks! But he was a wizard with the puck and what a teammate."

The win over the Flyers began a 16–1–1 stretch for the 1983–84 Capitals, which included a then–team record 10-game winning streak. Gustafsson finished with career highs across the board that year with 32 goals and 75 points.

Nearly a decade later, Bondra matched Gustafsson's mark on February 5, 1994, at USAir Arena in Landover. The Capitals beat the Tampa Bay Lightning 6–3 with Bondra scoring five goals, including four in the first period.

Not unlike when Murray shuffled his lines ahead of Gustafsson's five-goal outburst, Bondra's five-goal game came soon after head coach Jim Schoenfeld tweaked his forward trios.

Schoenfeld had just replaced Terry Murray two weeks earlier, and among his initial changes was partnering Bondra with Dale Hunter and Dmitri Kristich. On the night Bondra scored five goals, Hunter and Kristich had three assists each.

"Dale is a great player," Bondra told the *Washington Post* after the game. "He is everywhere and he will find you. He makes great passes, and if you're in trouble and someone hits you, he'll be there to help you out. Dima [Kristich] made great passes all night."

Two days shy of his 26th birthday, Bondra set multiple Washington records. His first three goals of the night came in a span of 2:06, which remains the fastest hat trick in team history.

He had four goals within 4:16, which also set a team record for the fastest four goals by one player.

"I was thinking for a long time about scoring a lot of goals while I was a growing up," Bondra said. "I scored five. That's unbelievable in the NHL."

With just three goals in his previous 18 games, Bondra was battling a rare prolonged slump before exploding for five goals against Tampa Bay.

"We've been on him about changing his stick," Schoenfeld said after the game. "So I asked him if he got that stick changed and he said, 'No, I brought a new pair of hands.' Not only was it great hands, but heart, determination, and great speed. That's as fine a performance as I've seen."

Bondra finished the 1993–94 season with 24 goals and 43 points in 69 games, but led the NHL in goal scoring one year later. Bondra had a league-best 34 goals in 47 games in the lockout-shortened 1994–95 campaign. He also led the NHL in scoring with 52 goals in 76 games in 1997–98.

96 Esa Tikkanen's Game 2 Miss

It took 24 years for the Capitals to reach the Stanley Cup Finals, but just eight days for the dream to come to a crashing halt.

Soon after Joe Juneau's overtime winner in Game 6 against the Buffalo Sabres secured Washington's first Eastern Conference title, the 1997–98 Capitals met their match in the form of the defending Stanley Cup champion Detroit Red Wings.

The Red Wings, who had seven future Hall of Famers on their roster plus the game's winningest head coach behind the bench in

Scotty Bowman, swept the Capitals in four games and hoisted the Stanley Cup at the MCI Center on June 16, 1998.

While the Red Wings were heavily favored, members of that Capitals team still wonder what could have been.

"It was a team that when I look back, I still believe that we should have won," said Brian Bellows.

"Guys came together, we went on a roll, and we were just wining. Then you get to the final and everyone is telling you how great it is, how fantastic it is, and it's easy to forget that you still have to go out and play that series and win."

Detroit took Game 1 at Joe Louis Arena 2–1, with Washington rookie Richard Zednik emerging as the answer to a trivia question after scoring the club's first goal in the Stanley Cup Final.

Two nights later, the Capitals carried a 4–2 lead into the third period and were well positioned to even the series at a game apiece. It had been 42 years since a team overcame a two-goal, third-period deficit in the finals.

Detroit's Martin Lapointe would cut the Capitals' lead in half with 11:52 remaining in the third, but the game, and potentially the series, truly turned two minutes later.

That's when Capitals forward Tikkanen broke into the Detroit zone, faked a shot, and beat a sprawling Red Wings goalie Chris Osgood, who was caught out of position. The only problem was that Tikkanen couldn't finish the play. The five-time Stanley Cup champion pushed the puck wide right of what was, at that point, a gaping open net.

"We were all standing on the bench and saw the open net and were about to explode," defenseman Mark Tinordi told reporters after the game. "But then he missed it."

"Yeah, I had an open net like three, four seconds, and I just missed the net," Tikkanen said. "The puck rolled off my stick, but that happens in the playoffs."

Tikkanen's miss set the stage for Detroit's Doug Brown to tie the score late in the third period and send Game 2 to overtime.

Former Capitals captain Bill Clement was working the ESPN broadcast that night.

"Should the Washington Capitals not win this game and the Detroit Red Wings go on to win the Stanley Cup," Clement said, "that miss could be the defining moment and the turning point of this entire series."

Head coach Ron Wilson recalled in 2017 having a similar thought behind the Capitals bench.

"That would have salted that game away and maybe would have changed the outcome of the series," Wilson said.

"We were playing really well in Game 2, and we [ended] up getting swept four straight. I couldn't believe that he missed it. He faked the goalie out, had an empty net, and he pulled the shot. It was unbelievable. I remember that very clearly. I remember thinking to myself right then when he missed the shot that that could be the turning point of the whole series. Turns out, I was right."

Instead of taking a 5–3 lead midway through the third period, the Capitals ultimately fell 5–4 in OT with Detroit's Kris Draper scoring the game-winning goal.

"That's a game you lose sleep over," Tinordi said.

Six periods later, the Red Wings were Stanley Cup champions. They beat the Capitals 2–1 in Game 3 for their third straight one-goal win in the series, before completing the sweep with a 4–1 win in Game 4.

"I think that we had a team that was good enough to do it," Bellows said. "But I really believe that when Tikkanen deked out the goalie in Game 2 and missed the empty net, it was almost like a sign of bad luck. After that it just seemed like we were half a goal short."

One year later, the defending Eastern Conference champions didn't even make the playoffs.

"It doesn't really sink until a handful of years later when you realize, 'Man, how hard is it get to the Finals, much less win the Stanley Cup?'" said Olie Kolzig.

"We went in the next year and we thought for sure that at the very least, we'd be a threat in the conference and try to make a run for it again. I don't know if we just had that emotional hangover because you realize, 'Man, we went all that way and we ended up like the 25 other teams.' The only thing is that we went a little longer, but ultimately, we didn't win it. It was a tough feeling."

97 Visit the Capitals' Hat Trick Display

Capitals fans have long embraced one of hockey's greatest traditions by tossing their hats onto the ice when one of their players scores three goals in a game.

This inevitably causes a momentary delay with the sounds of Run DMC's "Tricky" filling the air and the Capitals' ice crew coming out with barrels and buckets to collect the hats that reached ice level.

For years, fans wondered what ever became of those hats. Were they thrown in the garbage? Were they donated to charity? Could they possibly be retrieved by the original owner?

Dating back to 2008, the answer is none of the above. Beginning with the 2008–09 season, the Capitals sent all of the hats they collected from hat trick games to their practice facility in Arlington, Virginia, where they were kept in storage.

Six years later, with the Capitals celebrating their 40th anniversary during the 2014–15 campaign, the club unveiled a hat trick display on the main concourse level at Verizon Center. The exhibit has remained outside section 111, where the piles of hats amassed since 2008 are neatly divided into display cases and labeled with the players' names, opponents, and dates.

The exhibit also includes a large plaque that lists every hat trick in franchise history. For fans walking the concourse before games or during intermissions, it provides a nice look at some memorable individual performances.

20 Significant Hat Tricks in Capitals History

March 30, 1975: Ron Lalonde became the first player in team history to record a hat trick when he beat Detroit Red Wings goalie Terry Richardson three times at the Capital Centre.

"That's a milestone I'm very proud of," Lalonde said in 2016. "It's one [Alex] Ovechkin can't break—the first Washington hat trick. It was Easter Sunday, an afternoon game in Washington. We got out to a 5–2 lead. I scored two goals on one shift in the second period, but unfortunately, we ended up losing the game 8–5, which took some of the luster off that achievement. But I look back on it now and it's a point of pride for me that I scored the Washington Capitals' first hat trick. It only lasted a week—Stan Gilbertson scored four in the final game against Pittsburgh the next week. So I didn't have long as the only hat trick, but it still was the first one."

April 6, 1975: The Capitals finished their forgettable expansion season with an 8–4 win over the Pittsburgh Penguins in Landover. Midseason acquisition Stan Gilbertson became the first player in team history to score four goals in a game.

December 1, 1979: Rookie Mike Gartner netted his first career hat trick in a 7–2 win over the Quebec Nordiques.

April 5, 1981: Dennis Maruk became the first 50-goal scorer in Capitals history, thanks to a hat trick in the 1980–81 regular season finale. The Capitals beat the Red Wings 7–2 at Capital Centre as Maruk finished the year with an even 50 goals.

November 21, 1981: Maruk and Tim Tookey had three goals each in a 10–4 win over the Philadelphia Flyers. It remains the only double hat trick in team history.

February 24, 1983: The first hat trick in Alan Haworth's NHL career came in a 4–2 win over the Calgary Flames as the Capitals clinched the first playoff berth in team history.

January 8, 1984: Bengt Gustafsson became the first player in franchise history to score five goals in a game as the Capitals beat the Flyers 7–1 at the Spectrum in Philadelphia.

March 18, 1989: Less than two weeks after he was acquired from the Minnesota North Stars, Dino Ciccarelli scored four times against future teammate Mike Liut in an 8–2 win over the Hartford Whalers.

November 28, 1991: Rookie Peter Bondra recorded the first of his franchise-best 19 hat tricks in a 6–3 win over the New York Rangers at Madison Square Garden.

January 13, 1993: Kevin Hatcher became the first Capitals defenseman to net a hat trick when he beat Rangers goalie John Vanbiesbrouck three times in a 5–4 loss in New York. Hatcher finished the 1992–93 season with 34 goals, still the most by a defenseman in team history.

February 5, 1994: Bondra became the second Capitals player to score five goals in a game (and the first to do so at home) as the Capitals beat the Tampa Bay Lightning 6–3 in Landover.

October 8, 1997: Adam Oates had three goals and five points in a 6–3 win over the New York Islanders as he earned the 1000th point of his NHL career.

January 11, 2003: Jaromir Jagr had three goals and seven points as the Capitals beat the Florida Panthers 12–2 at MCI Center. It was the first of two hat tricks for Jagr during his Capitals tenure.

January 13, 2006: Alex Ovechkin scored all three goals, including the overtime game winner, as the Capitals beat the Anaheim Mighty Ducks 3–2 at Honda Center. It was Ovechkin's first career NHL hat trick.

December 29, 2007: Ovechkin notched the first four-goal game of his career in an 8–6 win over the Ottawa Senators on *Hockey Night in Canada*.

March 3, 2008: Ovechkin scored three goals in the first period to secure the second 50-goal season of his career as the Capitals went on to beat the Boston Bruins 10–2.

February 11, 2010: Following hat tricks from Ovechkin (February 7, 2010) and Brooks Laich (February 10, 2010), Alexander Semin scored three goals in a 6–5 loss in Ottawa. It marked the first time in team history that the Capitals had a hat trick in three consecutive games.

October 1, 2013: Mikhail Grabovski scored three goals in his Capitals debut and became the first Washington player with a hat trick on opening night. The Capitals fell 6–4 in Chicago, though, as the Blackhawks raised their 2012–13 Stanley Cup banner to the rafters at United Center.

December 13, 2014: Nicklas Backstrom recorded the first regular season hat trick of his career in a 4–2 win over the Tampa Bay Lightning at Verizon Center. Backstrom had previously scored three goals in Game 2 of the 2010 Eastern Conference quarterfinals against the Montreal Canadiens.

April 9, 2016: Ovechkin scored three goals in the penultimate game of the season to secure his seventh career 50-goal season. The Capitals beat the St. Louis Blues 4–3 as Braden Holtby matched the NHL's single-season record with his 48th win of the year.

98 20 Minutes of Fame

Capitals fans may not remember goaltender Corey Hirsch, but Hirsch will never forget his time in Washington. The journeyman goalie played for 17 professional teams in six different leagues over parts of 14 seasons. His stint with the Capitals was the briefest, but it remains his most memorable.

Hirsch was 28 when he signed a minor league deal with the Capitals in October 2000 before spending much of the 2000–01 season with their American Hockey League affiliate, the Portland Pirates.

Both Washington general manager George McPhee and Portland head coach Glen Hanlon had previously worked with Hirsch with the Vancouver Canucks.

Hirsch was recruited by the Capitals primarily to shore up their minor league goaltending. An opportunity to play in Washington seemed like a long shot, with reigning Vezina Trophy winner Olie Kolzig handling the bulk of the workload and veteran Craig Billington in his second season as the backup.

But when a hand injury sidelined Billington in early March, Hirsch was called up. For the first four games of his recall, Hirsch watched every minute from the bench. Kolzig and the Capitals won all four.

That was the backdrop as the Capitals prepared to host the Eastern Conference–leading Ottawa Senators at MCI Center on March 11, 2001. Washington was 13–1–1–1 in its previous 16 games, but the demanding schedule was starting to catch up with Kolzig, who was making his 15th consecutive start and his 27th over a 28-game stretch.

The Senators pounced, building a 5–2 lead through two periods with Kolzig allowing five goals on 26 shots. Hirsch, who had not appeared in an NHL game in 750 days, was summoned for the third period in what could only be described as mop-up duty on an otherwise lost evening.

"I thought, we're down 5–2 anyways," Hirsch recalled in 2017. "I thought we were going to lose, too. I just figured it was 20 minutes of practice. I wanted to get back into the NHL, that was the goal. But at that point, at that moment in the game, we were down by so many goals, my attitude was just to hold down the fort, don't embarrass myself, and try not to get scored on.

"But I remember, when Olie got pulled there and I go in for the third period, the players looked at me and they were probably scared shitless. I mean, really. Up until that point, the guys didn't know what to expect out of me because I had never really played for the Capitals. I was really an unknown kind of player. And then they throw me in there against one of the best teams in the NHL."

But minutes into his Capitals debut, Hirsch got everyone's attention with a glove save on Ottawa leading scorer Alexei Yashin to keep Washington within three. It also set the stage for one of more memorable comebacks in team history.

"That's probably what lit a fire under them in the third period," Hirsch said. "I make a glove save on Yashin, a really good save, and then from that point on it just kind of turned. The whole tide turned. They started scoring and it was like, 'Holy crap, we can actually win this thing.'"

Center Andrei Nikolishin provided the first glimpse of what was in store, beating Ottawa goaltender Patrick Lalime with about 14 minutes remaining. The rally was on, with the Capitals down 5–3.

Rookie Trent Whitfield pulled Washington within one with 6:41 left in the third period, before Sergei Gonchar tied the game at five with a slap shot from the slot with five minutes remaining.

"I really wasn't planning on that kind of comeback," head coach Ron Wilson told reporters after the game. "We're down 5–2, we get Olie out of there to give him a break. All we asked the team between periods was to work on a couple of things that have crept into our game."

Steve Konowalchuk completed the comeback with 1:28 left, netting his 20th goal of the season to secure a 6–5 Washington win.

"It just snowballed," Hirsch said. "We scored, I made a save, then we scored again and again, and then to come back and actually win the game, I remember thinking afterwards, 'Holy shit, did that just happen?' It's still one of the most wild games I've ever been a part of. I think for the guys, pulling Olie was a big kick in the ass. He was Olie Kolzig and if you let down Olie, you better pick your game up. That was the message that was sent—that they had let Olie down for those two periods. That was just the spark that they needed. And then they're probably looking at me thinking, 'Jesus Christ, we better start playing or we're going to lose 10–2.'"

While the Capitals exploded for four unanswered goals over the final 15 minutes, Hirsch was perfect, stopping all eight shots he faced in the third period.

"I'm walking around afterwards, just trying to be cool around the guys when really in my head I'm thinking, 'Holy shit, how'd that happen?' I knew that I hadn't played an NHL game in two years, so it was a special moment for me. For most of the guys it's just another game out of 82, but for me, it's something I'll never forget."

The celebration was brief for Hirsch, who was reassigned to AHL Portland two days later and never played for the Capitals again. Due to the brevity of his stay in Washington, Hirsch is the only goalie in franchise history who can claim a perfect stat line—a 1–0–0 record with a 0.00 goals-against average and a 1.000 save percentage.

Hirsch returned to the NHL two seasons later, finishing with a loss and a no decision in a two-game stint with the Dallas Stars. He retired from the NHL with a 34–45–14 record, with the comeback win in Washington serving as a memorable final victory.

"I would have loved to have played 1,000 games or to have been Marty Brodeur, but my path was different," Hirsch said. "But when I think back to that night [in Washington], that might have been the craziest game I was ever a part of. And that was, over the course of my life, one of the biggest moments in the National Hockey League that I had, so I'll never forget it."

99 The Chimeracle on 34ᵗʰ Street

Bruce Boudreau insists that he was set up for a can't-win situation. As the 2010–11 Capitals prepared for Game 4 of their Eastern Conference quarterfinal series against the New York Rangers, Boudreau made his weekly appearance on a classic rock station in Washington, D.C.

"They asked me which city had the better fans, or which was the better building," Boudreau recalled in 2017. "Well, what the hell was I supposed to say? I said the D.C. fans are by far the best."

That's not all Boudreau told the *Kirk and Mike Show* on 105.9 The Edge:

"Its reputation is far better than the actual building," he said of Madison Square Garden during the segment.

"I mean, it's nothing. The locker rooms are horrible. The benches are horrible. There's no room for anything. But the reputation of being in Madison Square Garden is what makes it famous.

Also, our building is a lot louder, too. So, I mean, they can say what they want, but it's not that loud there."

Suggesting that New York fans aren't especially loud probably wasn't in Boudreau's best interest. Thanks to the power of social media and an extra day off between Games 3 and 4, Boudreau's comments provided plenty of fodder for the Rangers' fan base.

Midway through Game 4, with the Rangers leading 3–0, they let Boudreau know.

"CAN YOU HEAR US?" they chanted at the Capitals head coach. "CAN YOU HEAR US?"

"I remember it was back and forth, 'Can you hear us? Boudreau sucks! Can you hear us? Boudreau sucks!'" he said. "I felt like [former Islanders defenseman] Denis Potvin."

Boudreau can laugh about it now, but with the top-seeded Capitals in danger of blowing a 2–0 series lead and returning to D.C. tied at two games apiece, the mood was tense on the Washington bench.

The Rangers were a perfect 29–0–0 when leading after two periods during the regular season. In Game 4, they led 3–0 at the second intermission and New York had 1:22 of power play time to begin the third period, thanks to an Alexander Semin boarding penalty late in the second. Had the Rangers converted with the man advantage and gone up 4–0, it probably would have been game over.

Instead, 85 seconds after the Capitals successfully killed the minor, Semin put the Capitals on the board with 17:13 left in the third. And just 55 seconds after that, rookie Marcus Johansson scored his first career playoff goal to cut the Rangers' lead to 3–2.

"We told them never to give up," Boudreau said. "You get one and you never know. When we got both goals quickly, we believed we were in it. I never knew. All I did was hope, but I tried to contain my excitement. I just wanted to be on an even keel, and the players, they felt there was a potential comeback in the making."

Johansson scored again with 7:53 left in the third to tie the score at three.

"It felt good for us," Johansson told reporters after the game. "No one expected us to come out with a tie after that second period, but we believed in ourselves and we went out and did what we were supposed to do, and that's how you win games. I think they got a little shaky after that."

As loud at Madison Square Garden had become in the second period, the Capitals managed to silence many of the 18,200 in attendance with an emphatic third-period rally.

After a scoreless first overtime, the Capitals would complete the comeback at 12:36 of the second OT. In transition, Capitals forward Jason Chimera took a shot from the right faceoff circle that ricocheted off defenseman Bryan McCabe towards the crease. When Marian Gaborik failed to clear the puck, Chimera pounced on it and scored the game winner from in close.

Chimera then sped his way towards the neutral zone for a one-knee, fist-pumping celebration, before he was eventually mobbed by his teammates.

"It's up there in your life," Chimera said of where his double-OT goal ranks. "Next to maybe getting married and having kids, I think it's the best thing that ever happened [to me]. I should say besides getting married. Kids are number one, but this is pretty up there. It's awesome. There's no better feeling in the world."

Chimera's double-overtime winner completed the Capitals' biggest single-game postseason comeback and secured a 4–3 win in Game 4.

"Chimmer was such a good teammate," Matt Hendricks recalled in 2016. "He was a great professional, a great player, so everyone was extremely happy for him to score that goal. What a huge goal for that team. It was a big win for us. It was a bit of a hostile environment after what Bruce had said, but that's part of the game. And with those teams, it was hard to count us out of too many games."

A year after blowing a 3–1 first-round series lead to the Montreal Canadiens, the Capitals eliminated the Rangers with a Game 5 win at Verizon Center three days later.

100 See the Capitals Win the Stanley Cup

Congratulations. You've made it to the final chapter of this book. It has been quite the ride, looking back at some of the moments and personalities that have helped shape more than 40 years of Capitals history.

If you've read all the way through, you are surely a loyal Capitals fan. And that deserves kudos in itself. It hasn't always been easy.

As any Capitals fan knows, the list of heartbreaks is lengthy. Just qualifying for the Stanley Cup Playoffs was a challenge early. If the top 16 teams in the league made the postseason, the Capitals finished 17th (1980 and 1981). When the format changed to four teams per division, they finished fifth (1982).

In 1985, the Capitals became the first NHL team to blow a 2–0 lead in a best-of-five series. The Capitals dropped the decisive fifth game at home against the Islanders.

Two years later, the NHL expanded the first round to a best-of-seven. Naturally the Capitals led three-games-to-one only to fall to the Islanders in Game 7…in the fourth overtime…on home ice.

Blowing 3–1 series leads has become old hat for the Capitals. They have done so an NHL-record five times—in 1987, 1992, 1995, 2010, and 2015.

There were also 2–0 series leads that ended in disappointment—in 1985, 1996, 2003, 2009, and 2013.

While other teams have gone longer without winning the Stanley Cup, few have lost in as excruciating fashion as the Capitals.

Their postseason history is a large part of their identity. Still, some suggest that what happened decades ago should have no bearing on what happens today.

"In [the Washington] market, it seems that everybody brings up the past," head coach Barry Trotz said during the 2016 postseason. "And it's funny, because the past, a lot of times, it's not relevant. It's just a story for [reporters]. It's really not relevant to the group."

Others argue that the ghosts of postseasons past can have an impact.

"I think that plays a big part in the pressure on our team," general manager Brian MacLellan said after the Capitals dropped an NHL-record eighth Game 7 on home ice in 2017.

"Your history's your history. You're going to feel it. I can feel it up in the box. That past pressure manifests itself in the present day. To ignore it, I think, is a mistake. I think you've got to acknowledge it and then you've got to work through it…. I would say all the past history matters to us, and that you can feel it in the building. You feel it in the crowd. It's in there."

Of the 20 teams that have played at least eight Game 7s through 2017, the Capitals (4–11) have the worst winning percentage (.267). Reminders of their playoff disappointments come up every spring. Veterans search for answers to how it can finally be different.

"Until we change the narrative, that's going to be the question," said defenseman Matt Niskanen.

And yet, Capitals fans come back.

They return every season with dreams that the next one might end differently. One of these years it will be different, and for the fans who stuck with them, it will be that much sweeter.

More than 60 former Capitals players and coaches were interviewed for this book. Many of them played for multiple teams during their careers. Yet, *unsolicited,* at least a dozen said there is little else in hockey they'd rather see than the Capitals finally raising the Stanley Cup.

"They'd be winning it for all of us," said Yvon Labre, an original Capital whose No. 7 sweater hangs from the rafters at Verizon Center.

"All of us who have worn the jersey before, we all would like nothing more than to see a team that has come so close win the Stanley Cup. The players deserve it. This city deserves it. And the fans deserve to see it. Hey, even us old guys deserve it."

"I'm pulling for them so much," said former Capitals forward and Hall of Famer Mike Gartner.

"I'm pulling for them to break through and to get into the finals and to win the Stanley Cup. Some of my best memories came from playing in Washington. I have great memories, but it would be so nice if they can make some new history and win it all."

"We're so close," said Dennis Maruk, who played with the Capitals from 1978 through 1983. "We're right there. It's going to happen."

This may be the final chapter of *this* book, but the best chapter in Capitals history is still waiting to be written. It should be well worth the wait.

Sources

Books

Boudreau, Bruce, and Tim Leone. *Gabby: Confessions of a Hockey Lifer* (Dulles, Virginia: Potomac Books Inc., 2009).

Cox, Damien, and Gare Joyce. *The Ovechkin Project* (Mississauga, Ontario: John Wiley & Sons Canada Ltd., 2010).

Dreyfus, Glenn. *The Legends of Landover* (Lulu, 2017).

Podnieks, Andrew. *Sid vs. Ovi: Natural Born Rivals* (Toronto, Ontario: McLelland & Stewart, 2011).

Starkey, Ted. *Red Rising: The Washington Capitals Story* (Toronto, Ontario: ECWPress, 2012).

Newspapers and Periodicals

Baltimore Sun
Medicine Hat News
Montreal Gazette
New York Times
Oakland Tribune
Sports Illustrated
The Globe and Mail
The Hockey News
Toronto Star
USA Today
Washington Post
Washington Star
Washington Times

Websites

AceBailey.org

Capitals.NHL.com

CapitalsOutsider.com

Capitals-legends.blogspot.com

CSNmidatlantic.com

DumpAndChase.MonumentalSportsNetwork.com

ESPN.com

HHOF.com

Hockeydb.com

Hockeyreference.com

GreatestHockeyLegends.com

Japersrink.com

NHL.com

NoVaCapsFans.com

RussianMachineNeverBreaks.com

Sportsnet.ca

TSN.ca

UPI.com

VividSeats.com

Yahoo.com

YouTube.com